FIREBIRDS!

For Rolande, my wife,
For Michel, my son.

FIREBIRDS!
Flying the Typhoon
in Action

Charles Demoulin

Smithsonian Institution Press
Washington, D.C.

First published in the United States 1988 by
Smithsonian Institution Press

First English language edition published in the United Kingdom 1987 by
Airlife Publishing Ltd.

Original French language edition published under the title
Mes Oiseaux de Feux in 1982 by Julliard.

Library of Congress Catalog Number 87-600396

ISBN 0-87474-366-4

Library of Congress details available.

Printed in England

Contents

Part Four: Crush Germany!

Part Five: Guest of the Third Reich

Dedication

I dedicate this book to my fellow-pilots of No. 609 West Riding of Yorkshire Squadron, Royal Auxiliary Air Force, who lost their lives during World War II 1939-1945.

Coming from all over the world, these pilots, who were my brothers-in-arms during those wartime years, gave their lives so that one day the world would be free again. They took with them into the infinite their tumultuous loving, their tremendous humour and their superb disdain of pettiness, cowardice and meanness.

As long as mankind can find outstanding human beings, prepared to defend freedom at the price of the ultimate sacrifice, the world will keep a sure hope of sunny morrows.

At war, everything is simple.
The only problem is to remain alive, day by day (one day at a time).

Acknowledgements

I could not have written this book without the help of my family and some close friends who suggested I publish these wartime memories and who encouraged me during a difficult task. My gratitude goes first to André Demoulin MD, of the Hôpital Français, and to his wife, Lucie Demoulin-Brahy MD, of the Pasteur Institute. I am deeply indebted to Mr. Munday, head of the Historical Branch at the Ministry of Defence, who provided those official documents without which certain events would have been difficult to relate with accuracy. Finally, the merit of the English translation of the main chapters lies with my very learned and good friend Mr. Peter Southall, Master of Law.

C.D.

Preface

On the torn pages of my old logbook the years have left a layer of dust. Long forgotten, buried in a drawer, the old witness testifies with brief notes, a few words hastily thrown on paper between two war-time operations. On every line, two or sometimes three words summarise hours laden with fire, blood and fear: Tiger tank destroyed, flak intense, engine failure, Focke-Wulf shot down, E-boat sunk.

On reading the faded ink, the memories rush back. The landscapes of the past return to life; the throb of engines, singing once again their wild song, escort my thoughts against a background of light blue sky. Familiar faces smile at me again and forgotten place-names snap like flags in the wind: Dunkirk, Biggin Hill, Manston, Normandy, Walcheren, Arnhem . . .

I push open the door of the Officers' Mess where, on the abandoned bridge table, the cards of an interrupted game still lie in disarray. On the radio the band of the Savoy Hotel plays a Gershwin tune as the bombs whistle down and London burns. At the local near the airfield we sip a tepid glass of bitter and all the girls we try to pick up are in uniform. The air raid sirens wail a warning as an ambulance speeds along the street. A house crumbles — a world, too.

At 400 mph I skim the green waters of the Channel, and the sea throws a film of spray upon the windscreen. At the cemetery, beside a neat rectangular hole in the yellowish clay, a guard of honour fires a salvo of blanks: a pilot is dead. On the shelf behind the bar we turn his silver tankard upside down for the last time. The Free French radio tells us 'The roses are red'; sending its message to the Resistance in France.

One morning, Group Captain 'Billy Goat', the mascot famous throughout the RAF, chews with relish my cigarette pack carelessly forgotten on a low table. Straight ahead, a Focke-Wulf 190 spitting a trail of black smoke explodes like an over-ripe pomegranate. With controlled excitement I dive into a wall of flak like gigantic fireworks at the shooting gallery of some satanic fair. Tiger tanks without their caterpillar tracks lie helplessly in the twilight of the Normandy plain while our rockets rip open the bellies of the hated SS.

Music in the air, the laughter of girls in a world of folly: liberation. I am lonely, for one is never so lonely as in a crowd noisily enjoying its rediscovered freedom.

It is so cold, so melancholy in wintertime, along the Rhine. Arnhem: I am falling, falling, towards those roofs of grey tiles. The SS, the field-grey uniforms, the hospital, the prison. My first escape, then the beating. I am so hungry. The disillusioned guards are quaking at the thunder of Russian guns. Berlin is dying. Hitler is dead. I am alive.

At the side of the road I pick a flower newly opened in the May sunshine, next to a corpse already stiffened. Like Agricola, the time has come to return to my distant home, in order to dig the earth, sow the seeds in the fields drenched with blood, and reap the rich harvest. I must at all costs keep my dreams, my illusions. All that's left of my youth has passed; left, before I ever realised it had gone away.

It was my honour to serve with the men in blue, and my privilege to share, above the clouds, a foretaste of a certain paradise that we named Shangri-La.

The old priest told me, with conviction, that God had spared me, with the help of the Holy Virgin, to whom he prayed so often. Thank you, vicar, on behalf of my dead friends! Then, in front of a gathering of my fellow citizens, the Lord Mayor gives me the medal of our good town; like an annual agricultural show, I am the prize bull; the others are dead. The music and the speeches sound flat.

'Hello Mother. Good morning Father.' This man who comes back was your child.

C.D.

Part One
Pilot in the RAF

Chapter 1
Dawn Patrol

On the airfield it was pouring with rain. I somehow managed to jump from the station-wagon as it stopped a few yards from the dispersal, and ran into the pilots' hut, completely drenched. It helped to wake me on that cold, dark early morning.

Awkward in his waterproof cape, Sergeant Hinchcliffe had already checked and carried my parachute to the aircraft, while Corporal Baker used his sleepy hand to turn the handle of the field telephone, hopefully trying to establish contact with the Ops room. 0430 hours. A cold front blanketed this side of the Channel, as was usual at this time of the year. It was my turn to fly the Met Recce, all the way along the enemy-held coast from the Belgian border to the estuary of the River Seine, taking off in the dark in order to hit the Boulogne area at first light. My instructions were simple enough: fly at 10,000 feet, slightly inland and following the coast, and describe by radio the prevailing weather conditions on that side of the Channel. Even if rightly called the 'English' Channel, there was at the time a strong dispute as to whom it belonged, and since the French collapse, the Germans most firmly objected to our visits.

Put in other words, it meant entering closely guarded enemy territory in full sight of his defences, infuriating the Huns for over an hour, and being pinpointed by all the radar stations of Fortress Europe. And, while flying in not too much of a hurry over the powerful flak defences, the chosen stooge was supposed to describe in plain language the exalting beauty of a French sunrise somewhat stained by the ugly black patches of Jerry's ack-ack.

'The Ops Room does not answer, sir. I reckon they are probably still asleep. But the grass runway will be lit seven minutes from now and the orders are unchanged.' The clerk on the telephone speaks in a monotone, his voice tinged with the professional indifference of someone who can do nothing about the contents of the message. His emotions have been blunted by long experience of a war that, for him, is fought between an impersonal voice on a field telephone and the changing faces of pilots who take off and do not return. I use the same matter-of-fact tone: 'O.K. Corporal. Please warn the coastal defences that I will cross at Dungeness at nought feet in about ten minutes. I hope those sods are asleep so that they don't get a chance to practise on my Typhoon. And make sure they look up their aircraft recognition books before they let loose their fireworks on my way back!'

'On your return? . . .' The clerk does not finish his thought. 'Oh, yes sir. As soon as I hear you on the R/T, I'll warn them!'

Time to go out into the wet dark night, barely protected by the umbrella brandished by a friendly fitter. After climbing onto the wing, I sink myself in the loneliness of the cockpit. The hood closed, I busy myself with the usual, by now mechanical actions: adjust the parachute straps, tighten the safety harness; snap in the radio plug, put on silk gloves, then leather ones; see that my Smith and Wesson .38 is firmly tucked into my right flying boot, and set the instrument panel lights to be not too bright. Then after going through the 18 checks laid down in the cockpit drill, I switch on the navigation lights and I am set to start the engine. Hinchcliffe, hidden under his umbrella, promptly gives me a thumbs up and, after priming the petrol pump twice, I fire the starter cartridge. A deafening noise shakes the airfield as the monster comes to life. Chocks away, I taxi to the grass runway, checking the mags on the way and get the sleepy control tower's permission to scramble. Turning quickly into wind I push the throttle forward to the gate, and soon the Typhoon becomes airborne. I lock the undercarriage up and reduce the revs to cruising speed. With eyes fixed on the instruments, I turn my aircraft towards the sea. Keeping down at sea level is imperative, in order to avoid radar detection for as long as possible. A few minutes gained now may mean that the German fighters sent to intercept will be late for the meeting. In some ways, my task is a bit like a reporter giving a running commentary of a sporting event on the radio: but somehow I feel more like a poacher trespassing on forbidden land than a hunter on his rightful ground. And I decline the challenge to meet single-handed the 2000 odd Nazi fighters stacked behind that hostile coastline. Needless to say, should one come my way by chance, I would not mind taking advantage of a well-aimed quick burst . . .

Having let down to sea level, I leave the Kent coast behind and sink into the night, busying my fingers with the necessary chores such as setting the correct course, lining up the gyro with the compass, undoing the cannon's safety catch and adjusting the gunsight brightness for the poor ambient light. By the clock, I have another 12 minutes at deck level before climbing flat out to 10,000 feet and crossing the coast at 300 mph.

How stupid can you get? I clean forgot to switch off my navigation lights. A neon sign up my tail would do as well to warn 'them' of my arrival! I have been too busy with my many little tasks to think about anything other than piloting my Typhoon, nursing and mentally cosseting the beast, as one would do with a thoroughbred. Now I have time to size things up, to let my mind wander over that hostile sky where the rising sun will soon replace the night.

My eyes skim across the dimly lit instrument panel, from petrol gauge to oil pressure, then back to the shadows: time now to climb at 3000 feet per minute using 2500 rpm, in rich mixture and gills closed. Time to make my entry into the coming dawn, creeping out of the night that still hides the earth below.

It takes a few seconds for my eyes to adjust to first light. Whenever I fly in the early morning I cannot help marvelling at the beauty of first light caressing the sky while Mother Earth is still deep set in the drowsiness of night. It is good to live such moments! And yet, how deceptive this peace can be; what utter loneliness one can feel as soon as the clouds break and one sits alone with just one's thoughts for company . . . There below, where the armies of the Third Reich are massed, a grey carpet of cloud hides the world. In front and above me, the sun rises to another day.

Ten thousand feet. Turn to the right and level off. Time to start my run, twisting my head around to keep a constant watch into the sun that will lie behind me for the whole trip. Jerry loves to jump on the pilot unaware of that deadly danger: I see in my mind's eye the poster stuck on the wall of the training school that reads 'The silly blighter did not look in the sun . . .' I am fully awake now; I know that the radars from Ostend to Le Havre are following my path yard by yard. I know that the alert is on and that the reception committee must be on its way. Where will they scramble from? Will it be St. Omer? Or Amiens Glissy maybe? In that case, they will be the 'yellow noses' of the Galland circus . . .

If they follow the usual ploy, they will send two pairs: one flying in full view, about the same height on a parallel course, but well inland and keeping just out of range, in order to catch my eye and induce me to have a go. If I fall for it they will gently dive inland, still keeping out of reach, until the other pair coming up behind will shoot me like a sitting duck. A typical German version of the old cat and mouse game, revised and copyrighted by Messerschmitt and Co. Cat and mouse, hide and seek, cowboys and injuns; funny how grown ups go on playing their games right up until death!

Then, to add spice I am supposed to report, loud and clear on channel A, the state of the weather over France. This should remove any lingering doubts about the ability of the flak computers to estimate speed, height and course of my aircraft and let their guns practise at my expense. With that in mind I start weaving every 20 seconds to make their task a little more difficult and at the same time to enable me to get a good look back in the dead sector behind my tail.

'Digby One to Schoolmaster. I am starting my run at angels 10. Got anything for me? Over.'

'Hello Digby One, nothing for the time being. You may start reporting now. Out.'

The sector controller, sheltered in his Kentish underground operations room, will record word for word my weather report as I fly along the French coast, then transmit it to all operational airfields in England.

'O.K. Schoolmaster, Digby One reporting. Dunkirk area ten-tenths up to 5 or 6000 feet. Cloudy inland. Clear sky above Boulogne area, coastline six-tenths around 3000 feet. Cloudy inland in patches up to 5000 feet. Slight haze in places further inland. Am on course. Out —'

The Germans must also be receiving me loud and clear, and I wonder why the flak is mute and no fighter has so far shown itself. They may well be waiting for the sun to rise higher, making it more difficult for me to keep watch. If so, the trap will spring between Calais and Gravelines. Yet above, the sky is clear, and of the tender blue one only finds at this time of day. The kind of blue that encourages reverie, with its whitish cloud carpet underneath and the beach showing its fringes through the gaps. Rain may be pouring down over England but here it is an early springtime morning about to dawn.

'Schoolmaster to Digby One'

The words explode in my earphones. Yet, so tense is my mind that not a muscle of my body moves and my hands and feet are ready for instant action. I am watching all sectors of the sky in a continuous sweep. Above, behind, where the most likely attack would come from. Below too. Nothing; I can see nothing yet. Even when I weave widely or just sideslip from side to side. Better acknowledge the controller's call: 'Yes, Schoolmaster, Digby One answering. Over.'

'Four bandits or more climbing over Amiens. Turning at 6000 feet inland. Keep a sharp look out to your left, Digby One. Out.'

'O.K. Schoolmaster. Out.'

The waiting is over, but the game has not started yet. Funny; I feel relieved. As always, the time spent waiting for something to happen is worse than the action itself. From now on I am going to be so busy that there won't be time for anything but, hopefully, doing the right thing. Gently, I push the throttle forward to increase speed to 330 mph indicated, with rich mixture — and I add 200 rpm for better engine response. My thumb rests ready, on the firing button. With correction for altitude, I am now flying at more than six miles a minute, making it difficult for Jerry to jump me or catch me unawares. Ahead, the sky is clear, and the coast below is perfectly visible. Far inland there are scattered clouds drifting over sleepy France.

'Digby One to Schoolmaster. Contrails 10 miles inland, parallel and slightly above my level. Probably a pair of 190s sniffing around. No sign of the other bandits. I am just passing Gravelines canal, still going west. The sky has cleared over the Channel but, from the coast inland, layers seem to hang at 6 or 7000 feet. Over.'

'O.K. Digby One. The other bandits are behind you, flying low, turning out to sea and probably trying to cut you off over the Channel. Do not, repeat do not follow the 190s inland. Over.'

'No bloody fear, Schoolmaster. I'm just keeping an eye on the bastards. But please keep me informed about those I can't see. Out.'

I realise that I am sweating, notwithstanding the freezing cold that fills the cockpit, and I must restrain a strong impulse to dive towards home — partly to seek the safety of our coast, partly also in the hope of bouncing the other pair somewhere on the way home. No! I must stick to my orders and fly another sixty miles due west to report the weather, as required. Boring perhaps but very useful. Keep going, Windmill.

Some distance away, inland and to the left, the bait is plainly in sight, teasing me in vain. Messerschmitt or Focke-Wulf, it doesn't matter which: they just sit there, watching my every move, hoping I will have a go at them. Then they would ever so gently dive inland, not too fast so as to induce me to follow them, but not slowly enough to give me the slightest chance of catching up with them. They just want to take me for a ride, leading me into the wolf's jaws, where the reception committee would happily attend to me. They would finish me off and the game would be over.

God, where are the other blighters? Even after a 360 degree steep turn, I can't see any sign of them. Waiting for me in mid-Channel would be the usual form, hoping to cut my escape route. But we both know the rules of the game and I have aces up my sleeve, for at this height the Typhoon dives a lot faster than they do. And, at deck level, it's a matter of skilled piloting to out-turn the enemy, and get your guns to bear. Of course there will be two of them, but that's not the end of the world. Anyway, there are friends waiting all along our own coast if I need to call for help. They would arrive within minutes, I am sure. I mean, I hope they would get there in time. Stop letting that mind of yours wander when you need to concentrate on the job in hand. 'Digby One to Schoolmaster. I am at the end of my run. Blue sky over here with about two-tenths inland at 2000 feet. Channel still covered by about five-tenths at 4 to 5000 feet. Out.'

'O.K. Digby One. You can come home. Steer 295 degrees. Maintain your angels for the time being. The other plot has faded but keep your eyes open. Out.'

As I turn gently for home, some distance away from Le Havre, I see clearly, sneaking along the coast, a six to eight thousand-ton cargo ship heading east, escorted by two E-boats. The tiny convoy leaves behind three wakes of whitish foam upon a dark green sea. What a tempting sitting-target for a hungry Typhoon!

'Digby One to Schoolmaster. Just below me, a cargo escorted by two E-boats, heading east, barely a mile off shore. Speed about 10 knots. Can I have a go?'

I can feel that my heart rate has increased, and the excitement must have shown itself in my speech, for the hurried voice of the controller comes back at me like a shot: 'Negative, Digby One, I repeat negative. Keep away. Just observe and report on return. Acknowledge. Over.'

Just my bloody luck! I should have known better and strafed the jokers first, then reported my attack! Now, I am stuck. It would be a breach of discipline, and that kind of 'black' would be dealt without doubt or delay. Now some other bright boys will prang the ship and get the credit!

'O.K. Schoolmaster, message received and understood! Coming home. Out.'

The disappointment must have shown in the tone of my voice, for the controller feels obliged to add, in a pretended cheerful way, 'Good boy! Keep on track. Out.'

On my way home I cannot get out of my mind the vision of a Typhoon diving with guns blazing, pumping incendiary and explosive shells at the rate of 600 rounds per minute. With pom-pom gunners collapsing or jumping overboard, a ship burning, and steam escaping from the guts of a sinking wreck! For good measure, I mentally add an E-boat raked with fire, lying helplessly on the sea with a dead crew on deck.

For a while now, I have been flying towards home, quite oblivious of the other fighters possibly hunting me down in mid-Channel. The fact that the plot has faded may mean that, disgusted, they have gone home, but it could also be that, flying below radar detection height, they are still around — somewhere between England and me. A sharp look-out is essential, for it's when nearing the stables that a horse thinking of oats can be caught unawares. Pilots also sometimes forget to look in the rear mirror while they long for that first cigarette after landing. Then over the news a short communiqué says: 'One of our aircraft is missing.'

Not for me. I am extremely watchful. Every five minutes I report my position and ask the controller if he has some gen for me, which apparently he has not, and I keep turning my head in all directions. In a moment I shall see the white cliffs of Dover looming out of the hazy dawn, while I fly on at sea level to cross the coast near Dungeness. Then I will forget about the treacherous sea, about the Focke-Wulfs, about a rough engine or unreasonable fears. I can let my imagination run wild again, finding myself amongst my friends at the bar with a pint in hand, shooting a line or talking shop, while Vera Lynn makes you dream that 'Only You' is addressed to you alone, and reminds you to date a lovely bird for the late NAAFI show . . .

Plain stupid again . . .! With that wandering mind of mine, I clean forgot to switch my IFF on! My radar Identification, Friend or Foe, sings like a canary; singing a sweet song of recognition to the ack-ack pongos who never miss a chance to let go at a Typhoon crossing the coast. So I'd better call Baker and tell him I am coming in. Only last week, they missed an escaping hit-and-run raider but managed to put a few holes in the pursuing Typhoon. The Battery Commander had the cheek to claim a 'damaged' — until their local pub was raided by B Flight pilots the same evening and our squadron unofficially credited with a good prang.

'Digby One to Schoolmaster. Approaching coast west of Dungeness. Angels zero. No fireworks, please. Out.'

'Cut the wisecracks, Digby One. Welcome home. Out.' The controller is not in a joking mood. Probably short of sleep. I couldn't care less. It's home, sweet home again, and time to set fine pitch, wheels down, flaps down — and glide on to Mother Earth.

My wheels kiss the wet grass of Manston, and I taxi quickly towards dispersal. The control tower sends me greetings in the form of a solid raspberry, mentioning the fact that I did not ask permission to land! Sorry, I forgot to ring the bell before putting the key in the lock! All the same, they are quite right and, joking apart, it was my mistake. I curtly apologise and make a mental note to be more careful next time. And I hope that Roland Beamont, the CO, will not tear me off a strip . . .

Engine cleared, switch off. After a 75 minute flight, I relax for a few seconds before getting out of the cockpit. The rain has stopped. It's first light in a world that has come to life. I enjoy that moment immensely . . .

'Cup of tea, sir?'

A little WAAF is waiting next to the wing with a boiling hot mug of tea and a lit cigarette in hand. A nice gulp and a puff that tastes like heaven.

Walking towards dispersal, I try to remember her name: Nancy? Or is it Joan? I forget. A mistake, for with a little care, she could be quite fun, that anonymous little WAAF. But of course everybody is beautiful, and life is wonderful when one returns from a dodgy op to live another day. The dew shines in the rising sun, Radio Calais dispenses lovely soft jazz music before making us laugh with Lord Haw-Haw's bombastic speeches, the porridge tastes sweet and the bacon and eggs complete the feast.

Forgotten, the disappointment about the cargo ship that was ignored. Forgotten, the dogfight that did not happen. Tomorrow is another day, and tomorrow holds many a fight to be fought and battles to be won. Tomorrow? All the time that lies in front of us, from here to eternity. But does one ever reach tomorrow, for we live but one day at a time? *Carpe diem.*

Chapter 2
A Vocation

That dawn patrol reveals just one corner of the sky in which I flew during those years of some 250 operational sorties. Many tanks burned out, scores of panzers destroyed, enemy ships sent to the bottom, troop transports of the Wehrmacht stopped dead on their way to the front line. Focke-Wulfs, Messerschmitts and Junkers shot down in long-lasting dog-fights. Barges, bridges, Nazi headquarters, V1 and V2 launching sites, all smashed by our rockets. SS hoodlums strafed at point-blank range. Never would I have joined in those ops had I not fulfilled the three basic prerequisites for a wartime fighter pilot: an urge to fly; the valuable training provided by seasoned RAF aces; and use of the most outstanding rocket-firing fighter of World War II — the Typhoon.

Even since the age of five or six, my dream was to be a pilot. Such a precocious ambition took root when Tcheffry, former pilot of King Albert of Belgium and hero of the first flight between Belgium and the then Belgian Congo, used to beat up our home in his slow noisy biplane. Soon after, Lindbergh crossed the Atlantic when I was seven and looking at the sky with childlike hope. Parents seldom realise how an idea can expand in a child's universe, that secret world where a vivid imagination can turn a dream into reality — provided one adds more than a pinch of determination to it. So much so that, when the 'phoney war' started in September 1939 and I was still a student at university, I made a secret decision to be a pilot in the Belgian Air Force. My father, whom I approached carefully on what I knew to be a most difficult subject, met my demand with a stern and categorical refusal. In those days, fathers' authority was not to be disputed, and had to be bypassed, with all the risks that involved, by sheer craftiness. This statement may sound dreadful to the ear of a Public-school-bred English gentleman, but when you belong to a peaceful country that has been overrun regularly over five centuries by powerful ruthless neighbours, you realise that the best chance to succeed against brutal force lies in the use of your wits. And you tend to forget about the 'morality' of things (just as politicians do most of the time) to concentrate on some 'practical' way to reach your perfectly honest goal!

In my case, this meant being admitted to the competitive examination of the Air Force Board at the War Academy, where the best 40 out of some 600 applicants would be allowed to go to Training School. But, not being of age at the time, I first had to produce a parental authorisation signed on an official application form bearing a 20 Franc stamp. The obvious thing to do was to copy my father's signature, which, after a little practice, turned out to be quite acceptable. Having forged a false but convenient signature, I was allowed to sit the examination and was then left to wait for the results for a while. And when the postman did not bring the hoped-for news, I naturally concluded that I had failed and relaxed my daily watch on the mail delivery. Which proved to be careless, as it happened. For one morning, my father, mail in hand and a very severe look in his eye, asked me what the official letter meant from the Ministry of Defence calling his son to report for a medical at the Air Force Board. It had been very careless of me not to watch for the postman, but who would imagine that the red-tape kings at the Ministry would ask applicants to pass the medical after the written examinations, so that half of the successful 40 brainy marvels were found to be either blind, deaf or lame? In the 54th position, I had qualified for the obsolete Belgian Air Force, apart from the fact that my father still had to have his say about it! And I soon found out that a father with the right connections could do a lot more than a young man with only his wits. After being properly admonished, the powers that be decided that I could only join the Air Force after finishing my studies, next July. With that compromise the family uproar died down, as usually happens when it boils down to a simple conflict between generations.

In 1939 little Belgium lived under a false sense of security, backed up by a declaration of neutrality that proved of little value when Hitler chose to ignore it. And yet about 800,000 men had been mobilised, armed with pea-shooters or the equivalent, but they were ridiculously underpaid, so that the morale of both the soldiers and their poorly fed families was at a low ebb. To the last day, a sheeplike population would live with the hope that the war would spare them. Next door to us, the French Army and the British Expeditionary Force were sitting more than cautiously behind the phoney Maginot line, fighting Hitler with leaflets and warlike songs.

The Belgian Army, led by a bunch of stuffy old generals, was preparing to fight this war brilliantly on the 1914-1918 pattern: our highly efficient army communication system was dependent on pigeons carrying messages, usually written in French for units who spoke Flemish, while our armoured division deployed Bren-carriers and sturdy bicycles. Luckily, horses were better fed than men, which pleased the society for their protection. As for the Aéronautique Militaire (a pompous name for an obsolete air force), the powers that be had elected to modernise it with the wonderful Fiat CR42, an Italian biplane fighter that was prone to having holes bored in its propeller almost every time its machine-guns were fired. Thank God the pilots had plenty of guts and were on the whole pretty skilful, as some of them proved after escaping and serving in the RAF later on!

This being said, the laugh should not only be on us, for our allies displayed a complete lack of imagination when they also chose to ignore the lessons of the Spanish Civil War and the invasion of Poland. Allied diplomacy was badly mauled when the Nazis and the Russians signed a treaty of friendship in 1939, giving Hitler a free hand in Eastern Europe and totally upsetting the balance of power in Europe. With the result that, after Poland, Norway and Denmark fell into Nazi hands like over-ripe plums.

What kind of future could a young man expect when nothing had been learned from the past, and the present contained all the ingredients of the end of the world? So when the war started — without trumpets but with live bombs — on the morning of 10 May, I found myself with my life in my hands, with my own decisions to take, and with loving parents bypassed by events. Face to face with destiny, at long last, I had the opportunity to do what I had always wanted, to be a pilot, and with an indestructible faith in ultimate victory I was going to fight, to win this war by myself if necessary, and in no time at all. This appreciation proved slightly wrong since it took five years and the help of a great many people . . .

War found me in bed at 4.30 in the morning, but by 7 a.m. I had persuaded the family to make a swift withdrawal to France in the family car, taking along grandmother and enough money to live for a while, so that, by 8 o'clock, I was totally free to meet the invaders on equal terms. Or almost. Jumping on my powerful motorbike, clad in leather jacket and shiny boots, and armed with an old 6.35 mm revolver retrieved from my father's desk drawer, I went to meet the German army.

I must have been one of the first guerillas, or, as they were later called, partisans, for I joined up by chance with the British forces that had crossed the border that night to take up positions on the Dyle River, making my home town of Wavre the pivot of the defence line. My war at this stage did not last long for, three days later, an unexpected meeting with a German panzer unit well inside our lines put an end to my warlike ambitions. Speeding along as guide with a British patrol on a country road, entrusted with the blowing up of some power plant, I was riding quite happily, when we met a German tank. The next thing I knew was that I was lying on the ground — and then, after watching the wheel of my bike spinning madly in the air, I quickly became unconscious. No pain, nothing, until I found myself lying on an operating table, in the St. Peter Hospital in Brussels.

After a rather lengthy operation, with my elbow smashed into 21 pieces and other flesh wounds that were less severe but still very painful, I spent three horrible days in a ward where some people died and many others suffered. Soon after, the electricity went off, few doctors were still around, and the nurses had their hands full. Chaos was rapidly setting in. My main and only worry, funnily enough, was not my health but how to avoid being taken prisoner. With the Germans only a few miles away, and everybody able to walk now fleeing, I knew I had little or no chance to get away.

On the morning of the day the Germans were to enter Brussels around noon, the young nurse who had been my guardian angel hurried into the ward with the secretary of the hospital, who was about to leave for the Belgian coast in his clapped-out Ford car. My British pass might help us to get through the roadblocks, so would I like to go with him, lying on a mattress in the back of his car? The miracle had happened, and we set off at 7.30 a.m. after the nurse had given me injections both for my heart and to reduce the pain. It took us ten hours to reach Ostend, with a few narrow escapes from Stuka bombs and strafing during the 60 mile journey. There the hospital was full, and I was allowed into a private clinic, after the nurses had overruled the nasty Matron's blunt refusal. With no doctor around, the only thing they did was change my dressings, and attempt to fight the infection.

Days went by, and the news came that the escape road to France had been cut and the Belgians were about to surrender. The only option left was to try and escape by sea, so when the walking patients got on the old local tramcar, I persuaded the nurses to heave my mattress on to the rear-platform, and we finally reached Ostend harbour. There a French troopship returning from Narvik took on board a mixed crowd of French soldiers, refugees and wounded. I was one of the lucky ones, for many stayed on the quay as we dodged the bombs and took to sea, with Dieppe as our destination. Once at sea, the ship was diverted to the Dunkirk area to help in the evacuation, and finally arrived in Folkestone in spite of continuous air attacks.

It was on a stretcher that I made my joyful entry into Britain. I had escaped capture, I was still alive, if in somewhat bad shape, but for the first time in days I could relax and hope. Lying in the Royal Victoria Hospital, the head surgeon looked at my infected right arm with a worried look in his eye and mentioned that it might have to be amputated. As best I could, I pleaded and told him I would accept any risk to try to keep it. But the doctors were overworked with the returning wounded just evacuated from Dunkirk, and while everybody did their utmost to help and keep us happy, it was a time when a man's life was held by a very thin thread.

After waiting for two long days, I was operated on for three hours and came out of the theatre with my arm encased in plaster — but still attached to my body. I woke up in a large ward, near a window overlooking a cricket ground, where men in immaculate white flannels played their favourite game in the warm spring sun. An amazing sight, almost unbelievable for someone who had just returned from Hell. Were our British friends that blind? Did they not realise that they had lost a decisive battle and what was at stake was nothing less than the very existence of our world? If my personal future did not look bright, the fate of my country was settled and the news of the fighting in France was alarmingly bad: it was obvious that the French were losing their heads and badly lacked fighting spirit. After bragging for months about hanging out their washing on the Siegfried Line they were running like rabbits, barely ahead of the German panzers, while their distinguished politicians blamed everyone but themselves in the vain hope of excusing their mistakes. With the end of the fighting in France in sight, lost in my rather sullen thoughts and a cripple at twenty years of age, I was evacuated to Bexhill Hospital, then transferred a week later to the Woodlands Cripples Hospital in the suburbs of Birmingham. I was to spend three long months there and go through two more major operations, superbly performed by the head surgeon, Doctor Henry, whose skill and daily attention managed to heal my wounds. Using a new technique learned during the Spanish Civil War, my wonderful surgeon rebuilt my elbow with silver wires and golden know-how, sealing my arm in plaster. Another six weeks passed before it was removed, and from under the plaster came a very thin arm, completely stiff. The doctor comforted me by saying that with time, a lot of trying and a lot of luck, I might regain partial use of my arm. When I told him that I was going to be a pilot in the RAF, he must have thought I was mad: he just shrugged his shoulders then, with a smile, said: 'Will can sometimes succeed where medicine has failed.' Even if it sounded at the time like a post-mortem, he added casually: 'It may take a bit of doing, I guess, but I hear they allow legless pilots to fly, so you stand a chance . . .'

When August came, I was convalescent and England was still in the war. The Heinkel 111s and the Junkers 88s had a nasty habit of raiding the area by night and by day, aiming at the Morris and BSA works not too distant from Northfield. But the worst was still to come when Birmingham and Coventry were chosen as prime targets for terror raids.

The Battle of Britain was in full swing in the south, and the BBC day after day kept the country informed about the monumental fight whose issue would be a matter of life or death for the country — and most probably for the way of life of a free world.

The invasion was expected at any time, and the plucky Home Guard had only their courage and knives and forks to oppose the Nazis' first-class weapons. But the people's determination and the cold-blooded will to fight to the last was such that we felt an unshakeable faith in final victory. Churchill's 'Sweat, blood and tears' had galvanised the British, and the long-haired boys in their too-few fighters had pointed the way towards better days. The exceptional behaviour of the Londoners during the blitz that lasted until 10 May 1941 would provide further proof, if that were needed, that such a nation would never be beaten.

I was bearing my enforced idleness as best I could, which was not very patiently, when one day a distinguished lady visited our ward, and introduced herself as a member of a charity committee, presided over my Mrs. Hastings-Orde, whose good deeds, amongst others, were to provide 'Godmothers' to lonely chaps — refugees like me. I accepted gratefully and, a few days later, the mail brought me a charming letter which from what I understood between the lines, came from a most charming youngster. She was aged 17, from Swansea, obviously keen to do her bit for the war effort. This did not exactly coincide with my personal idea of a 'Godmother', and I wrote to Mrs. Hastings-Orde, enclosing the girl's letter and explaining that I would rather have a more 'seasoned' Godmother, leaving my hands free as far as 'popsies' were concerned. I was wondering what kind of damage my answer had done when, a little later, a nurse brought me a heavy suitcase together with a letter written on top-quality writing paper. Astonished, I did not know whether to read the letter first or open the fine leather gift: I felt thrilled, like a child at Christmas. I opted for the letter, and discovered that my new Godmother was Lady Newton, wife of Sir Harry Newton M.P. and Baronet, and a director of Harrods. Sir Alfred Newton was a former Lord Mayor of London during the First World War and, I was to discover later, his full-size portrait as Chairman of the board was hanging in the main hall of Harrods. The very kind letter explained gently that Lady Newton was indeed 'seasoned'. She had three sons serving in the war, and she was pleased to adopt a fourth one, fully grown, for the duration. Jeremy, the eldest, was serving in the Middle East; he was killed later at Anzio as a gallant Captain leading his Company for the landing. Michael and Christopher gave very distinguished service, the former in the Army, the latter in the Navy. Lady Newton's brother Flt Lt Derek Grantham, was killed as a Typhoon fighter-pilot while her sister Nym wore her WRNS uniform with elegance.

From an orphan one day, on top of an invitation to spend my leaves on their estate at Westfield Place in Battle, with a railway warrant to take care of the financial side, I was to enjoy the affection and the tremendous kindness of my British family for many years. The suitcase contained a full set of clothes, both formal and for sport, with sets of shirts, underwear, socks, and shoes. In the space of a minute, I felt like a normal human being again. Later I succeeded in meeting the whole family and, although overawed by Sir Harry's uniform as a General in the Home Guard, I had the privilege of sharing their affection and becoming part of a family that has stayed close to my heart for a lifetime.

In September my recovery allowed me to be an out-patient at Woodlands, still totally unfit for armed service. Doctor Henry kept encouraging me to use my arm, to force the elbow to bend, in order to regain some flexibility. The process was painful and a lengthy business, but I was determined to make progress at whatever the cost. In order to visit the hospital for massage and physiotherapy, and thanks to the help of Dame Elizabeth Cadbury, I found a billet at 23 Elvetham Road, Birmingham, in the empty house of Mr. Lambot, a Belgian engineer who had fled to the country with his family and found it convenient to have his town residence looked after. Until, that is, I was bombed out during a November night, when I had elected to spend the air raid in the garden under an apple tree. I got up unscratched while the back of the house was blown to bits. That experience reinforced my decision never to go into an air raid shelter — partly out of claustrophobia, partly because I preferred to die in the open air if the worst came to the worst. For several weeks, therefore, I camped in a bombed house with an oil stove and my 20 years of age to keep me warm.

My financial position could best be described as parlous. Having during the months in hospital spent the thirty odd pounds I had on me when I was wounded, I was penniless. When I became an out-patient, I was totally dependent on the weekly 21 shillings dear Mr. Lambot paid me as salary to keep his house safe. In fact, he very generously gave me the whole 21 shillings he received from the British Government for billeting a refugee unable to work. I fancied one meal a week, at the then maximum cost of 5 shillings a meal plus cover charge in the Grant Hotel, just to feel like a human being once in a while. Otherwise I managed not to go too hungry on cheese, bread and butter for the rest of the week. But I did go short a few times when I invited a girl to dinner at my expense!

Then, one day, the Belgian Government in London decided that I was really an important part of the Belgian army at Tenby! And having tracked me down they ordered me to report there in the shortest possible time. I had a good look at the map to discover just where Tenby was, then, realising that I had no money for the train journey (I knew nothing then about railway warrants, which would have been provided on request), I left Birmingham, getting lifts all the way from kind motorists.

What I found when I reached that once lovely seaside resort would not be believed by anyone, let alone those who knew Tenby in normal times. The town had been partly evacuated for fear of invasion, and was used as a base for the remnants of the Belgian army. At the time it consisted of a handful of civilians hastily put into privates' uniforms with a mere dozen dead-beat regular NCOs, all having grown grey hair in various desk jobs, and about 120 officers of all arms and very divergent opinions as far as keenness to fight was concerned. The Atlantic Hotel was their hide-out. Old grandpa General Chevalier van Strydonck de Burkel, who was reputed to have escaped from Belgium with his dog and a pet canary, took his constitutional on the promenade every morning. The other ranks were billeted in lovely empty villas, where anything even looking like wood had long been dismantled and used as fuel for open fires. Luckily, the only furniture consisted of iron beds with straw mattresses, otherwise we would have slept on the floor-joists.

If the hordes of Attila had invaded Tenby, they could hardly have done better; but they would not have had one-franc coins. These could be used to empty the cigarette machine in place of shillings of the same size. One could hardly blame soldiers, whose pay amounted to one franc a day, for 'mistaking' the correct price; a pound was worth 175 francs, or almost six months' pay!

This is the world I discovered when I reported for duty, still wanting to become a pilot. And, still in civvies, I presented myself to what was supposed to be the duty NCO's office. Luckily, this was a reservist's job, held by a corporal old enough to be my father and a tramcar driver in civvy street, who sniffed at me with kindly indifference. He was efficient enough to issue me with a paybook, gave me a chit to obtain a photograph in uniform, announced that I was due 14 shillings and 2 pence for the time between volunteering in Belgium and today's date, and then proceeded to send me to the clothing store. There I was handed a battledress, a pair of shoes, a cap and a few other garments. Of course, the full kit of a brave young soldier must include his armament, which in my case turned out to be a 1912 model Enfield rifle. At least, that is how it was described to me, but I absolutely refused to carry such an artillery piece with a completely stiff arm! There followed some heated argument that included threats of terrible punishment on one side, and helpless laughter on the other. We reached a compromise when I decided to report sick on the spot, and I was allowed to leave my gun in the store — after signing for it! So both sides had their pride preserved until next day's sick parade.

Before that, duly clad as a warrior, I had to report to the Intelligence officer. Perhaps he was rightly described as intelligent by the British, but I would never have given this as a description of Lieutenant Aronstein, a lawyer in civvy street and little short of the prosecutor in my case. He started by interrogating me as if I were a Fifth Columnist, querying my story that I had gone to fight on the first day when, according to him, I should have done the right thing, meaning that I should have fled, and in any event, why was I so late in reporting for duty in England? At first I took it calmly, answering politely, and trying to make him understand that some people still believed in King, honour and country, and went off to fight quite naturally. But, after a while, I decided that he was either stupid or insane, and maybe both, so I stayed mute and became indifferent to whatever he chose to allege. At last, thoroughly disgusted, he threw me out of his office as a dead loss.

But I was not through with the flaming army, for I had the bad luck on the way to my billet to cross the path of a Major, armed with a stick and wearing the biggest moustache I have seen to this day. I just smiled at him, trying to convey both respect and sympathy; in return all I got was a sharp barked order to stand to attention and salute smartly! Can you imagine such a lack of courtesy when you smile at a perfect stranger? I gathered my wits fast enough to start undressing on the spot and, when it came to my arm, the bemused Major had to admit that even he would not be able to bend it into a smart salute. I failed to gather what he was mumbling through his teeth when he resumed his walk, but Major Maka must have had his doubts about the striking power of his pocket army.

I shared my room with two charming fellows, one named Levy, a most humorous chap, and the other called George Wouters, a lawyer who spoke in a clipped voice. Although our acquaintance did not last long, we had pleasure in meeting after the war, as both lived long enough to get home. My career in the Belgian army came to an end the very next day, soon after entering the sick bay. It began with what the services know as a 'Short-Arm Inspection'; bluntly, had I got V.D.? I was assured it was routine while waiting for the medical officer to arrive. As the inspection was unnecessary, according to the rather human orderly, I was allowed to dress again and waited an hour while the orderly went back to sleep at his desk.

At last, the doctor, a Captain, arrived, escorted by three chattering girls disguised as nurses and with officers' pips on their shoulders, and I was asked once more to undress, although I pointed out that my arm was the reason for my visit. It took very little time for the good doctor first to show his amazement, then to decide that I was unfit for duty in the armed forces. I would therefore be released and sent back to London for demobilisation. After what I had seen of the bloody army in Tenby, in the short time I spent there, I saluted that decision as a most welcome end to a pitiful comedy, and patiently waited for my warrant to go to London. Back in civvies, I spent most of the few days left in Saundersfoot, a lovely little fishing port a few miles from Tenby. Not least, I took away with me fond memories of kind gentle people, living in one of the prettiest parts of the British Isles.

When I arrived in London, I reported to 107 Eaton Square, which housed the office of the Belgian Military Attaché. In those days there was no proper Belgian Government in England. Recognised authority was in the hands of the Belgian Ambassador, Baron Cartier de Marchienne, and two Belgian ministers, Mr. Camille Gutt and Mr. De Vleeshouwer, the first to arrive via France. There is no doubt that our Ambassador was a great gentleman and a very good diplomat as well as a most respected man, known as a good friend of England. It is mainly thanks to him that Belgium stood firmly on the Allies' side, and helped the common war effort in no small way.

Mr. C. Gutt was the first to decide to leave the defeated French and continue the fight in England. He was a man of great integrity as well as a most efficient Minister of Finance and Defence. As a private pilot himself, he saw to it that his three sons joined the RAF as pilots, two of them being killed on duty and the third surviving to become a leading international solicitor. Mr. De Vleeshouwer was a distinguished Colonial Minister, who did not hesitate to put the resources of the Belgian Congo at the disposal of England when the Belgian Ministers who had stayed in France were still undecided, and the skies were dark to say the least.

Thank God we had those three men of international stature, far above the level at which politicians usually operate, who knew where their duty lay and showed the way to victory by their example. It did not cross their minds to beg the Germans for permission to return to Occupied Belgium, as others did, nor to wait in Occupied France until it was clear that Germany might lose the war.

It was some time in November 1940 that the Belgian Prime Minister Hubert Pierlot and Foreign Affairs Minister Pol-Henri Spaak stopped dancing their Hesitation Waltz and arrived in England. Their arrival in the country went almost unnoticed, apart from a few lines, hardly conspicuous, in the back pages of *The Times*, which read: 'The Belgian Prime Minister Hubert Pierlot and Foreign Affairs Minister Pol-Henri Spaak arrived yesterday in England, after crossing Spain disguised as peasants.' Unfortunately, the following week *Punch* — or was it *The Tatler?* — published a full-page cartoon depicting the fleeing ministers on horseback as Don Quixote and Sancho Panza, and below *The Times*' short paragraph was the even shorter caption: 'They needed not to.' Cruel humour, if ever there was . . .

This did not prevent Mr. Spaak, once he had chosen his path, from becoming a leading figure in the fight against Germany and, in later days, a man of outstanding stature in European and world politics. As for Count Hubert Pierlot, ennobled after the war as he quietly went back to private life, he was a very honest and decent man, who maybe was a bit too big for his boots.

But when I arrived in a London hit every night by the blitz, my main preoccupations were first to exist and then to restore my physical strength so that I might join the Air Force and fight again. I first had to report to the Military Attaché, Colonel Wouters, at Eaton Square in Belgravia. It had by that time become 'Belgian Square', as the whole of it was taken over by Belgian services of every kind. The Deputy Air Attaché, Commandant de Ryckman de Betz, was most sympathetic to my cause and, after issuing my release papers, advised me to meet Professor Timmermans, who would arrange for a scholarship at Birmingham University, and later at Jesus College, Cambridge, with the assistance of the British Council. He also mentioned that if later on my arm got better he would recommend me for the Air Force. An hour later, I was duly registered as a student reading for a Bachelor of Arts degree and granted a 21 shillings — one guinea — per week allowance, with which I was supposed to meet all personal requirements. For comparison, a single room at the Regent Palace Hotel then cost exactly one guinea per *night*, sirens and bombs included, so juvenile enthusiasm with make do and mend had to compensate for lack of money.

Still in London that night, with all of 8 shillings in my pocket, and dodging the bombs that Jerry scattered over the city, I found my way to Oxford Street, looking for a Belgian restaurant called 'Chez Maria'. It was in the basement of a half-demolished house, patronised by my compatriots in search of a rare steak as true beef-eaters like it. The place was lost in darkness, but the sign 'Business as usual' was proudly if dimly lit. When I pushed open the door, a pair of deep black eyes met me, sparkling in the dim light and cigarette smoke. They belonged to Maria, a middle-aged Belgian refugee with a keen sense of business and a heart as great as her culinary art.

'Hello there, newcomer. What's your name? Charles? You want a steak with chips, don't you? And a beer? They all do, because Maria's steak is the best in town.'

At first glance, Maria had seen through me, for she knew her trade. After weighing me up she quickly added: 'Tonight it's on the house. Have a drink first, then you'll tell me your story. Better sit here next to Michel.'

At a table, a sergeant pilot in Belgian uniform was chainsmoking and had obviously had a few beers already. He welcomed me with a rather thick accent: 'What the hell are you doing here? My name is Michel de Hepcee, and I am cheesed off. Been waiting for weeks to get back to training! What's your name?'

After introducing myself, I explained that I also wanted to fly, that I had to wait, that I was going back to university in the meantime. He told me he had been still under training in Belgium, that he was going mad waiting in London for somebody to send him off to qualify. His brother, Baron Charlie de Hepcee was a squadron commander. Neither survived; Charlie was later to become a top agent in the Resistance and die in the hands of the Gestapo; Michel was to die in his Spitfire over Belgium.

On that evening in London, in the dim light of a dive, a friendship was born. Michel offered to put me up for a few days in the mews house where he lived, brushing aside with his typical generosity my lack of money. Together we day-dreamed of coming victories, we rebuilt a world with the same words and the same hopes. When, much later and after many more pints, we weaved back to his flat, the sound of the All Clear filled the air of a cold dawn.

Back to Birmingham. My first visit was to Mr. Priestley, the Dean of the University in Edmonds Street, where I was to spend the next few months. A dozen Belgian girls and boys were also attending lectures there, thanks to the British Council, and neither staff nor students ever missed an opportunity to show us kindness and hospitality. The war was ever-present as the city was bombed every night, and established a common and strong bond among us all. With the local firemen and wardens overworked by fires, bombs and casualties, the university set up its own fire-fighting and first-aid volunteer unit, so that every night, from 6 p.m. until morning, a dozen volunteers camped in turn in the anteroom, with camp beds and fire-fighting equipment to hand. Shovels, fire extinguishers and hoses were stacked in a corner and sand buckets lined the corridors. The volunteers got a free cold supper, and off-ration eggs and bacon were promised for breakfast. That was exactly what I needed to help with the financial side of my precarious existence, so I arranged for my name to appear every night on the roster. Soon I became a very efficient fire-watcher, wearing a black helmet, putting out the odd incendiary bomb on the roof with sand, and visiting the kitchen larder with great regularity. When Professor Shapiro got wise to my nightly volunteering, I explained that I needed but little sleep, could use the library during the calm hours and, more than anything else, that it solved my financial and food problems. With great understanding, he immediately appointed me permanent warden, in charge of the team. When I left in the spring, the university was still standing, thanks partly to our efficiency but mainly owing to the inaccuracy of the German bombers.

During this time, my English had improved, and my arm did recover a little flexibility. Enough to give me hope, but not enough to be declared fit by the Medical Board at the Air Ministry, where I went once a month. Every Medical Officer was sympathetic but politely refused — and not without reason. Until one day when, entering the building that stood in the shadow of Nelson's column, I told myself that if Nelson had been a successful Admiral with a blind eye, there was no reason why I should not be a Spitfire pilot with a stiff elbow. Fate had it that the Medical Officer on that day remembered seeing me before, but this time I was armed with total confidence. I added a bit of smooth talking, to the effect that I was already a half-trained pilot (with my vivid imagination, I almost believed it myself!), and managed to transform his 'What, you again?' into 'Oh well, let's give it a try!' Fit for flying duties! I was at long last graded A1B, medically fit for aircrew — and thanks to the most sporting doctor I ever met, I was in the RAF.

Chapter 3
Royal Air Force College, Cranwell

I was now number 134769, an AC2 pilot under training in blue battledress and a cap with a white band. For a few days, I dreaded being sent to Canada, as it would have meant losing a lot of time before getting my wings, but luck was on my side and I was posted to the Initial Training Wing in Torquay. Our unit occupied a requisitioned three star hotel on the sea front, and from my bedroom window I feasted my eyes on the beautiful sandy beaches of Devon. Sometimes a pair of hit and run Messerschmitt 109s sprayed the town with their guns, dropping their two bombs at random and running for cloud cover even before the air-raid warning sounded. It wasn't really dangerous, but it reminded one that there was a war on.

For us, no flying yet. Plenty of drill, and strict discipline all day long, in order to make it sink into our thick heads that one must obey orders blindly, never speak to a superior unless spoken to, and that smiles must be wiped off our faces while we listened patiently to the utter stupidities falling from the lips of a regular Flight Sergeant with a pock-marked face. The great advantage of all that drill and exhausting P.T. was that it got us into top physical form, yet left one's head totally void of thoughts or even ill-feeling. If the NCOs could be mistaken for Dartmoor prison officers, the instructors were most interesting and succeeded in teaching us such topics as meteorology, mathematics, gunnery, navigation and Morse.

Our course was truly international, with a majority of British and Commonwealth subjects, but with representatives of many occupied countries, amongst whom were about 20 Belgians. We all mixed well together and there was friendly rivalry to be on top at the end of that ten-week course. Although I missed the Sword of Honour by a narrow margin, I was ranked second, with honours in all subjects, as a result of sheer determination to make up for lost time. Another reason for that keenness lay in the fact that another screening would take place at the end of the course, with the highest rankings to be trained in England, the rest going to Canada. The unlucky ones were posted to a transit unit, while I became part of the group scheduled for the Elementary Flying Training School at Stoke Orchard, near Cheltenham in that most lovely part of England, the Cotswolds.

Owing to bad weather, the course ahead of us was delayed in training. This resulted in blocking our posting to Stoke Orchard for many weeks.

During this time we were sent to 609 Squadron stationed at Biggin Hill, the most famous airfield at the time! To be in Biggin Hill in 1941; to see 'Sailor' Malan at a few yards' distance; to crowd the pilots' dispersal where a dozen Belgian pilots had already made their names in Spitfires of the famous 609 West Riding of Yorkshire Squadron — it was just heaven! From U/T pilots one day, we almost felt like operational pilots the next, trying to make ourselves useful, anticipating the slightest desire of our gods, sometimes making ourselves a nuisance by getting in everyone's way, but all the time feeling on top of the world. The day Paul Ritchie allowed me to sit in the cockpit of his Spitfire, and dedicated for me his marvellous book *Fighter Pilots*, I looked upon my colleagues with a certain condescension that earned me envy to say the least.

The squadron was then under the command of Sqn Ldr Michael Robinson, a truly great gentleman. He was later killed as a Wing Commander in South East Asia with his friend and No. 2, Flt Lt Christian Ortmans, also a member of 609 in 1941. His brother-in-law, Paul Ritchie, DFC, was a Flight Commander, and had fought gallantly in France in 1940. Wounded in the last days and hospitalised in the American Hospital in Paris, he had barely escaped capture and fled in civilian clothes to the unoccupied zone of France. Meeting a Belgian Air Force unit there, operating an 'unprepared withdrawal', he was given a uniform that helped him to get back to England safely. This help was later repaid when Paul Ritchie, sitting in a first-class railway carriage in England, met by chance three Belgian pilots who entered his compartment; they said they were hoping to serve in a British fighter squadron. At once Paul said he would fix it for them in his own squadron, which is why Belgians were always welcome in 609, to the point that three of them actually commanded this legendary outfit in 1944. They were Sqn Ldr Manu Geerts, DFC, Sqn Ldr Raymond Lallemant, DFC and Bar, and myself.

For weeks, our urge to fly was sharpened by the presence of our 'aces', by the rushes of scrambles, and by the landings in the twilight with the smell of cordite floating in the air from uncapped machine-guns. We lived in the shadows of our gods, happy if Duke Dumonceau de Bergendael smilingly allowed us to carry his chute to his plane, swallowing every word of Pike Offenberg's combat report, listening to the careful debriefing of François de Spirlet, DFC, and trying to learn something of the art of fighting in the air that was daily demonstrated in front of our hungry eyes. There was the grim humour of Vicky Ortmans, the mad Belgian DFC with more than five kills in a few weeks. He went twice into the drink on the same day and was rescued by the same launch, whose skipper remarked, 'What, again?' Vicky answered with a grin: 'See, if you don't weave, they get you! And even if you weave, they still get you!' Vicky's luck ran out the third time he went in the drink. Wounded, he drifted for two days in his dinghy, to be rescued this time by a German patrol boat and ended the war in a prison camp. It was written that Vicky would meet his fate in the air for, a few years after the war, his pet dog became entangled with the controls, and his small aircraft crashed.

Then there was Roger Malengrau, always neatly dressed, looking impeccable, quietly spoken, who fought this war as if he were there for drinks at a cocktail party. A true gentleman, one could expect him to become the distinguished ambassador that he is today. Neither Pike Offenberg nor François de Spirlet lived through the war. The latter was killed when Sergeant Lallemant's aircraft collided with him on take-off although Lallemant escaped death. Pike Offenberg was also victim of a mid-air collision with a young pilot. Already credited with two victories during the 18-day campaign in Belgium, and with further victories during the Battle of Britain, Pike was a legendary figure in the RAF and an outstanding pilot amongst his peers. Maybe one day he will be recognised as the true hero he was; his example should inspire the generations to come.

I devoured books like *Fighter Pilot* by Paul Ritchie, one of the best books ever written on the subject at the time. And Richard Hillary's *The Last Enemy*, which was probably the most human book ever written about the fate of a gentleman who gave everything for King and country — including his young love so as not to impose the burden of a terribly burned face on a beautiful girl. Soon after, we enjoyed the English version of Saint Exupéry's *Flight to Arras*, a book published in the USA where the famous pilot-writer had sought refuge in 1941. It describes perfectly the feelings of a man who was both a fantastic pioneer in the air and a most gifted writer. Saint Exupéry chose to meet death on a last flight in 1944, maybe to make up for his years away from the fight, maybe because it was, for him, the logical way to go. Maybe, too, it just was not his day. As far as I am concerned, he will always remain the 'Little Prince' and the world has lost one of the greatest human beings that ever lived.

During those weeks of waiting in 609 Squadron, I had the privilege of getting to know Joe Atkinson, DFC, and to serve for a while under him when I later returned to the squadron as an operational pilot. Joe was still there, as if time or danger had no hold on him. Of great refinement, Joe was always even tempered and fought his war with determination, instinctively concealing his bravery behind his natural shyness. No wonder that later, after a distinguished career as a top civil servant, Joe was ennobled by Her Majesty the Queen.

Last but by no means least, there was 'Ziggy the Spy'. As Intelligence Officer, Fg Off Frank Ziegler, a few years older than most of us and formerly a journalist in Fleet Street, had served with the squadron since the 1940 days. Quite naturally, he had become the custodian of the squadron's traditions and, with gifted pen, had recorded the everyday life of the squadron in his daily reports. A close friend of Joe Atkinson and endowed with a keen sense of humour, Ziggy was both trusted friend and confidant to all the pilots. He saw several generations of pilots pass through 609 during the four years he served — with great distinction. He was mentioned in dispatches and, later, deservedly awarded the OBE. Probably more than anyone else, he was responsible for the spirit that animated 609 all through the war. Many years later, he wrote an account of those years which became a best-seller under the title of *The Story of 609 Squadron Under The White Rose of Yorkshire*, published by Macdonald.

Just before our posting to Biggin Hill, the squadron had acquired a mascot in the person of Pilot Officer Billy Goat. Our friend Fg Off Vicky Ortmans was responsible for this recruit. While driving the Belgian 'Barouche' in the small hours of the morning after a beery visit to the Wellington Club in London, he missed a turn in South Bromley and landed, without damage to the car or passengers, in the back garden of the local vicarage. He, full of alcohol, promptly fell in love with a seven-week-old goat, which was rather frightened at the intrusion until Vicky took it in his arms and drove away with it. The vicar calmed down when the Squadron Adjutant offered compensation and a special hut near dispersal to shelter the new pet. He grew rapidly in size and in the affection of all pilots, who fed him with every delicacy available. Domesticated to the point of sharing the pilots' life in dispersal, Billy developed a marked liking for the most unexpected food, such as newspapers, cigarettes, draught beer, and pure oxygen from our oxygen bottles. However, he proved to be very choosy, for he refused the *Daily Mirror*, and also disliked Woodbines, but he learned to open the tap on oxygen bottles and sucked until, with a belly full, he was almost about to take off. Invited to all parties in the Officers' Mess, he sometimes disgraced himself by not holding his beer properly. I remember one evening when, having been promoted to Wing Commander sometime in 1943, he got so tipsy that he went to sleep in the deserted WAAF anteroom. When discovered in the morning, he had been wide awake for sometime, and had played havoc with the WAAF Officers' knitting, magazines and curtains. The damages were recouped through our Mess bills, but Billy got away scot-free. By the end of the war, Billy had followed the squadron to Germany, wearing on his horns the broad ring of an Air Commodore. He finished his life at a special Home that looked after service mascots and was pensioned-off with most of the gongs one could win for distinguished service.

Finally the day came when we moved to Stoke Orchard, and had our first taste of the old Tiger Moth. At long last we were flying. On alternate days we had lectures in the morning and flew in the afternoon; next day, it would be the opposite. In the evenings, we studied or played games, so that time flew by. Only on Saturday nights did we get permission to leave camp, provided we were back before midnight. We did not mind, as our only concern was to qualify for the next school, where we would fly modern aircraft. My instructor, a tall middle-aged Rhodesian, trusted me to go solo after a few hours dual, and I started piling up the hours, hungry to fly and to get experience. So much so that I discovered a way to fly more than the others — by missing the bus taking us back for lunch and then asking my instructor's permission to fly instead of waiting for the 2 o'clock bus to come. As I had made a pile of sandwiches at breakfast, I did not go hungry, and after a few times, my instructor just signed up for my flight with a conniving grin. The result was that by the end of the course I had accumulated over 30 hours more than anybody else and easily got an 'above average' assessment for flying aptitude. For ground subjects I could again get no better than second. Maurice Van Neste came first, as usual.

A few students had been washed out, but I was lucky again. I was not to go abroad, but was selected to go to the RAF College, Cranwell, for the Service Flying Training School. In peacetime, Cranwell was, and is, the RAF Academy, where regular officers are trained. So the few lucky ones selected to enter this Mecca of the Royal Air Force got there with a feeling of achievement and with a sense of dedication akin to that of novices entering a monastery. Inaugurated in 1923, Cranwell bred all the great names in the Royal Air Force.

As one enters the imposing building lying between two adjacent airfields, one is caught by a certain majesty, built from a tradition and *grandeur militaire* that was almost surprising in such a young service. On the walls hang the portraits of the men of the Royal Flying Corps, as the Air Force was known until 1918. Models of all service aircraft reminded us that our fathers fought in Camels, Sopwiths and even French Spads. They might look like toys compared to modern aircraft, but they nourished the dreams of adventure, the hunger for glory in my generation. We felt very proud to belong to an elite, but knew we still had to prove our worth.

Future fighter pilots were trained on the airfield in front of the College, flying Miles Masters, while the quieter bomber chaps were relegated to the airfield at the back, flying sturdy twin-engined Oxfords, and sharing the airfield with the radio trainees on tricky Proctors. As we arrived, another severe weeding-out took place, and a number of pupils from our course left us to go on bombers. Our ranks had been thinned to only a third of our starting strength still on the nominal roll. Again we found ourselves part of an international course, though with a majority of British and Dominion subjects. Then, to our surprise, we were joined by 20 Turkish officers speaking little English and wanting to be fighter pilots. A neutral country at the time, Turkey also sent 25 officers to Germany to train on Messerschmitts, just in case . . .

For the first time, I was flying a modern monoplane, with a retractable undercarriage, and an in-line engine that gave it the looks of a fighter aircraft. It cruised happily at 130 mph, loved aerobatics and forgave quite a few mistakes — except only a flat spin.

In B Flight, my flight commander was Flt Lt Horsley, having his official rest after his first tour of ops. He was my instructor and at once we hit it off. About 28, absolutely charming and a marvellous pilot, he devoted himself to making me a good fighter pilot, giving me the best tuition I could dream of and adding the many personal tricks learned on ops that were not to be found in any flying manual.

On my side, he had a pupil avid to learn, keen to fly and with an urge to prove himself amongst the best — not only in flying but also in ground lectures, and in physical fitness. Tennis did a lot of good to my arm; I ran 100 and 200 yard races; I played centre-forward in the Belgian football team in England. As we played the other Allied nations, this let me travel and meet lots of people. And to get an 'international cap' although, in view of the scarcity of players, it was not difficult to represent one's country. I enjoyed the games and valued the few trophies we won.

So we lived, flew, studied, and played; forgetting easily the harshness of our life and pledging ourselves to fight as soon as possible. The hours were piling up in my logbook, building up my self-confidence. As the course was nearing its end, we moved to a satellite airfield for night flying. This exercise was often interrupted by bad weather, and sometimes by enemy raiders. The Germans seemed to sniff out inexperienced pupils making circuits and bumps in the moonlight and fired short bursts of incendiaries at pilots on the last leg of the landing procedure. I cannot remember anyone being shot down by intruders but it sometimes became quite dicey when the dimly lit grass runway went suddenly black, and we had to fly in circles round a beacon, with no radio on board, waiting for Jerry to leave the area. As I had spent lots of my own time in the Link trainer, I rather enjoyed instrument flying, and it proved useful at such times. This was not the case with the Turkish pilots who, for reasons best known to themselves, created havoc on the circuit as soon as the lights went out. Some of them got lost, either landing wheels-up anywhere straight ahead, or more often just baling out in total panic. Quite a few killed themselves, and soon the Turks were forbidden to fly at night so that at least a few would stay alive to go back to their country.

It was about this time that a gentleman of colour was told by his instructor to fetch a Miles Master from the Repair and Inspection hangar, and taxi it to dispersal. His royal father, a member of the Commonwealth, had decided that his son should be trained as a pilot, and in return had offered to pay for a squadron of Spitfires. Climbing into the cockpit in the crowded hangar, his face lit by a wide grin, he forgot to check the throttle, which was stuck in the wide-open position. Our U/T pilot switched on and started the engine. The immediate result was that he shot out of the hangar like a rocket and took off unstrapped, at right angles to the runway where a number of pupils were taking off or landing. Totally amazed at being airborne without a parachute, and clinging to the control column, he then proceeded to switch off the engine, close his eyes, and wait for things to happen. A few moments later, after missing the controller's caravan by a few feet, he crashed in a potato field nearby. He got out of the wreck, didn't wait for the crash wagon and ran all the way back to dispersal. His face was an ashen-grey colour and, with his eyes rolling in all directions, our good friend was shaking like a leaf. We never again saw this aerial acrobat but we heard that he had been returned to his Royal Daddy as fit to become Commander of his private air force. As the African sky was less crowded than ours, it was a wise decision that removed a standing threat to the RAF.

With the autumn, the long awaited day arrived: we were qualified pilots, and were to get our wings! Somehow, little by little, we had grown into responsible human beings, trusted with a man's job and filled with a new confidence. At long last, the time had come to fly Spitfires, to be an operational pilot, to get in the fight, and prove that we could do the job we had trained for. It was a great moment in my life; but one tinged with sadness, caused by a gap in our instructors' ranks. My Flight Commander, Hugh Horsley, who was also my friend, was loaned for a 1000 bomber raid over the Ruhr, and did not return. Captain of a Wellington, he went to avenge Coventry by giving Cologne a taste of their own medicine. The Red Cross informed his young wife that no one had got out of his crashed aircraft.

The Passing Out Parade took place in front of the College, presided over by an Air Commodore who reviewed the cadets, making them proper pilots as he pinned the wings on their tunics. Once again Maurice Van Neste was top of the course and was awarded the Sword of Honour, with best overall results in ground subjects and 'above average' assessment in flying aptitude. To keep up with tradition I was second also, with another 'above average', but he and I were the only two of our course to become officers. We left Cranwell as Pilot Officers while the others were Sergeants and had to gain their commissions in their squadrons. After the ceremony, I impatiently opened my logbook to read the assessment signed by Group Captain MacPhearson, in charge of training. It said: 'Recommended for fighters'.

With my wings on my chest and the narrow ring around my sleeve, I walked slowly back to my room. It had been a long journey, painful at times, but I had been filled with determination and the kind of will-power that turns a disabled volunteer into a fit pilot, and makes a child into a man.

Before leaving Cranwell to report to the Operational Training Unit in Grangemouth, we were given a welcome 10 days' leave. Most of us went to London, where we spent one night having a celebration party. There were lots of girlfriends, to be forgotten as soon as we left them, and lots of drinks that made for a monumental 'morning after'.

Fortunately, I had a home to go to, and was soon on my way to

Battle, where Sir Harry and Lady Newton welcomed me warmly to Westfield Place and made me feel that I was a son in their home.

Those days spent in the quiet countryside — like all the other leaves I was to enjoy there — made up a wonderful time, with tennis played on a well-cut grass court, shooting pheasants with the gamekeeper, and rowing on the lake. In the dining room Sir Harry sat at the head of the fine Chippendale table, but rationing was strictly observed, although there were farms on the estate. However, it seemed that an exception was made for me, and I felt rather uneasy to see on my plate every day what my hosts didn't eat in a week. But my new family said that it was really quite all right and brushed my scruples aside. Yet tradition was kept alive; even though the family yacht *Ocean Rover* was serving with the Royal Navy and the only car in use for both Home Guard and household was an old Morris Eight, we changed for dinner every evening. Sir Harry produced a marvellous sherry as a starter, a noble 1928 Haut Brion was carefully poured into crystal glasses and he crowned it with a vintage 1923 port, which he had carefully uncorked and added a few drops of brandy annually.

But the war was never far away. Air Marshal Sir Trafford Leigh-Mallory, a friend of the family, reported that Derek Grantham, a Typhoon pilot and brother of Lady Newton, had failed to return. Later, when Jeremy, the heir, fell at Anzio, their terrible grief was contained with the great dignity that only the British can muster in such tragic circumstances. But the sorrow marked the patrician wrinkles on Sir Harry's face, and Lady Newton's eyes glistened sometimes for a few moments. But life went on, and the war still had to be won.

That evening, Sir Harry called me into the library, where he kept the marvellous first editions he had collected for years. Then, in his simple matter-of-fact way, he offered me a fine leather-bound book in which he wrote: 'Your book, my son'. Few words were spoken but, in the dim light of the desk lamp, I knew at once that I was close to the bosom of his family.

My leave was over. A brief goodbye on the platform at Folkestone station and I was on my way north, the clattering wheels of a smoky train carrying me to the OTU in Scotland. Lost in my thoughts, I was caught between the marvellous feeling of belonging to such fine people, and the dreams of what lay before me as a fighter pilot. Every mile on that cold night brought me nearer to my long-awaited Spitfire.

Chapter 4
Spitfire

A language that sings. The men rough as the climate, and the women with skin tanned by the wind from the sea, with clear eyes and a lively gait. A sky overcast, monochrome, over a bare landscape with grass fields almost too green. That was the Scotland I discovered when I reached Grangemouth and the last stage of my training for war.

At the station, a Morris van driven by a cute little WAAF was waiting for me. I was greeted by a lovely smile, an endless flow of words meant as a welcome, and a pair of big blue eyes under curly blonde hair: enough to make one forget for a moment that the Spitfire was top priority for me!

At the airfield, I soon found myself amongst a rather odd lot. The final stage of our training had been entrusted to a bunch of Polish pilots with a glorious past, loaded with well deserved medals and experience, all hardened veterans of the Battle of Britain who had also previously fought in Poland and France. Their names were not easy to pronounce: Brzeski, Nunsche, Lipinski, Machoriak, Chodek . . . Not easy to spell either, and a lot more difficult to follow in the sky! On the ground, one needed a strong constitution to keep up with their ability to down the liquid consumed every night in the local. So, unless we chickened out (and then be likened to schoolgirls) we had to go through a crash course in 'elbow lifting' — quite appropriate in my case — to keep up with our instructors.

What human warmth, what tremendous fighting spirit filled those exiled fierce fighters, always dreaming of killing Krauts at breakfast, bumping Jerries off at lunch time, and mowing down Nazis after dinner. They would have done anything to be back on operations, and soon let us know their feelings on the subject. Escaping to England, the only luggage they carried with them was their gallantry, their immense love of their country, and their hatred of Nazism. Understandably, they failed to express much sympathy for Stalin, who stabbed them in the back.

The Poles lost no time in making it quite clear that we were there to fly; to fly and to kill. The time for theory was over. 'Spitfire? Easy. Just get in the cockpit, and show me what you can do with the aircraft!' Is that all? 'Come on, follow me, get on my tail . . .' God, where is my instructor? I look all over the sky . . . then I hear a deep laugh in my earphones: 'You . . . boom, boom . . . dead!' Yes, I am dead; my instructor is sitting on my tail, and I am a dead duck because I never saw him getting there! 'Do it again! Keep turning, keep climbing, that's better . . .'

After a few days, and a number of times when I felt that I had been 'dead' too often, I realised that combat flying was very different from the niceties of perfect aerobatics, and that it was hard work to keep out of the way, let alone to get your guns to bear. This was the last chance before the real thing, and it had to be learned fast! The orders given in rudimentary English with a strong Polish accent did not make it any easier, but somehow most of us survived those weeks in good spirits. We lost an instructor and his two pupils, who flew in close formation into the side of a hill and were found only six days later. An elderly Belgian Captain spun into the sea and four pilots were washed out before the end of the course.

Finally, despite the many chances taken by our daring instructors, 18 of us managed to qualify with the help of Providence. But, with hindsight, that may have been the secret of our survival; for going through such training makes one both confident and experienced in the shortest possible time.

The last three weeks at OTU were devoted to live firing and we moved to a satellite airfield, Balado Bridge, to join the Air Firing Squadron to learn the rudiments of air gunnery. The time was spent alternating between mock dogfights, using camera guns, and firing with live ammunition at a target towed by a Harvard.

Deflection shooting is a basic principle of air-firing and it hangs on the elements of a complex trigonometric problem. A fighter, fast moving, has several fixed guns which are synchronised to have the bullets converge at a point 400 yards in front. The target is also moving fast. The pilot's job is to assess correctly, in a split second, in his head, all those changing factors as he flies his aircraft so that after he has pressed the trigger his bullets, and the enemy machine, will both reach the same point 400 yards ahead — at the same instant! I had been brought up with a gun in my hand, shooting game since my early teens with my father, and I had spent a lot of time on the clay pigeon range during our training. But I soon discovered that this was a different game altogether. The secret is to estimate the range accurately then coordinate perfectly smooth flying with the 'follow-through' of correct aiming. And the excitement of hitting your prey is replaced by the cold-blooded concentration required to keep the target perfectly positioned.

For the first few days most of us got poor results, then, after hard work, we began to score. By the end of the course five of us were assessed as above average, which seemed to please our very keen instructors. But not the poor target-towing pilots, for whom more than once I felt sorry. Most of them were pilots removed from operational flying, either for lack of keenness or skill, and they were exposed to the biting humour of their comrades on the ground, and to the wild firing of the over-keen trainees in the air. On more than one occasion, if the target was completely missed, the towing aircraft was riddled with bullets, and a rather shaken pilot came home after a narrow escape.

Although I never heard it said, I am convinced that, deep inside, they reckoned it might be safer fighting the Germans!

The tuition was bearing fruit. I had added over 50 hours of Spitfire flying time in my logbook, and I felt that my plane and I were one, that we were going all the way together, and I was totally convinced that the Spitfire was the best fighter in the world — even if the planes we flew were in fact old Spitfire 1s and 2s, survivors of the Battle of Britain with a short life to live.

Then one day towards the end of the course, I was sent up for an altitude test. That meant climbing as high as the plane would go. Far above the beautiful scenery of the Firth of Forth I could see almost the whole of Scotland and a good part of England and the North Sea. At 29,300 feet, my old Spit reached its ceiling. Up 50 feet, then down a hundred, climbing again at full throttle a few feet — to drop at once a few more feet. I wanted to get to 30,000, just to do better than most, but the more I tried, the less my Spit responded: the old warrior was exhausted, done. I refused to torture my kite any longer and dived gently towards home, admiring a dramatic landscape in a peaceful blue sky.

It's a funny feeling, dreaming and enjoying life in a world at war. You are face to face with yourself, trying to reason why you are training to kill when life could be so promisingly wonderful. I was born to love, to live, to learn, to listen and to laugh — not to kill. On the other side, surely people feel like me? Are there people flying planes with the same ecstasy when they discover the beauty of the sky, the prettiness of the earth, the fakery of politicians lying to mankind for their own benefit? And yet, who are ready to kill because there is no other choice?

Better stop daydreaming; this is no time for philosophy. Especially when your windscreen is suddenly splashed with scalding oil and your revs go over the limit! Diagnosis instantly, is: the constant speed unit has gone for a burton! Just like a car without a gear box . . . completely deprived of power, engine useless, the Spit glides gently towards the ground from 3000 feet, not far from the airfield. With the windscreen covered in oil, I can only see sideways and I must soon decide what to do. Either bale out while there is still time, or choose a wheels-up landing if I can make it to the airfield.

I open the cockpit hood and, putting my head out, immediately get my goggles covered in hot oil. Goggles removed and side-slipping. Visibility zero. Losing height fast. Better forget the useless engine and think fast. Decide, you clot! I think I can make it. With a bit of luck, I could even land the old kite wheels down, and save it from being scrapped. Provided it doesn't go up in flames on the runway. I suddenly realise that I love my old kite, I don't want it to die. I want to live and keep the Spit with me, that old friend who has been part of me for weeks after living through so many previous battles. I trust it with my life; I won't jump. I won't land wheels-up and hurt her. I'll try to get the wheels down and land on the runway; it's against standing orders which specify that I should either bale out or land wheels-up. No engine, no flaps, no power for the undercarriage. So, let's pump the wheels down, side-slip and hope for the best — with my eyes clogged in oil that I wipe as best I can. Steady now, nose up, a last line-up with the runway, and wait till the speed drops. A light touch-down, on the wheels, wait a while, then stick hard back, touchdown, and some gentle braking. Slowly, the Spit loses speed as if grateful for being saved, then skids quietly onto the grass and comes to a halt without further damage.

Slowly, painfully, I pull myself from the cockpit, cleaning my stinging eyes as best I can, while the crash wagon speeds along the runway and the firemen stand by. I suddenly realise I didn't call the tower, and have broken all the rules. Too busy, yes; no time for regulations in an emergency. But the rules are clear and I know I am for it. To hell with it! I am alive. My old Spit is saved. Maybe 'they' will understand. If it were to happen again, I would do the same. And probably break my neck. Which would prove that rules are made to be obeyed.

After being taken to the sick bay where the M.O. washed out my eyes and put soothing cream on my face, I had to report to the Wing Commander. I walked slowly to his office, with what could best be described as mixed feelings: proud, yet fearing the wrath of God.

I hadn't even finished saluting, as smartly as I could, before the words lashed into me, exactly as expected: 'Can you tell me, Pilot Officer Demoulin, what the standing orders are in such a situation?'

'To jump or to land wheels-up, sir, if possible.'

'So why didn't you?' The tone was inquiring rather than reproving — unexpected from a Wingco addressing a mere sprog.

'I judged I had a good chance to save the kite, sir. And I rather liked that old Spit, if that's any excuse, sir.'

'And so you nearly broke your stupid neck, is that it?'

It was more a statement than a question, but the words sounded more like a smack than a flogging, so I ventured to state the obvious, that both my lovely face and the Spit were in one piece, and surely that might be taken into account when we are short of aircraft. And, of course, pilots.

'Right! For this one time only, I will overlook this breach of discipline. For your own sake, don't do it again!' Then, after a pause, and almost as an afterthought, he added: 'Not a bad dead-stick landing, really, and we've a Spitfire that will fly again.'

Two days later the course was over. I was fairly confident that my assessment would be good, but my heart beat fast when the Wingco stopped in front of me, handed me my logbook, and just smiled as he said: 'Above average as a fighter pilot' then passed on to the next man. Furtively, I opened the book and discovered on the last page a green endorsement that read: 'Saved his Spitfire under difficult circumstances.' A commendation instead of a punishment, what more could I wish for? Six words do not amount to much, but in this case it taught me a lot — always take a calculated risk when it is worth it, and have the guts to stand up for what you believe in.

I was now a fully qualified fighter pilot. At least, that's what they said. Now I had to live long enough to prove it. Which, as they say, is quite a different kettle of fish.

Our last night in Grangemouth! Tomorrow, we shall get our postings. Where will the wheel of fortune send me to meet my fate, to fight my war, to help liberate my people?

I did not have to wait long to find out. With Maurice Van Neste, I was called to the CO's office and we were told that we would be posted overseas, to a new Belgian Squadron being formed in . . . Sierra Leone! As the roof fell in, he said it was a special request from the flaming Belgian authorities! This of course was the end of everything for both of us, and at once we decided to fight it to the bitter end — never to go to that non-operational area, nor to go to a Belgian Squadron. RAF we were, RAF we would stay! And damn the bloody Belgians in the UK! Enough of this pantomime, what we wanted was 609, and with above average assessments we had a right to express our wish!

Somewhat infuriated, but also rather pleased by our stand, the CO finally promised to send us to 609, ignoring the demand from Belgian HQ but saying that what might finally happen was out of his hands. We had won the day, thanks to the understanding of a very human Commanding Officer, and escaped the humiliation of being posted thousands of miles away from the fighting. Now was the time to celebrate with our wonderful Poles in the craziest night of our young lives . . .

After a first session in the Officers' Mess, we piled in to ancient battered private cars fed with stolen high octane aviation petrol and driven by lunatic instructors at speeds unknown in Scotland, towards pubs that were supposed to have closed hours before. But Scottish hospitality is not a myth, especially if one contributes to it financially, so that doors opened without problem as soon as our Poles gave the password, and we found ourselves thrown into a mad party before we knew where we were. We sat on old oak benches, with smooth Scotch whisky on rough wooden tables. Then my Flight Commander pushed me to a battle-scarred piano and the singing started. Folk songs carried by the winds of the Baltic Sea, filled with the nostalgia of the Polish soul, alternated with Scottish, English and more vulgar French songs till late in the night.

Leaning against the open piano, my pretty little WAAF driver stared absently; it may have been my imagination, but was there at times a tinge of regret in her eyes? Tomorrow, other pilots would take our places — while we would leave to fight a war.

Chapter 5
The Typhoon

Grangemouth and the Firth of Forth disappeared into the grey sky of a Scottish winter as the cold Anson took off for the south. In my breast pocket, I had my official posting: 'P/O C. Demoulin will report to 609 Squadron at Manston, Kent.' I was delighted. Only my friend Maurice Van Neste and I were going straight to an operational squadron. And what a Squadron! The others were posted to a reserve pool from which the different operational squadrons drew to replace their losses. But I was going to fly the famous Typhoon, the latest RAF fighter. I had never even seen a Typhoon, but I supposed that it would not be beyond my capabilities, even if it was reputed at the time to contain a few gremlins. The important thing as far as I was concerned was to be on ops, to fight, to succeed and, hopefully, not to get shot down . . .

As the old Anson droned the many long miles to the south, I found myself dreaming — shooting down a Focke-Wulf, dog-fighting with Messerschmitt 109s and flying over France and Belgium as their liberator. After all, for more than fifteen months I had flown every day to that one end. Now that that was done, Tally-ho, Tally-ho!

A quick refuelling on the way down and we crossed many airfields on our route. England — the whole of the British Isles — had become a gigantic aircraft carrier, and more than 1000 airfields were now in use. Lincolnshire and East Anglia harboured the 'heavies' that flew mostly at night. In the Midlands were the American bombers, Flying Fortress, Liberator, Mitchell and Marauder medium bombers, operating during daylight. The south was the land of the British fighters. We overflew Gravesend, Biggin Hill, and finally landed at Manston, the nearest airfield to occupied Europe.

Not far from Margate, facing Dungeness and right on the sea, Manston was just a field with a few hangars, and a lot of fighter planes spread all over the place. On the left were the twin-engined Whirlwinds of 137 Squadron and to the right, 609's Typhoons. Suitcase in hand, I jumped from the plane and made my way to the dispersal, which looked rather deserted. I stopped to admire PR-K, a seven-ton monster. The famous Typhoon at last! It sat on a wide undercarriage, with its four 20 mm cannon protruding from a wing much thicker than that of the Spitfire. My first impression was of sturdiness, of brutal strength, of terrific power from a huge engine flanked by 12 exhaust stubs.

A mechanic busied himself feeding 20 mm shells into the open gunbay and then screwed down the cover on the wing. He turned his head towards me, pretending to notice me for the first time. 'You the new pilot, sir? My name is Hutchinson, LAC Hutchinson.'

'Hullo, Hutchinson. Yes, I'm the new pilot. Where's the adjutant?'

'First office on the left, sir, next to the CO — but both flights are off duty today. The pilots are in the Officers' Mess at Doon House.'

'Thanks, Hutchinson. I'll report to the adjutant.'

After knocking at the door, I entered an empty office with white wood furniture. Through an open door I saw a non-aircrew Flying Officer busying himself with coloured charts. I introduced myself: 'P/O Demoulin reporting for duty, Sir, posted to 609 Squadron.'

In clipped French and with an amused smile on his lips the answer came back. 'Charles Demoulin? "Windmill Charlie" then? Well, Windmill, I am Frank Ziegler, the Intelligence Officer on 609. Most people call me Ziggy, which I prefer to the more usual "spy". Anyway, welcome! I'll give you a lift to Doon House, the Officers' Mess. It used to be a girls' school.'

A likeable man Ziggy. Getting on for 35, not much hair left, but elegant, with intelligent sparkling eyes and a humorous approach to life. We climbed into his car, a 1939 Opel. 'Do I remember rightly? Weren't you one of those U/T pilots who came to 609 in mid-1941, pending training? So! You succeeded in getting back to the squadron. Well done! It's an honour to be selected for 609 and quite a distinction to belong to this gang. By the way, do you know any of the Belgian pilots who fly with us?'

'Well, a few, yes. But not very well. And as for being posted here, Ziggy, I am the proudest man on earth. I did work hard for it, but it was worth it!'

Doon House was quite a comfortable place — a huge mansion with a lovely garden — its girls' school femininity was now replaced by the usual Officers' Mess club-house atmosphere. A batman took my suitcases and checked my room number with the Mess Secretary, then advised me that tea was served in the anteroom from 4 o'clock and the bar opened at 6 o'clock. Just time to unpack, freshen up and, after a look round, find my way to the bar.

There were a few pilots there and I introduced myself to a three-ring character who looked even younger than me — I soon discovered that I had bumped into my own CO, Squadron Leader Roland Beamont, DFC and Bar, the man who had given the kiss of life to the Typhoon by convincing, at the age of 22, a bunch of doubtful air marshals that the Typhoon was just the aircraft the RAF was waiting for. Next to him was Flt Lt Joe Atkinson, B Flight Commander, then old Ziggy, together with Jean de Selys-Longchamps and Mony Van Lierde, two more Belgians. A few words of welcome, a few questions and the ice was broken. By the look of it, I did not put up a black and was accepted — but on probation, I guessed.

Next morning, I was keen to get to dispersal as soon as possible, so I had an early breakfast. When I got to the dining room, surprise: quite empty, apart from someone seated at the head of the table and hidden behind that day's issue of *The Times*.

My first mistake was not to notice the four big rings on his sleeves. In a cheerful voice, and trying to appear very self-assured, I volunteered a bright 'Good morning, Sir', and sat down a short distance from the reader. It then struck me that four rings meant a Group Captain, and that there couldn't be many of those around here, apart from the Station Commander. A few seconds elapsed. Then the newspaper was slowly lowered, revealing a rather severe face showing astonishment and some annoyance. Two words shot out. 'Is it?' Then, without waiting for my opinion, the reading was resumed and a heavy silence fell. A little late, I remembered that one never addressed a high-ranking officer first, but merely awaited his pleasure. I had the shortest breakfast of my young life, and retreated noiselessly, making myself scarce and wondering if I was often going to 'boob' as a young 'sprog'.

When I finally reached dispersal, after finding the duty office-caravan, I discovered that the pilots of A Flight had already flown several patrols that morning, and I reported to my flight commander. Then I went through the usual procedure on arriving at a new squadron: drawing a Mae West, a parachute that had to be measured and adjusted to my size, a Smith and Wesson .38 revolver, a pair of operational flying boots, plus helmet and goggles. This took most of the morning. Then I had to read the flying instructions, memorise the password of the day and, most important of all, learn by heart the section 'gen'.

I was looking sadly at those Typhoons through the window, but there was no indication that I would be allowed even to get anywhere near one of them. So I waited patiently, introducing myself to each and every pilot as they came along. After lunch, Ziggy cross-examined me on aircraft recognition, a very wise precaution in an area where one fast-flying aircraft could easily be mistaken for another, and friend shot down instead of foe. Finally, Joe Atkinson must have realised that I was at a loss. He explained: 'First day, all new boys must get their bearings. Then you do a sector recce on the old clapped-out Hurricane before you go solo on a Tiffy. Before that, you'll go and see Jackson, the engineering officer, who will give you all the gen about the engine. And then, off you go — OK?'

Right. Off we go to fly that old Hurricane. It looked as if the sector was quiet enough, but I took off with many questions unanswered: What is Dover like from the air? Can I see the French coast today? When shall I fly a Tiffy? And so on. So much so that I found myself airborne almost without realising it. I flew around for an hour getting a grip on the area. It was my first flight in a Hurricane and I found it slower and heavier than the Spitfire, but quite easy to handle.

During that first hour I was really busy: pinpointing the landmarks that would come in useful for getting home in bad weather, memorising the local radio codes, listening to the controller issuing orders to the standing patrols; so busy that time flew very fast. I had to concentrate on my landing which would surely be watched by my flight commander.

All went well and when I returned to dispersal I found the CO himself waiting for me: 'OK, Windmill, so far so good. I hope you realise where you are? In 609, we want only the best and I hope you will make the grade. The Tiffy is the best aircraft there is of its kind, but there are still a few problems to be solved, so have a good look at it, study the Pilot's Notes carefully and tomorrow you can do your first solo. One more thing: Dover balloon barrage is a death trap in low cloud, and we get plenty of that around here. Plenty of 190s nipping in and out along the coast, and the Channel too, so keep your eyes open! Good luck!'

Beamont was not the type to use two words when one would do. I felt that he was more used to firing his guns than making speeches. We were about the same age, but he was already one of our top aces. And it was he, and he alone, who saved the Typhoon at the very moment when the Air Council was about to scrap its production. As a test pilot lent by the RAF to the Hawker factory, he had gone through all the troubles experienced by this monster and had done more than anyone to set them right. On top of that he had asked to be able to prove his point by taking command of 609, one of the first squadrons to be equipped with the Typhoon for operations. So, at the end of 1942, there were only Nos. l, 56, 266 and 609 Squadrons testing the Typhoon in action. 486, 183 and 198 were still being converted to the Tiffy and, like the others, experienced many difficulties in overcoming its faults.

The truth at that time was that the long-awaited fighter, the one planned to replace the Spitfire, was in fact a cruel disappointment for the RAF. Although by far the fastest from ground level to 10,000 feet, the Typhoon lost most of its power at altitude where much of the combat took place. This was an unsurmountable set-back for, even with its supercharger, the huge engine of over 2200 hp could not compensate for the seven tons it had to move about the sky — against a mere 3.5 tons for the Spitfire.

Then there was, at that time, its rather bad habit of losing its ailerons in a steep turn, and, for good measure, the tail rivets would not stand the stress of a power dive. To add to those problems, the Napier 24 cylinder sleeve-valve engine suffered from a mysterious malady and had an average life of about five flying hours before it packed up without warning. It took months to find the remedies and, as far as the engine was concerned, although the cylinder sleeves causing the trouble were changed more often, and even replaced by another kind of steel, the reliability was never up to the standard of Rolls-Royce engines in the Spitfires. No wonder that many pilots asked to be posted back to fight on Spitfires rather than to die accidentally on Typhoons. Quite honestly, the great hopes that had been pinned on the Typhoon melted away when it first went into operational service and proved itself to be totally unsuitable for high altitude combat. But there was nothing else better for dealing with the low-level, hit-and-run raiders, the FW190s. In that role the Typhoon was a wonderful war machine, with its formidable armament of four 20 mm cannon firing at more than 600 rounds per minute and its level top speed of about 410 mph. A new kind of warfare was found for this monster: low-level fighter sweeps, low-level attack, dive bombing and, later, rocket-firing and intruding at deck level.

Last but not least of its vices, the aircraft had to be held hard with full rudder on take-off to counteract the torque and oxygen had to be on at all times because the cockpit filled with exhaust fumes! These may have been minor troubles compared with the others, but nevertheless they required even-tempered pilots to put up with them.

So this was the situation Roland Beamont found (and very well knew) when he took over command of 609 Squadron and tried to prove that the Tiffy was a good aircraft. He was well served not only by his considerable flying skill and his immense faith in the plane he had nursed and christened but also by luck.

His luck was that the Typhoon, and under his leadership, proved very successful against the Fw190 hit-and-run raiders that nipped in and out along the south cost at the end of 1942 and the start of 1943. The Typhoon was the only plane capable of catching them, and 609 practically put a stop to these intrusions by making the penalty too heavy for the Germans to pay. The success had another consequence: it boosted the morale of the pilots, and hastened the solutions to the chronic troubles in the fuselage and engine. So it can be truly said that it was Roland Beamont who saved the Typhoon, at a time when the Air Council was about to stop its production and to remove it from operations. Instead, some 3300 Typhoons were produced during the war and played a great part in the victory, especially when used in 1944 as rocket-firing tank busters in Normandy. It was probably the most versatile plane of the war, for it was used as a low-level fighter, a long-range intruder with extra tanks, a dive bomber with two 250 and later two 500 lb bombs under the wings, a low-level attack aircraft with eight rockets, and an anti-flak shipping hunter. Life in 609 was never dull, and as the war went on, we were entrusted with every possible kind of operation, and, on rare occasions, impossible ones!

So next day I got the green light to fly a Typhoon. It was old PR-K and, as I suspected, a spare aircraft not allotted to a particular pilot, probably because no one fancied it. There is always in a squadron one aircraft that pilots want to avoid, perhaps because it's vicious, or old, or even unlucky.

I was a little afraid of the brute as I stood in front of it. I felt it was something mysterious and dangerous and I longed to master the monster, to break it in, like a thoroughbred horse. I wondered if I would be able to hold it straight on take-off with full rudder.

Settled on the runway, I set the trims and opened the throttle. The aircraft raced across the grass as if impatient to free itself from the earth. Then, suddenly, the nose lifted and pointed high towards the blue sky.

Wheels up, throttle back, revs at 2200 rpm, and a few words on the radio to report that I was airborne.

What a magnificent beast! Free from its chains, my Typhoon cut through the air gracefully, the engine neighing happily and the altimeter climbing rapidly. If there had been no war on, I think I would have gone straight to heaven. The euphoria of space, freedom from worry, a feeling of mastered power. The certainty of destiny accomplished, a fate fulfilled. I had my reward for those years of hard work, victory over a broken elbow and I was enjoying it immensely. There was a moment of total communion, between my Typhoon and me, a wonderful feeling of togetherness. We were one, and only one, thing, tool and craftsman united, depending upon each other and therefore destined to the same end.

I was totally alert, watchful, and handled my fire-bird with much respect, knowing that he would not forgive me if I were careless. I could see the huge balloon barrage around Dover and my eyes darted over the sky and earth, watching out for Jerry stalking a dreaming or over-confident pilot. I skimmed the odd cloud lost in the blue sky, and my thumb gently caressed the gun button. I wanted that moment to last for ever: my dream had come true. The time had come at last to fight, to win and to suffer — but to win at any cost. I wanted to be alive when victory came. I wanted to be there for that great moment, before going back to being just another man in the street.

With the same care that one takes when caressing a woman's skin, with sensuality and gentleness, I pushed the stick slightly forward. Adding a bit of throttle, I left the ether and dived towards Mother Earth.

A turn to the left, straight and level to lose speed, then, on the radio: 'Beauty aircraft to base, joining the circuit. Permission to pancake, over.'

'OK, Beauty aircraft, come in on runway 23. Out.'

With a tinge of regret, I was coming back to earth. A part of me was still lost in that hazy world I had explored for just a short while. The fear of danger, the discovery of the unknown, the voluptuous sensation of conquest belongs only to the select few of whom I am now one. My entry into that special world made me wildly happy.

'Flaps down — get your speed down to 140. Fine pitch — wheels down, trims set, bucket seat up — hood open and start turning in towards the runway.' I talked to myself to bolster my confidence and land this racer in the best possible way, for I was sure that at dispersal a dozen pairs of eyes were watching me with interest.

'A bit of throttle just before touch-down. That's a good boy — easy — now, keep straight, level off and stick gently back.' The ground came up at me at 120 mph. Relax, old man, relax! I touched down with the same soft caress as one kisses a loved face — what a sensation! The aircraft rolled on nicely, jumped lightly over a few grass patches like a horse trotting up after a gallop and showing his pride when one pats his neck. A burst to clear the plugs — off the runway, and I'm back at dispersal. Another short burst before switching off.

Slowly, voluptuously, I opened the cockpit cover wide, removed my helmet, unplugged my radio lead and oxygen tube, unclipped my straps and climbed onto the wing before jumping down to the ground. Then I took off my gloves to feel the metal skin of the fuselage — a caress, as if to promise myself to that monster with whom I was going to share my life. To express my gratitude, my friendship — for better or for worse . . . I did not know then that in fact it was going to be for both.

But I knew that the Typhoon would never deceive me.

Chapter 6
Baptism of Fire

To belong to a top fighter squadron, based on the nearest airfield to Occupied Europe and manned by brilliant individuals belonging to different nationalities melded together in the same craving for victory, is a wonderful inspiration to go beyond one's limitations day after day, and to cultivate the art of staying alive after daily meetings with the grim reaper.

Some flirt openly with death, as if they want to prove that they have their share of courage, but my approach to becoming accustomed to danger is rather different: I try at all times to be methodical, to improve every day the knowledge of my trade, to analyse my best chances of staying alive. My one and only rule is to take any risk when it is necessary, and *none* when it is not. It did not take me long to realise that there are many brilliant pilots, but few old ones; everyday life offers enough risks without adding carelessness or senseless bravado.

So my attitude when I met my baptism of fire was composed of a mixture of a wish to be one of the best, and my personal rule of strict self-discipline. As foreseen, my first meeting with the enemy came by chance and on the spur of the moment. Three days after my first solo on the Typhoon I had managed only four hours on PR-K, in the vicinity of base, when suddenly, at dusk, control ordered the squadron to scramble for an interception of E-boats near Boulogne harbour. There were reports of a small naval battle between a flotilla of British torpedo boats hunting in the Channel and the German E-boats based at Dunkirk and Calais.

The squadron had been released from readiness a little earlier, and only seven or eight pilots were still around in the dispersal. The senior pilot was Fg Off Peter Raw, a tall rugby three-quarter, built like a tower. Peter rapidly gave his order of battle and wrote on the board the names of the pilots to fly with him. In fact, he named all of them except me, for I was not yet 'operational'. As the squadron was far from complete, I had scrounged my way into the team, it being understood that I was 'reserve' or 'spare', and that I could take off only if one of the chosen formation went U/S before take-off.

Everyone ran to his aircraft, the mechanics already starting the engines. Hurrying, we taxied while plugging in radio and securing straps. As we came to the runway and the first Vic took off, I saw that the leader of Blue section had stopped with a burst tyre.

This was my chance. Without hesitation, and keeping the sacrosanct radio silence, I took off and opened the throttle wide to catch up the seven aircraft already airborne. I rapidly joined up with them and positioned myself to the left of the formation, making myself as inconspicuous as possible, fearing I might be sent back to base.

At dusk, low on the water, it was quite a job for me to keep good formation, guess what to do, and also master that almost unknown aircraft in which I was about to fight in anger for the first time. I realised I hadn't a clue about what was going on, and I was far from confident — but there must be a first time for everything. The dice had been thrown, now I must try not to disgrace my instructors!

I was so busy trying to solve all my problems, one of which was the poor visibility — and getting poorer, that I didn't notice at first that our mile-wide formation had veered to the right, cutting in very close to the French coast. Lagging behind, and alone, I turned steeply to catch up with my fast disappearing friends. I did not realise I was in the middle of Boulogne harbour. Under a sky turning slowly to a velvety black I witnessed a grand display. All around me were big black shapes, which I so mistook as to break radio silence and shout 'Red leader, obstruction ahead!'

By a mixture of reflex and stupidity, I thought I was warning my friends that we were entering the balloon barrage! I am sure they are still laughing today. Those big black forms were not balloons but the explosions of 88 mm shells fired point-blank and at sea level by the German gunners. Nobody acknowledged my warning — no surprise at that — and so, fully aware of my stupidity, I swallowed my shame and, followed by the bursts of flak, hastily rejoined the disappearing formation in the coming darkness.

But we flew straight into a marvellous firework display that illuminated the sea all around: we were smack on the E-Boats, who let go at us with everything they had. No time to make a planned attack: within a second the Tiffies were diving, turning, climbing and diving again on their prey, all guns firing and with the radio full of laughs, warnings and chatter.

I followed suit, fired a short two-second burst, missed my target hopelessly and turned away steeply to avoid collision with a Typhoon surging out of nowhere. Then I tried to get my bearings while keeping out of range of this free-for-all. Peter Raw came on the air to sort out the shambles: 'Shut up, for goodness sake, and concentrate on the burning ones!' The radio fell silent, and discipline came back to the excited warbirds.

In a more orthodox way, the Tiffies liquidated the burning boats one after the other. I scarcely had time to join in and let loose with a long, better-aimed burst when the order came over the air for my section to go back to base to leave Peter and his wing men to finish the job.

I managed to join Payne and Blanco in the dim light that was left, and the three of us set course to base where we arrived in complete darkness. Navigation lights on, I was told to land first and stopped in front of dispersal where a crowd of pilots had gathered after being told that we had gone for a show. Soon after the others landed, unscratched. The trip was worth it: on our side, no one hurt or hit; on the other, two E-Boats sunk and two others left ablaze.

The CO was there. So too was Ziggy with his notebook, trying to sort out a more or less coherent combat report from the excited chatter coming from all the pilots. Nobody referred to my hasty intervention and it was purely through the kindness of my friends that my nickname 'Windmill' was not changed on the spot to 'Balloon'. On the contrary; Peter Raw, in front of Roland Beamont and with a grin on his face, said: 'O.K. Charlie, now you know what it's all about! Good show — keep it up!'

Yes Peter, I know what it's about — well, at least I've had my first lesson, but there is still a lot to learn. The day after, my name went up on the board among the fully operational pilots: I had made the grade.

Part Two
The Big Circus

Chapter 7
609 Squadron

Low-level patrols in the Channel. Keeping a close watch on our convoys. Hunting the 190s that sneak along the occupied coast, looking for prey unaware of the rules of the game. Our hunting ground extends from Dungeness to Folkestone, along the deserted beaches of Kent, and we also dash across the Channel — up to Walcheren and down to Gravelines.

At times, we escort medium bombers who cautiously penetrate as far as St. Omer or Amiens. Just short of open provocation, we tickle the Germans in order to judge their reactions, to size up their strength, to test their defences. The time has come to go on to the offensive, after that long period during which we just reacted to their raids. Since the bulk of the German army is engaged in Russia, the initiative has slowly become ours. There is as yet no Second Front in the west. So it's up to the Air Force to keep in contact with the enemy, and it will be up to the RAF and the USAF to wage war against Occupied Europe, right up to the time of the invasion in 1944. The North African campaign has been won at long last and the invasion of Italy will in fact have little bearing on the final issue — the downfall of Germany. The other great battles in progress are the deadly struggle against the U-boats in the Atlantic, with the very life of the British Isles at issue, and of course the Russian front where Hitler is demonstrating the tremendous power of German armour.

As our duty takes us daily across the grey and cold waters of the Channel to hit the enemy in the occupied territories of northern France, Belgium and Holland, we all acknowledge the courage of those sailors who man the convoys to Murmansk in an attempt to take guns, armour and munitions to our Soviet allies. Exposed to all kinds of attacks from U-boats, from naval vessels based in Norway, and to air attacks that last for days on end, those convoys are badly mauled and the survivors have little chance of being rescued from freezing waters where a man cannot live for more than a few minutes. When a ship is torpedoed, the convoy, or what is left of it, sails on: strict orders are that there is to be no stopping to save anyone in the sea, for it would only mean losing another ship in the process and add to the terrible toll. I have the highest respect for those sailors — and my sympathy also goes to the pilots, all volunteers, who fly old Hurricanes carried on a catapult fixed to the cargo decks, launched on a one-way trip when a shadowing Fw200 is detected. After shooting down the intruder, their only salvation — highly unlikely — lies in parachuting into the ocean and hoping to be picked up by an escort vessel. It takes tremendous courage to do such jobs, and their sacrifice should be honoured as the highest mark of human devotion to duty.

For me, in 609, my way of life is most rewarding. For though I get plenty of fighting and a daily dose of danger, I also get the compensations of a comfortable life, with all the amenities, and a taste of civilisation, which we enjoy all the more because our life expectation is short. Such things as a hot bath, a decent meal and a personal car with enough petrol to get about, the opportunity to mix in the friendly ambiance of a pub in the evening, the decor of a night club where on leave we have brief encounters soon to be forgotten — all those 'little things' make up for the risks that we take every day.

When I am given a job, I am happy to fly, keen to fight and I take life as it comes, day by day. I give little value to earthly belongings; friendship and human warmth are more important. The war has taught me the vanity of material wealth — and, so far, I have never heard of a safe following a coffin . . .

We have learned a particular philosophy. We know how to admire a sunset, to appreciate the softness of sunrise, to give without expecting to receive in return, to offer what best there is just for the joy of giving — an art of living that has followed naturally from the harrowing years we have gone through in the early stages of manhood.

It was in the cockpit of my Typhoon — amid the flak, skimming the top of the waves or coming out of the clouds or even in the loneliness of a suddenly empty sky — that my philosophy was born, was added to and developed into a set of rules for living. A living that at the time was based more upon hope than on statistics.

When Roland Beamont left us for bigger things, he gave us a last display of his inimitable flying technique — what he could do with a Typhoon went beyond imagination. For him normal practice when landing was to fly low over the middle of the airfield and then pull an Immelmann turn, that is a half loop followed by a slow roll, during which he got his wheels down and then landed straight ahead with a perfect three-pointer. This was not exactly the way prescribed in the flying manual and, needless to say, not encouraged by those who wrote King's Regulations.

Roland Beamont was replaced as CO of 609 by Squadron Leader Alec Ingle, AFC, a regular peacetime RAF officer, who had distinguished himself in other fields. I suppose that every CO has his hobby-horse, and when getting a command is keen to try out his theories. With Beamont it had been to demonstrate the value of the new aircraft against the Fw190s at low level. For good measure he had added a new sport — train busting. One of his favourite pastimes was to go over on 'rhubarbs' — low-level intruder work done by a single aircraft over occupied territories and to shoot up railway engines. He soon got the whole squadron to volunteer for that performance, with the result that a good part of our spare time outside patrols and escort work was devoted to locomotives. The Germans soon objected to this by putting a flak wagon next to the railway engine — and another at the end of the train. The sport therefore became a deadly one but, undeterred by this, 609 destroyed many dozens of engines in a short period.

Alec Ingle had obviously to invent another sporting demonstration to put his personal mark on the war effort. So we became kings of the flak-ships that infested the Dutch and Belgian coasts. The squadron more or less took the shape of a private enterprise, a kind of limited company with an 'à la carte' service. We enjoyed in the RAF a kind of special status, outside normal fighter activities such as sweeps, patrols in the Channel and escorts to bombers, where we could propose our own targets to HQ and get authority to go on our 'private' war. I never discovered if Alec hated whatever floats on the sea, but he definitely took a sadistic delight in sinking anything to do with the German navy. In so doing, he demonstrated that the Typhoon was not only a fighter, but could also be a fighter-bomber — and an assault aircraft very suitable for ground and sea attacks. For the anti-shipping strikes, the form was to scramble in complete darkness, and fly at deck level to reach the enemy coast at sunrise. Four Typhoons would each carry two 250 lb bombs under the wings and another four would precede them, to rake the vessels with cannon fire, silence the flak, and open the way for the bomb-carrying Tiffies who would, theoretically, sink the defenceless ships.

So, based at Manston, we skimmed the Channel after our prey. With success, I agree. But also at the price of bullet-ridden aircraft, losses and frights that balanced the damage done to the enemy. It was just a suicidal enterprise, and after a few months of this mad pastime, I definitely took a dim view of that kind of mission.

The technique was not very elaborate — I would even call it simplistic. We took off in the dark, flew at low level up to the Dutch coast and systematically searched the area in the early light so as to spot the ships before they reached the safety of a friendly harbour. When a convoy was found, the ball started. But soon the Germans got wise to us and after that we could never catch them unawares. Before the bomb-carrying Typhoons could get at their target the anti-flak section had to silence the defences and they always had their flak-ships at the ready. Against guns of 20, 37 and 40 mm (called Pom-Poms) and a fair number of twin, heavy machine-guns, all firing from deck level to 90 degrees, we just had to go through the wall of flak with all our guns firing and hope for the best. Doing so, most of us got hit, and we were lucky not to lose too many planes and pilots at the game. The part I hated most in that Russian roulette contest was the prospect of ending up in the water . . . It seems silly, but I always felt more at ease over land than sea when offering myself as a target for those pom-poms — but I suppose it had to be done, and we had great faith in our lucky stars. It took some practice to keep cool, take careful aim and try to kill the gunners before they scored a direct hit. It was a must to clean the place up to give our friends a chance to bomb with accuracy. But going into that inferno several times a week did not provoke a wave of enthusiasm amongst the pilots. Although after a month or two we had sunk a dozen ships, and damaged another dozen, we were not really sorry when the decision was taken to stop those nerve-racking attacks. The price we had paid was not heavy, for although many aircraft were hit only two were lost and two more destroyed in forced-landings. The coastal traffic was greatly reduced, but even so, I am not sure that it was worth the risks. The only positive consequence as far as I was concerned is that I enjoyed life even more when it was over.

Maybe I am prejudiced, but it was not always the enemy who was the greatest danger on some occasions. In fact, one dawn, as we were taking off in the dark in formation and with navigation lights on, my own section leader, whose name I choose to forget, swerved to the right, sending me at 150 mph into the barbed wire fence bordering the airfield. Too late to use the brakes and not quite enough room to get airborne, I just had to hope for the best and take-off through the barbed wire. The Typhoon went gracefully on, taking no notice of this obstacle, but when I tried to lock the wheels up, the undercarriage refused to retract fully. With red warning lights on and at reduced speed, I flew low round the circuit for half an hour, keeping radio silence until the boys had reached the Dutch coast. Only then, in the little light that announced the day, I flew slowly past the control tower warning the duty officer of my predicament. The news came back that my wheels were half-locked and that I was trailing about 50 yards of barbed wire fence behind me. Those spikes are not the best thing there is for tyres and I had to decide whether I would crash land wheels-up or try to get the wheels locked down. Eventually, I chose the latter, and, although the red light kept blinking I made as gentle a landing as I could, without trouble. When the Typhoon stopped, it took the whole morning for a team of airman to cut away the thorny tail.

Another clever idea at the time came from higher circles. We were to fly during the full moon period as night fighters, patrolling the Kentish coast to intercept German fighter-bombers — mostly Fw190s that were causing casualties in the nearby towns and cities. The brass-hat who thought that one up should have been promoted for such a bright idea — two Typhoons flying at different heights and patrolling about 70 miles of coastline up and down for one hour before being relieved by another patrol.

So for about a full 10 days a month, we added that night flying joke to our daily missions. Needless to say, we never came close to a Jerry but we were ourselves caught many a time by our own searchlights and had the closest attention from our own ack-ack batteries. Luckily they were rather inaccurate. The more we yelled on the radio that the plane was a Typhoon, the more the mad sods would bash away and we had to dive steeply to escape the lights while the pongo gunners had the time of their lives. Eventually, after losing two or three Typhoons, Fighter Command decided to stop the experiment. We in 609, having proved that we could fly at night and escape the friendly ack-ack, spent the full moon periods of the following months on intruder work over enemy territory.

Life went on, and op followed op — Channel patrol bomber escorts — sweeps — shipping attacks — night rhubarbs: experience grew, and with it came weariness. A few months of exhausting operations mature a man. Almost without noticing it, I found myself in the middle of the seniority board, acquiring more responsibilities and becoming a senior section leader. Younger or newer pilots follow you, trusting your ability, even though you are full of self-doubt and consider yourself as less than perfect.

Come July 1943, and we are to leave Manston for a short period and go to the east coast, to Matlask, in order to operate mainly over Holland. Just before leaving Manston, I made a last night rhubarb over Belgium. Since we went freelance, I chose to patrol the railway network of Ottignies, south of Brussels, and take a look at the nearby airfields of Evère and Beauvechain, used by the Germans for night flying. Secretly, I hoped also to fly to Wavre, my home town, only ten miles distant from those targets. But it was not to be my day, for as soon as I got near the railway station, all hell broke loose and the sky filled with fireworks. Discretion being the better part of valour, I rapidly sought a quieter area — and got lost. By sheer luck, a few minutes later, I saw puffs of white smoke and spotted a goods train moving slowly across country. The engine threw up a torrent of smoke and sparks when I kissed it goodbye and, following a rough course home, I climbed to 10,000 feet, to cross the coast and land at Manston without further trouble.

The day after that almost abortive mission, we flew to Matlask, a lovely little airfield not far from the North Sea. Soon after landing, we were welcomed by a bunch of enthusiastic WAAFs and found that the nearby big estate had a beautiful mansion, the property of Lady Walpole. The Officers' Mess was in an old watermill alongside a small river where trout fishing became Ziggy's main activity. The old mill had been beautifully restored, decorated and furnished with exquisite taste — low ceilings, old oak beams, orange brick walls, and pillars. Some of the bedrooms even had four-poster beds. The place was a haven of peace and a thing of beauty, set in a park where there were hares and pheasants by the hundred. We were in for a good time!

I shared a room with Ziggy at the back of the mill. From the window sill, Ziggy cast his fly and even caught a trout once in a while. For hours on end he would stay there, absent-mindedly sucking a pipe gone cold, choosing the right fly, pulling up the rod, getting the line caught in the branches, but never giving up. As for me, I went shooting in the nearby woods, together with my old friends Mony Van Lierde and Poupa

Jaspis. Lady Walpole was kind enough to lend us two beautiful Purdey 12-bores which helped to keep the mess supplied with game — partridges, hares and pheasants. I wasn't sure that the game season was open, but the good lady gamekeeper closed her eyes on that matter. The Mess Secretary did not open a single tin of bully beef, and we thoroughly enjoyed 'la vie de château'.

But there is an end to all good things. A few days later, we flew again and this time we participated in the rescue of Squadron Leader Charles of 611 Squadron, shot down near the Dutch coast in a choppy sea. All day, with eight aircraft in turn, we kept a constant watch above the unfortunate pilot until at last, the sea having calmed down, a Walrus amphibian came down and picked up our friend before the Germans could get hold of him.

There are lucky days when everything goes right, where the impossible is feasible, where the maddest enterprises succeed. To snatch a pilot from under the very nose of the enemy, with an old slow unarmed aircraft, was a deed that comforted us. We, pilots, knew what it meant to fly above water all the time.

Matlask was a lovely change — even if we had to cross a lot of sea to get to Holland. But such a cushy life was not good — we might get used to it and forget that the war was still far from being over.

Chapter 8
Once Upon a Time

Dark clouds of smoke billow from the fires that eat at the roofs of the small red-brick houses. In the empty streets field kitchens lie next to abandoned, sabotaged guns. In single file on the pavement, harassed men wander, rifles on shoulders, empty looks in their tired eyes, waiting their turn to move to the beach. It is June 1940: Dunkirk is dying from the repeated blows of the Luftwaffe as 300,000 beaten men try to board the ships that reach the pier, load their human cargo, move out and go flat out for England. Here and there, a pall of black smoke marks the end of a ship hit by a dive bomber. Groups of exhausted men fall down at the water's edge or hide in the dunes. Some are mowed down by the machine-gun fire of a low-flying Messerschmitt 109. The Royal Navy, helped by Sunday afternoon sailors with their yachts and fishermen with small fishing boats, are trying to save the bulk of the BEF, while the French soldiers wait with resignation.

Moving through the human tide, a Belgian officer wearing the uniform of the legendary 1st Guide Regiment makes his way to the water's edge where a British major is sorting out the embarkation of his men. A long line of Tommies wades waist deep to board overloaded lifeboats making regular trips at high tide between the coast and the waiting destroyers.

Stopping the Belgian officer with a gesture of his hand, the Major says: 'Sorry, British only. You'll have to stay out of this queue. Those are my orders.' The words are short and sharp, and that lifted arm holds a revolver. The beach commandant takes no joy in seeing that his orders are obeyed, but war and personal feelings do not mix well. As a kind of excuse, he adds: 'Allied troops are to embark at the West pier.'

Baron Jean de Selys-Longchamps looks with tired eyes at the revolver that stands between him and freedom. He has come from the West pier, and he knows that there are no more ships there — only a mass of beaten men, waiting for the end of their nightmare. For four days he has walked, ever since that terrible 28th of May when he refused to lay down his arms; a Selys-Longchamps does not surrender. With a small kit bag on his shoulder and his gun at his waist, he walked, with rage in his heart, towards Dunkirk, among the retreating British units. To serve his King, to fight to the end, and to come back one day to free his country.

So, calmly, and determinedly, Jean de Selys-Longchamps looks straight at his British colleague and walks slowly past him, saying quietly: 'Shoot if you have to! But I've got a war to win.' Then he enters the water beside the orderly Tommies moving as if on manoeuvres, while the astonished Major lowers his arm.

Son of an old noble family, Baron Jean de Selys-Longchamps was 29 when he landed in England. Twenty-nine, and 18 sad days of war that ended in inevitable surrender. But at no time did he accept defeat. A Christian knight of a King who can no longer defend himself, Jean obeys only his own conscience. He must fight and win, and since the days of the cavalry are passed, he will join today's equivalent: the Royal Air Force.

Now, in 1943, he has been for several months a fighter pilot in 609 Squadron, where several of his compatriots and friends — de Hemptinne, de Grunne, de Spirlet, Offenberg — have paid with their lives. Jean has managed a posting to the thick of the fighting, and flying the new Typhoon with which he will distinguish himself.

Desperately keen to revenge the past, and impatient for a present where he can give of his best, Jean sketches for himself a future in which his dreams can be fulfilled. Already he has had victories, shooting down Fw190s over the Channel. But his real dream is to do something extraordinary — an impossible deed. For him, war is a private fight — single combat — and he has no room for compromise.

So one day Jean comes to dispersal with a grin on his face and a light in his eyes. He busies himself at the wall map showing the landmarks of the known German defences on the Belgian coast, then his eyes shift to Brussels, his home town. His finger traces a route, crosses a park, follows a street — then stops dead. 'Yes, there it is.'

'What?' asks a fellow pilot.

'The Gestapo HQ in Brussels!'

He has decided. Alone, he is brewing a crazy plan. He will prepare it with great care, to the last detail, to a split-second schedule — all alone, as fits his character. Through contacts he has personally maintained with Occupied Belgium, with the help of de-briefing escapers arriving in England, with his knowledge of the building where the Gestapo has its HQ in Brussels (in the Avenue Louise, where they torture Belgian resistance fighters) with all this he can now put together the pieces of his jigsaw.

At low level, a plane could get to the building and have several seconds to rake it from cellar to roof top with a long burst of cannon fire. At a rate of 640 shells per minute per gun and flying slowly so as to have a better chance of accuracy, he could fire about 200 shells in that short period.

To succeed, the raid needs three conditions to be met: first, complete secrecy; second, not to be detected on the way in; and finally, to identify the target immediately, for it would be very unhealthy to stooge around after the alarm has been raised. As far as the flying is concerned, there is nothing special to worry about: for months now, 609 pilots have been trained to penetrate the occupied countries at nought feet single-handed.

Authority to carry out the mission is requested by Jean through the usual official channels, but without telling his fellow pilots. Weeks go by with nothing heard. Ziggy, the intelligence officer, who is obviously in on the plan, has personally approached HQ 11 Group to hasten the decision: the brass say nothing; but there is a whiff of disapproval to be discerned in that silence — the staff at HQ does not usually justify its decision, or the lack of it, to pilots on operations. RAF discipline is strict, and pilots of His Gracious Majesty are not encouraged to bypass it.

And yet, this is exactly what Jean does. On the 20th January 1943, around breakfast time, he takes off from Manston for the Ghent area, but instead, after sending his No. 2 back to base, he flies alone to Brussels. His cockpit is filled with small British and Belgian flags, and, to enrage the Germans further, a larger Belgian flag that he intends to drop there.

Thirty minutes later, after faultless navigation at low level, Jean can see his target. He turns around the Boitsfort racecourse, an excellent landmark, and flies down the Avenue des Nations at roof-top level. Only five hundred yards now separate him from the criminals' den.

A little left rudder brings his gun-sight onto the basement. Jean presses the button and fires his cannons as he eases gently back on the stick. The shells slam into the building, climbing up the front, wrecking each floor, smashing windows and bringing death to the men in black uniforms. The whole building fills his sight and Jean pulls sharply back on the stick, barely missing the roof. He takes his leave — but not before scattering the little flags over the city and letting the huge flag descend slowly from the Brussels sky.

Those Germans still alive do their best to hide the damage and to remove the victims quietly. All traffic is stopped in the Avenue Louise. Passers-by and the curious are brutally pushed away. Like a fire, the news spreads through the city and crowds of happy Belgians arrive from everywhere. Soon all Brussels and Belgium itself will feel themselves part of the affront inflicted on the pride of the dreaded Gestapo.

Jean is now on his way back. A long solitary 35 minute trip at low level, then the coast crossed in cloud and, finally, the welcome sight of Manston airfield. Seventy-five minutes of an unforgettable flight, crowned by success! The combat report arrives at HQ at the same time as messages from the Belgian resistance are reaching London, and Flt Lt Baron Jean de Selys-Longchamps, A Flight commander in 609 Squadron, is soon to be decorated with the Distinguished Flying Cross by the Air Marshal Commanding No. 11 Group for his courage.

But at the same time he is demoted from Flt Lt to Flying Officer and posted to No. 3 Squadron — for disobeying orders.

Only later was the whole truth revealed, and the silence of the RAF explained. For amongst the high-ranking Gestapo officers killed in the action against the Gestapo HQ, (some thirty of them) there was a certain Colonel Muller. On his body, in the top right pocket of his uniform, the German Secret Service found the complete list of a resistance network. The Gestapo Colonel was in fact an important British agent.

Many brave Belgians fell into the hands of the Gestapo after that dreadful discovery. And almost all of them died in Nazi concentration camps.

Is it not a sad irony of this war, that such a feat of arms can at one and the same time galvanise a whole nation fighting for its freedom and sacrifice in the process some of its best men?

So, posted to No. 3 Squadron, also equipped with Typhoons, Jean de Selys-Longchamps goes on fighting with the same keenness and probably a little more discipline. On the evening of 15 August 1943, we met again at Manston, from where we were to take off for a night intruder mission. He told me of his life in his new unit: I felt that he missed 609 but he was in top form and confided that he hoped soon to be made a flight commander, as soon as his 'black' was forgotten.

After dinner we walked together to the old station-wagon, 'The Barouche', to drive to dispersal and inspect our respective Typhoons, each loaded with two bombs. It was almost 11 p.m. when we took off one after the other to go for our individual targets. His was in Belgium, mine in Northern France.

The moon gleamed from a clear sky, and the sea was like a mirror; there was no sign of wind, the Channel like a lake. I crossed the occupied coast at Bray-Dunes, as usual. Then I turned right, towards Amiens. Over the deceptively sleepy French countryside, I presumed that the alert had been given to the defences, now just waiting for a chance to catch the intruder in their searchlights.

Flying a Typhoon at night is not for a beginner, especially at low level. On top of piloting, which is not easy at deck level, one has to navigate and try not to get lost. There is no question of using radio at that height, for its range is less than 15 miles. And the searchlight trap is often deadly, for the simple reason that it blinds the pilot, who can easily lose control of his aircraft. Then if one has to take violent evasive action, the instruments such as the giro and the artificial horizon spin crazily, and are useless for many seconds. On top of this, when one fires the guns, the flash momentarily blinds you, creating what we called a 'black hole'. That was why we took the precaution of climbing slightly before we dropped our bombs, especially if they were fused for a delay of only one or two seconds. And that was the opportunity for searchlights and flak to give us a warm welcome.

But on that night calm prevailed all around — strangely — up to the moment when I came smack over an airfield without the slightest warning, and not even knowing exactly where I was. A quick glance around and I saw an open hangar with a few dimmed lights. I made a climbing turn and dived towards it, releasing my bombs. Then I kissed the unknown airfield goodbye, not really interested in seeing the results and exposing myself to the reception committee that would by now be wide awake. As expected, batteries of searchlights skimmed the sky and the flak fired blindly, but I was already miles away. Goodbye, stupid Jerries: I took my leave and made myself scarce, climbing north to reach a patch of cloud. Dead reckoning navigation for a while, then, in the general direction of the coast.

When I was at what I hoped was a safe altitude I noticed a veritable firework display illuminating what I reckoned to be Ostend, far away to my right. It blazed away ferociously and, for a few seconds, I saw a brilliant spot, a prisoner of the searchlights. It must be Jean caught in the lights and I imagined him at eight or nine thousand feet diving at full speed to escape the trap. A few minutes later, as I approached Manston at 2000 feet, I heard a familiar voice in my earphones. It was Jean contacting the control tower: 'Solex aircraft joining the circuit. Permission to pancake, over.'

'O.K., Solex aircraft, you are No. l. Come in, over.'

I slowed down and maintained altitude in order to leave Jean clear to use the standard 1000 feet circuit height and land first. I would contact the tower and ask for landing clearance only when he had touched down.

Then suddenly, about two miles away, there was a huge bright flash not far from the runway.

A horrible premonition came over me and I heard myself yelling into the radio: 'Beauty aircraft to base: an explosion right in front of me. What are your instructions? Over.'

No answer for a while. I heard the controller calling Jean but there was silence. My fear changed to certainty: that explosion could only have been my friend's aircraft hitting the ground. When the tower called me and gave me the O.K. to land, I landed promptly, my heart pumping. I taxied quickly to dispersal, where it was confirmed that it was Jean who had crashed. It was a horrible sight. But, so far, no information about the pilot. Was he safe? Probably impossible at that height, but maybe he just managed to bale out in time?

There was no miracle this time. When the crash crew reached the wreckage they found the broken body in what was left of the cockpit. Death had been instantaneous.

The inquiry was never able to assess with certainty the reason for the crash. The fact that the tail was found some distance away from the fuselage led people to think that it had broken off when the pilot lowered his undercarriage. That was always a nerve-racking moment, for the Typhoon shuddered until the wheels were locked down. Maybe the tailplane had been damaged by flak, or maybe it was just metal fatigue, the old Typhoon disease? It was to remain a mystery; the experts could only guess, never be certain. I thought about the Ostend flak I had witnessed: perhaps Jean was hit without him even being aware of it?

Dawn was breaking over the sleeping airfield as Doc MacKechnie, that Scotsman with a big heart, together with his first-aid team laid Jean's body on a camp bed in Sick Quarters. The blood-spattered uniform made a stark contrast with the white sheet. The room was empty, like a monk's cell. The first rays of a timid sun seemed to caress the peaceful face, and the closed eyes seemed to add serenity to death.

For a long moment I stood beside that still-warm body, trying vainly to understand the secrets of life and of death. But maybe generations to come would recount to their children, in the evening, in front of an open fire, the epic story of a gallant knight: 'Once upon a time. . .'

Chapter 9
One of our Aircraft is Missing

Autumn on the Kent coast had slowly replaced summer with a combination of humid haze and a touch of frost. Perfectly camouflaged at the back of the chalky cliffs behind Folkestone, some cleverly dispersed Nissen huts sheltered a team of radar controllers for the southern approaches. Not far away, tall pylons supported aerials that day and night probed sky and sea in search of any unidentified object. Depending on its altitude, a plane could be detected up to 100 miles away. Only aircraft flying at deck level would escape — they could be detected only at a distance of a few miles.

That Sunday morning, the Mayday wavelength was Trudy's responsibility. 'Mayday' is a code word, a phonetic version of the French 'm'aidez' that means 'help me' and, appropriately, is used to identify (even today) all calls coming from aircraft in distress. Fighter aircraft were then equipped with a VHF (Very High Frequency) radio set with four frequencies, selected by four push-buttons. Button D was permanently tuned to the Mayday frequency. Provided he had sufficient height and could transmit for a minimum of ten seconds, a pilot would be heard by a WAAF at this control radar station. Then, using a goniometer, she would take a bearing on the transmission, which was displayed on a map.

That first approximation gives only the direction and not the range of the transmission. To get an exact pinpoint on the distress signal it needed more than that, so two more radar stations, one located to the east at Dungeness, the other near Tangmere to the west, also received the distress signal at the same time, and each determined the direction of the call as they heard it. It was then a simple problem of geometry, the point where the three direction-lines crossed gave almost exactly the source of the signal. Within seconds the rescue units, both sea and air, were scrambled to patrol the area and recover the ditched aircrew.

Those were Trudy's responsibilities when the pretty 19-year-old reported for duty at 10 a.m. that Sunday morning. For a year she had been training and had finally been entrusted with a high degree of responsibility: a second's inattention, a wrong move, and a human life could be lost.

At Hawkinge the airfield overlooked the sea and 91 Squadron, equipped with the Spitfire IX, shared the station with a special Air Sea Rescue unit under the command of Squadron Leader Wade. An old hand, Wade; he flew with the Royal Flying Corps during the 1914-18 war! But his outstanding airmanship and sheer determination forced the authorities to allow him back on active service again. His special duties were rewarding; he saved lives — fishing pilots out of the drink. With six old 1940 Spitfires, each equipped with a droppable self-inflating dinghy, he maintained a 24-hour guard on the Channel. The routine went like this. As soon as a pinpoint was obtained, the pilot at readiness took off within seconds and followed the courses given by the controller to the ditching or the bale-out. There, normally within the half-hour, he started a square search at low level and, if the pilot was located, dropped the dinghy as near as possible and reported the position to base. The dinghy, double the size of those we carried with our parachute, was equipped with survival rations, a first-aid kit, a 25-yard long rope and a sail.

But flying alone in a virtually obsolete plane, prey to German fighters and not under the protection of the Red Cross, needed great courage and a particular kind of self-denial. Though the daily task was not a spectacular one, it provided a great sense of satisfaction to snatch a missing pilot from the sea.

At Dover, in the inner harbour, a flotilla of high-speed launches was at permanent readiness to go to sea. These were the 'St. Bernards' of the Channel — the Air Sea Rescue unit. Flying the Royal Air Force ensign, these boats were manned by men who would rescue pilots shot down in the sea by day or night. The crew was a Flight Lieutenant in command, his second in command and two airmen. About 50 feet long, the boats were fitted with two big Hispano-Suiza engines of some 1000 hp, and were armed with 20 mm cannon. With a top speed just short of 40 knots, those sea racers went out in all weathers and did not hesitate to go almost to the enemy coast. Often they met with their German equivalents that were hunting for their own pilots — or ours — and it sometimes happened that a battle was fought over the rescue of a crew. In practice, there was a gentleman's agreement allowing each side to rescue their own pilots, particularly if they were within their own waters. But as we strayed nearer and nearer their coastline, that agreement often went by the board.

On Sunday 26 September, on board rescue boat No. 32, the crew was skippered by Lt Tony Grantham, a big bearded fellow. The refuelling had been done and a Morris van had completed the victualling by 11 o'clock. Fresh fruit, prepared food and, as is normal for seamen, a cask of rum had found its way aboard. Every fifteen minutes, Tony switched on his radio for a routine contact with the duty controller and then went back to his thriller whodunnit. Another monotonous Sunday was going by, as empty as the sea that slapped against the hull.

At Lympne, on the airfield, the wind from the Channel gently moved the grass on the runways as the duty riggers made their daily inspection of our Typhoons. With three other pilots, I was at readiness: it was my turn to scramble, if the controller gave the word with Flight Sergeant Martin as No. 2. Not yet seasoned, my Australian friend Martin had been posted-in only two months ago, with barely 25 hours on the

Typhoon, and of those only 15 on ops. But what a man! Over six feet in height, with powerful muscles, a mane like a lion, thick-set features, and his dark eyes shone with malice. This was a man to be wary of; one could sense an air of anger ready to be unleashed. As the local was closed on Sundays, we were just as well spending Sunday on readiness rather than messing about in a deserted Officers' Mess.

Chiefy Hanson brought me the Form 700 to sign. It was a sacred routine; standing orders stipulated that this document, proving that the inspection had been carried out and everything was serviceable, must be signed before take-off. As Martin snored away next to me, I also signed his F700 and then returned to my Sunday paper. A real treat, that Sunday paper! About 60 pages, with interesting articles and a puzzling bridge problem. Martin's favourite paper was the *Daily Mirror*, and I think his choice had more than a little to do with Jane, the cartoon heroine who was usually only half dressed!

'Scramble!'

Hinchcliffe fired the Very pistol and yelled at the same time. The red ball of fire sketched a gentle curve in the sky. Within 30 seconds, we were in our cockpits with our helmets on. Then, with the engine at full bore, we were airborne, wheels up, coarse pitch set and starting to turn towards the sea.

'Hello, Control, Beauty Red One airborne 11.52 hours.'

'O.K. Red One. Investigate bogeys at 0 feet, vector 110 degrees.'

'Roger, Control. Out.'

I dived to sea level, followed by Martin flying on my right, and went at high speed towards the Belgian coast to intercept those unidentified bogeys. How many? Where are they going? I hoped the controller could tell me more as soon as he got the gen — it was up to him to steer me to the target.

The sea was choppy — short waves topped in white. After a little mental arithmetic I reckoned that it would take ten minutes before we could intercept the bogeys, and that meant near the enemy coast. Always providing we had been given the right course and got there in time . . . Just in case, I set the revs at 2400 and opened the throttle slightly. The airspeed rose to 335 mph. At that speed, we feared no one at deck level for we were on average a good 30 mph faster than the Germans — and we had 40 minutes additional endurance, thanks to our auxiliary petrol tanks which we would jettison so as to be lighter in action as soon as we contacted the enemy.

'Hello Control, — Red One. No gen for me?'

The controller volunteered the opinion that the bogeys were heading for Boulogne and gave me a new vector of 130 degrees.

Good God! Only two alternatives: either they were friendly and control should know about it and, more, with their IFF they should have seen identified; or if they didn't squawk they must obviously be bandits.

'Hello, Red Two, keep a sharp look out. Switch on your gunsight, arm your cannons, over.'

'O.K.'

Martin was tense. His answer was sharp, concise, like a whiplash. I sensed that he was strung like a bow, ready for action. With that Aussie, no problem. Even single-handed against ten of them and in spite of only having 25 hours' experience on the Typhoon he would go at it as though on an exercise. In fact, there was a problem: was he too keen and would he mistake haste for courage? Well, we would see, but I was confident. I would rather a fellow like him than someone who would lose me as soon as the ball started.

We were near the coast. Nothing in view — what to do? I turned left, slowly, and flew parallel to the French coast with eyes wide open.

Suddenly, a few miles ahead, I saw a bunch of planes climbing flat out towards France. In that grey sky, and at that distance, it was difficult to decide what they were. They were at 2000 feet, slightly to my left, and we were about to fly underneath them. They hadn't seen us — we were lucky to have seen them first. Nine of them — so the score was to turn and climb hard unobserved, then shoot the odd one down before they reached France. With surprise, we could then dive towards England before they woke up and reacted.

'Red One to control. Nine bogeys climbing towards the coast. Tallyho!' Then, 'Red Two, line astern. Full throttle, and don't fire until we've identified them. Out.'

We dropped our auxiliary tanks and turned left, climbing hard. The Typhoon was jumping like a thoroughbred under the whip. From the corner of my eye, I could see Martin glued to me, while I tried to identify the aircraft. Seen from this angle, and from below, they looked to me like Spitfires. As the gap narrowed we got within firing range: 'Don't shoot, Martin! They look like Spit 9s!'

A stream of oaths issued from my earphones, then 'Not a single one of those bastards ever saw us! We could have shot the sods down without them ever knowing what was happening!'

I was furious.

Time to blaspheme once more before we skidded to left, drawing level with nine Spitfires, quite amazed to find two Typhoons flying in close formation with them, as if coming out of nowhere. To add to their stupidity, the clots were on another frequency, which made a slanging match impossible. Acting like tourists, they hadn't warned control about their trip and they had kept their IFF off. A really good show!

It was about lunch time, it was Sunday, and we had been scrambled after fools who couldn't even fight a war according to standing orders. Someone was going to get a raspberry when I got back.

Speaking of home, it was time to think about that. The comedy was over, but we were flying over the Pas de Calais and for five minutes had been over France instead of intercepting over the sea as planned. There was no question of flying along with jokers we couldn't talk to and didn't know where they were bound for. And, the Typhoon flew like a sponge at the Spitfire's standard altitude, we would soon find ourselves like two lonely orphans if the Spits climbed above 20,000 feet, which was their usual form. At that height, even with the supercharger in, the Typhoon was pretty clumsy. The only manoeuvre it liked then was a 45 degrees dive, when, thanks to its weight and power, speed built up to over 500 mph, but then the controls got stiff, and any harsh manoeuvre to pull out might well result in the tail rivets being scattered about like a boxer's teeth. It was strongly recommended to limit speed to 500 mph, which in any case was fast enough to escape enemy fighters.

After a rude sign to the distinguished gentleman leading the Spitfire herd, we dived away towards Mother Earth and crossed the coast at deck level near Berck-Plage. It wasn't advisable to lurk about as a pair at 10,000 feet, because we would be sitting ducks, and discretion at times can be the better part of valour. To keep us company, the flak boys let go happily, but at our speed it would have taken a lucky shot to score a hit. So we kept on the deck, heading towards Folkestone and home.

About three miles out to sea, my engine cut dead. No warning — just going one second, then dead the next. I transferred to main tanks although my wing tanks were still almost full. I pumped the starter but nothing happened. A quick climb with what was left of my speed. While doing so, an R/T call: 'Red One baling out. Mayday!'

No time for more — oxygen mask disconnected, helmet and earphones discarded, harness undone, jettison the canopy and jump. Five seconds. That's all the time there was to reach 400 feet, where my Tiffy would stall and plunge seaward. It took more than 300 feet for the chute to open — provided the ripcord was pulled at once. In theory one should count slowly up to 3 when jumping, in order to get clear of the tail. Never mind counting! I had barely left my seat before I was pulling hard on that ripcord, hoping for the best . . .

A sharp blow — straps cutting my shoulders and a white silky canopy ballooning above my head. Just time to look down before I hit the sea. To add to my problems the white silk chose to fall over my head. I struggled to reach the surface, drinking a full cup of salt water in doing so, but fighting with the ropes did nothing but drain my meagre strength.

Up to then, everything had happened so fast I had no time to be frightened. Too fast to get rid of that parachute that hid the sky from my view, and pulled me deeper into the sea. Too fast to have time to inflate my life jacket. Finally, heavy with my boots, soaked uniform and parachute, I managed to get my Mae West inflated, which helped me to float, but didn't protect me from the waves that broke in my face. That damned chute was drawing me deeper and deeper, and I couldn't undo the harness.

Theoretically, it was easy: just turn the central knob and hit it with your fist: the straps fall free. But with the harness at belt level, and your body in the water, just try to use your fist: the only result is a little splash and nothing else.

I was freezing, and swallowing salt water. I was so clumsy, and panic was setting in. Calm down. Think. 'Try to get on your back, swim with your legs. Turn the knob, get your thumbs behind and squeeze it with your fingers in front.' One try, then another — thank God, the straps fell apart. The silk floated away slowly. O.K., I could see the sky — and Martin, my No. 2, flying around me. I was sure he had seen me. He must be giving a fix on the R/T. They would be coming to rescue me — just a matter of time. Yes, everything would work out all right.

'Get in your dinghy.'

Ah yes, the dinghy! It was like a cushion, linked to the Mae West by a strap, and I just had to free the folded dinghy from its pack, then inflate it with a CO_2 cartridge.

My right hand found the strap, followed it down once, twice, where the dinghy should be, while I swam with my left arm. But nothing was there — the strap floated with nothing on the end: my dinghy had sunk with my chute!

All at once, I felt a terrible cold in my bones. As if all the winters of the world had met for a rendezvous in my chest. I felt terribly alone; alone with the noise of the sea, the slapping waves, quite alone. A part of me seemed to have gone, and despair added to my weakness.

I knew that my injured arm would not be strong enough to fight the sea. I was too cold. And I began to wonder if my time had come. Already the salt water was burning my eyes, blinding me, and I was coughing — my lungs half full of water.

Suddenly I found myself thinking about many things — or rather, very clear images, some long forgotten, flashed before my eyes, impressed themselves on my wandering mind. Can the stories about a drowning man be true?

Just as I felt that the last of my strength was ebbing away, something else surfaced from what was left of consciousness. An inner voice urged: 'Die if you must, but at least go down fighting!' With renewed fury, with the last vestiges of strength I could muster, I began to swim again. I fought to breathe; I suffered. But I fought.

Martin had been gone for a long time; the sea was empty and the sky a dirty grey. But I was swimming. Swimming madly towards England. To avoid becoming a prisoner. To be warm again. To get away from that hostile coast so close behind me.

I wasn't scared any more. I was beyond fright. I began to tell myself stories. They would come. They would not give me up. 'The English?' Of course, yes, the English. 'They never give up. They never surrender.' So, I just had to keep going. Hold on! Hold on against that bloody sea. Against that f...... cold! Against that dirty wind bludgeoning me. It was a man with a temper fighting now, not a girl crying over herself. 'You *will* hold on; hear me? You *will* hold on, even if you die doing it!'

An hour and a half later — but I had lost track of time, was it an hour, was it a day? — I heard the noise of an engine. Was I dreaming? No, I was sure I heard it — it was a Merlin, a Spitfire engine. Quick, look around. There he is, 100 yards away. He turned — and flew away, only 60 feet above the sea.

He had not seen me.

Was God blind? No, he came back, he *had* seen me! He waggled his wings and, as he passed by, he dropped the dinghy — and the wind blew it away. I hadn't the strength to make a sign, but I could see the pilot giving me the thumbs up.

Let's go. I must swim and find that dinghy full of air and hope. I have to find it at all costs.

Sometimes, perched on the crest of a wave, I could see the yellow dinghy, about a hundred yards away it seemed. Then it disappeared again in the perpetual up and down of the tide. Then I swim, with all that's left of my strength, towards the spot where it disappeared. For a long time I try, then I stop, I look — but it's always just as far as when I last saw it. It must be the current, but I *have* to reach it or I am a goner.

I swim again — then, suddenly, my hands find a floating cord. Saved! I catch it, I pull on the cord and at long last, I reach the dinghy. There it is, a beautiful bright yellow. But upside down.

Ten times, twenty times, I try to turn it the right way up to heave myself on board. Nothing doing; it's too heavy for what remains of my strength. After a while, I have to face the fact that I won't be able to climb on board. But I can pull the cord through the straps on my Mae West, make a knot and use it as a buoy — and wait.

I waited for hours.

I couldn't feel my frozen body, and my mind began to wander. I had to do something. Tossed about like a cork, I held on to my memories, made up stories of fast boats rescuing me, imagined a Walrus amphibian landing nearby and pulling me on board — but I knew that the sea was too rough to allow that. Wishful thinking. But what of it! 'They' will come, I am sure. 'They' will try anything . . . everything . . .

My head got heavier and heavier and my eyes hazy. I swam less and less — I was frozen. All feeling left my arms, legs and hands, as if my whole body was becoming one with the cold of the water.

I thought idly of the coming of darkness — soon now. I managed to switch on the small light hanging on my Mae West, but who could see a glow-worm on the sea? My thinking was no longer clear — my mind was slowing down, sinking into the torpor that had taken hold of me, enveloped me, weighed on me. I just floated like a cork, hanging on to the dinghy. Sleep! I wanted to sleep! 'If you do, you fool, you've had it! You will die from the cold before they can find you. Move, swim, think. Dream of a pint of beer. Think of a girl. But think, for God's sake!'

I dreamed on. The thunder of an engine. A dark low shape approaches on the water. There is a change in the rhythm of the propellers. It comes. It goes. It rattles — then it comes nearer. I imagine things — I can hear voices. 'Can you here me?' Obviously, English is spoken in heaven too. The engines are throttled back, just ticking over, the roar is almost a murmur, as the shapeless mass closes in and pitches about near me.

'Can you swim this way?' It's the Air Sea Rescue boat that is hanging over me, and the man who speaks is real.

I heard, I saw, but my feelings were too strong. I was speechless, unable to react. I waited, as I had for nearly seven hours; and I intended to go on waiting, just in case it turned out to be a mirage. The Queen of Hearts! I should have finessed the Queen, and the slam would have been a laydown . . . Idiot! A bit late to find the solution now. Make a note for the next game. And sleep, sleep for ever.

Two airmen dived in to rescue me. Gently, they pushed me towards the rope ladder hanging on the lee side. No strength left to climb, so one pulled on my Mae West while the other pushed behind. Then I found myself on a bunk soaked by the water that drained from my uniform.

'Sleep, old boy! You'll be O.K. in a jiffy . . .'

It was a bearded man who spoke — I noted that he had kind eyes. Later I learnt that he was the skipper. Right now, I was content just to lie in silence, while they undressed me and massaged my body with the rum that warmed my skin, then penetrated my body.

The engines roared away, the boat hit the water and shook me like an apple tree, but I let myself slide into a sweet euphoria. To me, that spartan cabin looked like the Palace of the Thousand and One Nights. The coxswain was at the wheel, and smiled at me occasionally. My uniform looked like a bundle of wet rags on the floor. A big white woollen pullover, a pair of sailors' trousers, woollen socks and a pair of rubber boots were handed to me. I came back to life. I was thirsty. Let's have that tumbler of rum. Horrible stuff that hits my stomach. I managed to keep down the brew and it warmed me little by little.

The lighting in the cabin was dimmed and I dozed off. Then the radio spoke: 'Mailcoach 32 to base. Pilot rescued and in good shape. ETA 2330 hours. Out.'

'Well done, 32! Reception committee laid on. Out.'

Engines idling, the rescue boat glided on the calm water of the inner harbour. Ropes were thrown to the ground crew. Then silence . . . Earth, the good Mother Earth was waiting for me. I got up, helped by the sailors, and thanked those men who risked their lives to save mine.

Apparently, I had been in a sea of floating mines. But they did not hesitate to go in, to search for me and fish me out. I take off my hat to you, Lt Tony Grantham.

'Think nothing of it, old boy. We enjoyed every moment of it. But next time, just stay with us a little longer!'

'No thank you! Many thanks, but it's not for me. The sea and I will never be on speaking terms again!'

The 'Barouche' is on the quayside, as are the Hillman, the CO's car, Pat Thornton-Brown with half a dozen pilots, and Doc MacKechnie with the soft Scottish brogue.

The party starts. I am whisked away from the hands of the port medical authorities who would like me to go to hospital, but my friends insist that the bar of the Officers' Mess offers better treatment. The CO orders drinks. Martin is there too. Tonight, officers and NCOs are together — all pilots — a big family that almost lost a member.

Doc hands me a huge pint filled with a nondescript liquid. 'Bottoms up, old man,' says he, lifting his beer. I swallow it and, before I get half-way through, hit the deck like a pole-axed ox. Good old Doc has filled my glass with whisky, gin and beer, a lethal mixture that puts me out for 36 hours.

Chapter 10
Fear, my Companion

I woke up next morning with a hangover, but otherwise feeling fine. Life was wonderful — I was hungry, that must be a sign of good health! A bath first, a shave, and my best blue, then off to the mess. In the bar Ziggy and Doc were sipping their beers. I, awaiting my pals, joined them to try a hair of the dog . . .

The 'Spy' told me the full story of my rescue. When I ditched, Martin orbited the spot for 15 minutes but could not see me. He just orbited the oil slick left by my stalwart Typhoon. But he gave them a radio fix before he had to leave, short of fuel. From then on, it was the young and efficent Trudy's job to pass on the exact pinpoint to the Air Sea Rescue units. She was sure that she had got it right, that her calculations were sound, but the fact remained that no dinghy had been seen . . .

Squadron Leader Wade had personally taken on the job of finding me. He was first to take off and start the search, that famous 'square search' at low altitude. Without bothering about the enemy fighters that could arrive at any time, he searched the sea — like looking for a needle in a haystack. An hour went by, but he carried on, nose at deck level like a cocker spaniel. He was determined to find me — and he did, after an hour and a quarter, just as his fuel was running low. Once the dinghy had been dropped he gave another fix to confirm to control my new position, and came back to lead the rescue boat. I had by then drifted some distance, due to a strong current parallel to the French coast. But sailors know all about currents and what the wind can do. On the report made by the Mailcoach 32, the intersecting lines indicated a pinpoint 9 miles off Berck-Plage. Water temperature 45 degrees Fahrenheit. Brrr. Time of rescue 1839 hours. Just a few minutes before darkness.

A medical board: Doc is grinning. 'As strong as a horse, Windmill! No visible damage. Cat A1 as far as I am concerned, but you'd better take a few days' leave. I'll send my report to the boss.'

Pat Thornton-Brown welcomed me with his usual smile. 'Good show, Windmill. Just take your car and clear off on leave. Come back in top form.'

'No, Sir!' No question. It was clear as daylight to me. I had just realised that if I went on leave without flying first, and at once, I would never fly again!

'I feel scared, Sir, yellow!'

It was true. I had the jitters. I explained my feelings as best I could. Either I flew again at once, and overcame my fear, or I would never again dare to venture over water.

Pat listened carefully and thought for a while. He weighed the pros and the cons. Then he spoke on the phone with the Doc. And his face split by a beaming smile: 'O.K., Charlie — I think you are right. Take my own kite and have a go. But don't overdo it if it doesn't go well. Good luck!'

There were only a few people at dispersal. Two pilots took no apparent notice of me, pretending not to see that my face was tense. It's a sixth sense, intuition, that counts at a time like that. They were well aware of my problems. They knew I was laying my future on the line. Hinchcliffe had already kindly fetched a new parachute and adjusted the straps to my size. The fitters were shining the fuselage of the CO's plane as one grooms a thoroughbred. Chiefy Hanson himself fussed around me like a mother-hen and helped me to strap myself in.

'This kite is a beauty, Sir. No problem with this one!'

Good old Chiefy. What human warmth in those few words, meant to give me a boost. What delicacy not to mention my anxiety when it must have been perfectly obvious!

Thumbs up, and the engine started. I taxied towards the take-off point then quickly checked the instruments, did a last cockpit drill and took off towards the sea.

I found myself at 1000 feet — with my tail towards the Channel. Subconsciously, I had turned away, refused to cross the coastline. I was chicken. Big drops of perspiration, of acrid sweat, that smelt like mould. A smell that stuck to me and seemed to fill the cockpit.

Hell! My hands gripped the stick and throttle too strongly. It took all my will-power to turn back towards the sea. I forced myself to fly towards France, ten feet above the water. I was dead scared. I could feel panic setting in, I was sure I was about to give up.

Minutes went by — but I held my course, my mind blank. Ten minutes, then twenty minutes and my view ahead was all the French coast. I turned slowly, without haste, and started on my return journey at cruising speed. I was sweating less, and my heart rate was almost back to normal: I even sang to myself.

There was the airfield. I beat up the dispersal, then made a perfect three-point landing, sure that many pairs of eyes were watching my Typhoon. A few bursts of engine to reach the tarmac, and then switch off. A pat on the stick, then I jumped on to the wing, taking a good look round. Cured — I was cured! Gone, the fear. I knew then that everything would be as before — Thank God.

Every human being, whoever they are, has known fear, but it's too simplistic to talk about fear or an absence of fear. There are different degrees of fear. There is basic fear; anguish, fright, apprehension, and panic-fear too. Panic fear banishes all self-control, and often induces a fatal reaction. But a pilot, apart from being a volunteer, has been through an intensive period of training that familiarises him with fear, and that gives him, as long as he's in good physical shape and his psychology is right, the means to master it relatively easily.

Very early in his career, a pilot experiences danger, and danger brings about a normal (and useful) reaction — apprehension. Danger comes from three main things, difficult meteorological conditions, such as storms, fog, clouds, icing and sleet; mechanical failures — engine trouble, fire, shortage of fuel; finally, human error — lack of experience; over-confidence, blacking out in steep turns, not keeping a good lookout, carelessness; and of course, for good measure, in war time, add the enemy to those factors, flak and fighters.

All those things together produce stress and fatigue — a weariness of the mind and body. The usual external sign of this was called the twitch. For no apparent reason a pilot would develop an uncontrollable tic, an unconscious muscular contraction which was in fact a loss of control. In the RAF it was considered that one hour's flying on operations corresponded in nervous energy to eight hours, physical or intellectual work. In about 50 per cent of the cases, losses on wartime operational sorties were caused by factors other than enemy action.

There is also a lie that should be refuted: it says that pilots were always hitting the bottle! Or worse, that we were pepped up with pills or drugs. It is true that there were a few cases where the odd one drank too much, but then the medical officer would send him for a rest as soon as it was apparent that the man was a bit off balance. But, more often, a sharp warning that he would be removed from his operational squadron was enough to stop any excessive drinking. As far as stimulants were concerned, apart from a few vitamins given when necessary, I never saw any signs of drugs in an RAF squadron. The only ones were sealed in a survival kit that we carried in our Mae Wests. That kit had Horlicks tablets, concentrated food with vitamins, and a few benzedrine tablets (six if I remember rightly) designed to give a quick burst of energy in case of emergency. A morphine shot was also available to help with the pain of a wound. But, as said before, this was a sealed kit used only in an emergency, and being strictly personal and rationed, could not have been used for other purposes. We also had in the kit 2000 francs in French and Belgian currency, and two silk maps to help us to escape if we were shot down over enemy territory.

In 609 Squadron, we often used to go out to the local pub for a few beers. Two or three, never four. When in the mess, we would have one or two drinks during our bridge game, and if there was a party those who were not flying the next morning might get high once in a while, but our mess bills saw to it that things were kept in check. Although our RAF pay wasn't bad, it didn't run to lavish drinking.

Fear as a topic was taboo amongst us. A matter of shyness, I guess, but respect, too — maybe because we had learned to master it. Before an op, waiting for take-off, we were sometimes tense. But as soon as we went into action, everything was different. From the moment we were strapped in the cockpit, when the Very light went up prior to scramble, all our faculties were sharpened — acutely. Combat added to this mental sharpness, quickened our reflexes and left no time for thinking about ourselves.

The pulse rate of pilots was normally around 60 on the ground. In action, it would step up to 80 per minute, and higher for short periods. This rhythm would sometimes be kept up for a long period of tension, and tiredness would be the normal feeling that resulted. We had to be in top physical condition to counteract its effects. Our reactions were honed by experience and long training to respond to emergencies and combat conditions. It was a full-time job for the junior pilots to follow their leaders without losing sight of them, and they were so busy that there was no time for fear. As for the leaders, there were so many additional tasks and responsibilites that they had no room for fear either.

But sometimes, on returning after a particularly hairy operation or if one had been hit by flak (which was quite common in our trade) or if the fighting had been fierce, there was a kind of 'decompression', a slackening in the tension which produced what I would call retrospective fear. It lasted only a short time, but the passage from action to inaction could produce a kind of flash-back of events, that in turn produced delayed fear. It was as if one became conscious of a retrospective perception of danger. In aerial combat, the action is brutal but lasts only a short while; the pilot's mind is totally concentrated on flying, firing, taking avoiding action, and keeping a look-out. However, from 1943, the problem changed. With the production of new weapons, such as the rockets with which our aircraft were fitted, coupled with the fact that the German fighters were withdrawn either to Germany or to the Russian front, the Typhoon became more and more an assault aircraft — a rocket-firing fighter or fighter-bomber that was to be the most useful aircraft of all in Normandy in 1944. Making attacks on flakships, or the V1 doodle-bug launching ramps, or striking at low level enemy airfields, or blasting the German tanks, our specialisation was now against ground targets. We had to press home our attacks through a wall of fire that the flak laid in front of us. Some of our targets needed several attacks, so on a single operation we might dive again and again to destroy the target. The common practice was to fly down on the deck, or in a shallow dive; aim at 600 or 700 yards, then let go at close range, sometimes 250 yards, with cannon and rockets together. Either way, one had to go through that wall of flak on the way in, and then again on the way out. Playing this new game constantly made some pilots 'flak happy' — a phrase that disguised the stress we experienced . . . Diving six or seven thousand feet to ground level through that defensive fire, or flying at deck level for almost a mile towards a target protected by every kind of flak that follows you for another mile on the way out — it is the kind of feeling that a man has in front of a firing squad. Any human going through that experience lives with apprehension. He becomes worn down in proportion to the number of operations he has done.

Most of the old hands on Typhoons had done between a hundred and two hundred ops of that kind. Small wonder that our losses were high — nor is it strange that the survivors showed a strong affection for their Tiffies, the metal monster that soaked up punishment much better, relatively, than any other plane. No one should be surprised when I say we had a lot of respect for the German gunners, who fired at point-blank range and fought gallantly to the last. I know from experience, for I talked to some of them when later I became a prisoner, that they feared us tremendously. We had every reason to be wary of their devastating fire and they knew that we would also go for them with all our might: it was us or them, it was total war — impersonal, savage, primitive, stupid — but fought with absolute commitment on both sides.

Fear is a hard school. It is also a challenge — but one lives daily in the company of fear, when death and life mingle to the point that one returns from one to continue uncertainly in the other, then fear becomes a kind of drug. One feels its withdrawal when things get back to normal. Strange and paradoxical, sometimes, to miss both danger *and* fear . . .

Chapter 11
The Messerschmitt of
Beauvechain

In the autumn of 1943, 609 Squadron was still operating from Manston under the command of Pat Thornton-Brown. Our Squadron Leader had succeeded in tuning up the group: the tool was well honed, a war machine working smoothly. The Typhoon had just about overcome its early problems and the team of 30 pilots had gained wide experience and were as keen as mustard.

As for me, I had passed the 50 operational mission point and I was now a seasoned warrior, with the slightly wider Flying Officer ring on the epaulettes of my battle dress. Alas, my friend Maurice Van Neste, who came to 609 at the same time as I did, was no longer with us. Just a month after joining the squadron he had engine failure at low level, near Dover, and the green waters of the Channel now held both plane and pilot.

Maurice had bad luck. He chose to ditch his Typhoon in the sea rather than to bale out at low level. It is a tough decision, but he was attempting the impossible; the huge radiator hits the sea and the plane flips over at once, giving no chance for the pilot to get out. Although the Typhoon's ailerons were more reliable and the tail unit now seemed to hold together, we were still at the mercy of an engine whose working life was unpredictable.

By day and by night, I had accumulated some 400 flying hours and stored up enough experience to feel confident in my ability as a front line pilot. It was still true to say that, though one was unlikely to live to be old in the RAF anyway, one was inclined to die young in 609. Maybe it was because the squadron was required to carry out such a great diversity of tasks and pilots were required to assimilate the different techniques in a very short time — mostly by trial and error. One of our jobs was to fly standing patrols along the coast and protect convoys in the Channel against low-level attacks from Fw190s. We also did unsuccessful night-fighter work during the full-moon period. Then, in addition to these ops, we spent some months doing anti-flak and anti-shipping strikes along the Dutch and Belgian coasts. That sort of operation was suicidal. The flak-ships were festooned with guns covering every angle of attack, so that striking aircraft had to go through the barrage on the way in and on the way out. The density of fire was murderous, ranging from heavy machine-guns to 20, 37 and 40 mm four-barrel guns. We only had four 20 mm cannon to counter these so our losses were bound to be heavy. Even though we often silenced and even set on fire or sank those vessels sometimes, pleasing our HQ by doing so, I am not sure that the game was worth the price we had to pay. Then there was our escort work, where we became the sheep dogs of our bombers operating at medium range; sometimes we escorted the Flying Fortresses and Liberators as far as the German border on their way to or from Germany. Positioned to the side of and slightly above the big formations, we kept a sharp look-out for enemy fighters and didn't ignore the sun where the danger nearly always came from. So positioned, we could see the ground on a cloudless day and pick out the flashes of the opening shots from the flak. A difficult moment was always when the formation of bombers turned back after releasing their bombs — the Huns seemed to favour that moment for diving out of the sun. I also used to watch the bombs go down when over the occupied countries, hoping that they would hit Germans and miss the poor people living down there . . .

Another kind of op was particularly exciting. The code name was 'Rhubarb' — why on earth, I never discovered. We had to fly alone at deck level for a few hundred miles over enemy-held territory, hopping over roofs, passing under high-tension lines, shooting at railway engines, strafing German transports or attacking any German aircraft caught unawares. This was great sport. Flying at nought feet is thrilling and requires a great deal of expertise, but in fact it is less dangerous than one would think. It catches the enemy by surprise, and makes it difficult for the flak gunners to get their shots in. At about 330 mph the landscape whistles past quickly and allows no margin for error. I must admit that shooting up railway engines was not my favourite cup of tea, for the simple reason that the poor fellow driving it had little chance to jump clear. The Germans added a flak wagon in front and at the end of those goods trains, and even set booby traps by stopping a train next to a concentration of flak, in full view and with smoke billowing to attract an unwary pilot. I learned about these tricks and preferred strafing airfields or stalking the German aircraft flying around them.

On 30 October 1943: I teamed up with Manu Geerts for a 'Rhubarb' over Belgium. 'Old' Manu came to 609 shortly before I did. We were both Flying Officers, with about the same seniority. There the similarity ended. For Manu could have been my father; he had been a Warrant Officer and instructor for many years before the war in the Belgian Air Force, and had several thousand flying hours to his credit. Manu was almost 40 years old when he escaped to England and joined the RAF as an officer. He looked almost like a grandfather when he first joined the squadron and got a rather doubtful reception. But, totally impervious to this, Manu soon put the matter right. On his first solo on the Typhoon, he set the scene: a steep turn on take-off, upside down at low level over the airfield, a slow roll followed by another over the runway, then a series of loops finishing between two hangars where he disappeared in the valley. It wasn't aerobatics, it was a wizard demonstrating his witchcraft. Everyone was outside, watching with amazement this bird-man who, with his deceptive grandfatherly ways, proved himself to be the very best pilot there ever was in Belgium — to this day.

So, today I fly with Manu. Needless to say, I could hardly find a better partner. He knows every church steeple, every railway station and cross-roads in Occupied Belgium, so naturally he will fly as leader and I will be his wingman. We agreed our tactics before take-off. After approaching at sea level we will cross the coast in cloud at 2000 feet by Bray Dunes; then we will dive towards Furnes, visit Wevelghem airfield where Manu was an instructor before the war, fly around his house where his wife still lives, then on to Waterloo and circle the Lion. From then on, I will lead to visit Wavre, my home town, where I shall have a look at my house while Manu keeps watch on my tail. After that, he will resume the lead and we will head for Brusthem airfield. As the German night fighters stationed there make their trial flights every day around lunchtime, we hope to add a few scalps to our belts — and then come home.

Take off at 12.30. Return around 14.00 hours. Perfect weather with a thin layer of cloud at about 2000 feet. Visibility good — temperature fresh, wind light. Our flight plan is filed, and we climb into our aircraft. Usual cockpit drill, oxygen full on, then take off on the dot. R/T silence, so I keep close formation with Manu so as not to lose him when we cross the coast in cloud.

At 12.43 we dive out of cloud at full speed to the deck. It is always a nervous moment when one pops out of cloud. The Jerries have had plenty of time to pinpoint us on their radar; if by bad luck we deviate a little and cross the coast near a flak post, we are sure to have a reception committee. But with Manu, no such problem: he hits the Furnes area as planned and we are now moving fast over open country. Course set for Wevelghem where we arrive in a few minutes. The airfield is empty. Climbing a little, Manu flies around, then beats up his house as if on a training flight, then does it a second time. We are only a mile away from that enemy-held airfield, yet he seems to fly as comfortably at 200 feet as if he were taking a walk on the ground! I cannot help wondering when the Jerries will come and, although I have full confidence in my leader, I expect the bloody Luftwaffe to jump us anytime now.

Another two or three minutes of that game before Manu decides to stop his merry-go-round, waggles his wings and leads towards Waterloo — thank God. I feel better and get ready to lead, thinking of my home, which I will soon see.

Is it thoughtlessness? Is it just sheer stupidity? My radio is set on button B and Manu is on button A, which means that we are on different wavelengths. But we don't realise it because up to now we have observed R/T silence. But it's my fault, and it is to lead to serious trouble later on.

13.06. I can see Waterloo and the big stone Lion. I take the lead and fly towards Wavre. A beat-up over the roof of my house, a sharp turn left and another beat-up a few feet above the roofs, looking down the street. Surprise! I can see my father standing at the front door. My heart jumps: I wish I could signal to him. But everything happens too fast. I can only try another beat-up, hoping to make my father understand that it's me — then I have to go, for the war goes on.

I look around for Manu. Nobody!

Quickly, a call on the radio. 'Manu, where are you?'

No answer.

Then another call, while I fly towards Louvain. 'Manu, I am leaving Wavre — where are you?'

Of course, no answer — but, on my right and climbing slowly at an angle of 30 degrees, there are a dozen Me109s showing their blue-grey bellies and obviously unaware of my presence.

What a piece of luck! Immediately, I veer towards them without another thought than to get myself a brace of these pretty birds. At the same time I realise that I am near Beauvechain, from where they must have taken off. It would be wise to call up Manu, so as to have his support in the messy affair to come. So, at the same time as I open my throttle: 'Manu? Quickly — Beauvechain. Twelve bandits, angels one climbing on 240 degrees. Tallyho!'

No answer from Manu; he cannot hear me, but I still don't realise why. I keep catching up the 109s who are assembling in close formation. I decide calmly on a line astern attack from below. Under them, I shall pull up sharply, aim at the leader and spray my gunfire around the centre Vic. With a little luck, at that range I should hit two or three of them and, taking advantage of the panic that's bound to follow, I will climb into the clouds to go home happily, richer by a few scalps.

Let's go! I am completely at ease. I have but one object: to fire into the pack, steadily, from left to right, not wasting a second but without haste, then profit from the resulting shambles, by leaving before they come after me.

I climb slowly, in order not to overshoot my prey and in order to aim with complete accuracy. Eight hundred yards; not close enough yet. Better to start firing at 400 yards so that my guns are properly trained and every shell will count.

The 109s dance around the red-lit central point of my gunsight, grow bigger and bigger . . . 'Look out behind you, clot!'

Of course! The last check before the attack: you must make sure there is no one behind you, in that dead sector below the tail. Time and time again during training I have been warned that the danger always lies there! I screw my neck around and see with amazement half a dozen furious wasps darting after me, with black smoke pouring from exhausts; a tell-tale sign of their chase at full boost.

I dive down to the deck, throttle right through the gate for full power, and stick to the tree tops; hide myself in a valley, play hide and seek behind a hill top, hoping to shake off my followers. Goodbye my brace of 109s! I have got to shake them off, lose myself in the countryside before the barbarians settle my destiny. Fly fast and straight ahead to put plenty of space between them and me. No use climbing towards the clouds for the simple reason that there are none around.

A few hectic minutes, then I look behind anxiously to find that no one is in sight. Before me, the landscape has changed: a few hills, a large river, a high-tension line under which I fly at top speed: the Meuse river! In my precipitate escape, I have gone far south, and I must turn right towards the west, then north west, if I want to reach base! Still nothing behind. My pulse is just getting back to normal when something shows up in front of me — a Messerschmitt 110, twin-engined fighter. I can't believe my eyes, but yet it's really there! It's flying quietly at 2000 feet, about a mile away and right across my patch. This time I am not going to be had for a sucker. I describe a wide arc to my left, keeping my prey under close observation while I search the sky behind me, to make sure that this time my way is clear. Then I turn right, still at nought feet, and start stalking my target. I am not going to miss my Jerry this time.

As my speed is far superior to the Messerschmitt's, I throttle back slightly and check the dead sector carefully once more. Then suddenly, as I start a gentle climb to close in on the tail of my 110, I see his undercart come down, as he prepares to land. Good God! No more waiting . . . Forgotten now, my carefulness. I must get this one, at all costs.

Flat out again and, closing in rapidly from 660 yards, I spray the target that soon fills my gunsight. At the same time, flak opens up on all sides, and both Messerschmitt and Typhoon are in the middle of the fireworks. I must be in the Florennes circuit, and tracer comes from all sides as I overshoot my slow-moving Jerry. A big kick on the rudder to side slip, just missing the Messerschmitt, then a dive towards the ground, turning in a north-westerly direction. A column of black smoke billows up to the sky, marking the spot where the twin-engined 110 has fallen, burning fiercely.

Everything happened at once, and not exactly as planned. But this is not time for reflection: I got my Hun, I am alone, petrol is low after my wild chase and I must get home. But my engine roars beautifully, I still have plenty of rounds in reserve and a nice layer of white clouds form a protective blanket in front of me.

A big town, Charleroi maybe. I am not sure, but my course home must lie at about 310 degrees. Let's go. Climbing fast, I pull through the clouds and reach sunshine at 2000 feet. Full sun on my left, projecting my shadow on the white carpet a little ahead and to the right. I skim the top of the clouds, ready to hide in them if need be.

And Manu? What happened to him? He must have gone to Brusthem and may also have been lucky enough to shoot something down. I am amazed that I lost him, but it happens often during a fight and there is now nothing to be done about it. The important thing is to cross the coast without further trouble, for they will be waiting for me.

I cannot yet fully appreciate my victory; I am haunted by mixed feelings: a flashback of the recent events, expectations of flak on the way home, fear of possible waiting fighters ahead, solitude in an empty sky — all this makes me feel both happy and a little flat. For it would have been a field day to shoot down a few of the first 109s. With a bit of luck, I could have achieved the dream of any fighter pilot in the world. As it was, within a matter of seconds, and thanks to the other Messerschmitts, I had to run when I was so near to triumph. What a bag of emotions for a single day!

13.50. I must be over the sea by now. Let's go down to see what goes on. Flying on instruments, I dive gently and the Typhoon goes into cloud. The altimeter unwinds slowly: 2000, 1500, 1000, 900 feet — the sea is there, with white foam on the crests of greyish short waves.

The coast is there too. I see Dungeness, and the IFF is switched on while I contact base. It takes a while for the answer to come, then the controller tells me to change to button A. It comes to me in a flash that I have been the whole time on channel B — and I expect that therein lies the reason for Manu's silence! Something tells me that I will, quite rightly, have a strip torn off when I land . . . Well, with a Jerry to bargain with, I may be let off this time . . .

Wheels down, flaps down; I land gently on our grass runway and park my aircraft at dispersal next to Manu's, who has returned before me. He also had a good time, bagging two railway engines and shooting up a bomber on Brusthem airfield. Then he came home, thinking that my radio was unserviceable — a technical hitch that happened sometimes.

But when I tell him that I had been on channel B he looks at me with incredulity, then, fixing me with his mocking eyes for a long moment, lets me have it: . . . 'and to think that such a bloody clot pretends to be a pilot!'

To the list of the squadron kills, Ziggy adds a Messerschmitt 110: it's the 197th Hun destroyed by 609 West Riding Squadron since 1939.

Chapter 12
A Cobblestone in the Wing

Number 609 Squadron now shows its wings at Lympne. Stationed alone on that lovely grass airfield surrounded by little hills, our squadron enjoys a special autonomy, unique in an organisation as structured as the Royal Air Force.

Under the keen leadership of Pat Thornton-Brown our squadron has become a unit entrusted with all kinds of special operations, partly because we are now equipped with long-range tanks giving us an endurance of about $2\frac{1}{2}$ hours, but mostly because we are fully trained to fly at deck level and penetrate deep into enemy-held territory on 'Ranger' missions. The difference between 'Rhubarb' and 'Ranger' is that a Rhubarb was a single-handed low-level operation at medium range while a Ranger was a squadron-strength deep penetration low-level op. These are mostly on special targets, such as an attack on an enemy airfield, catching enemy planes in their own circuit as well as playing havoc with the airfield equipment and personnel. Or, perhaps, a planned attack on a German headquarters such as Rommel's or von Rundstedt's, based on messages from the Resistance to British Intelligence. The joint attack, with Mosquitos, on the prison of Amiens to set free French Resistance fighters is a good example.

But, best of all, we enjoy a rare privilege: we propose our own operations, mostly freelance sweeps deep into France, Holland and Belgium. We can choose our targets and jump an enemy taken completely by surprise. Intelligence reports are studied, and German airfields used by bombers or night fighters become favourite targets for our squadron. We know that Germans always flight test their aircraft in the afternoon, so we try to give them a surprise. Of course, it means flying all the way at 20 or 30 feet, to avoid German radar and ground defences. To reach the target undetected, navigation is most important. Pinpoints fly past at 300 mph and detailed map reading is not recommended when one needs to avoid tree tops and church steeples. Flying low on a five or six hundred mile round trip over unknown hostile territory can be fun, and full of surprises. Such as dodging low-flying birds that sometimes collide with us, making holes in the leading edges of our wings and slowing down the aircraft dangerously — as happened several times when hitting a flock of seagulls. It's a hazardous venture at best, but we all enjoy Rangers, whose code name reminds us of the Royal Canadian Mounted Police.

Today Pat leads nine, in three sections tight around him, to Venlo just past the Belgian frontier on the German-Dutch border. I am in charge of Blue Section, with Flt Sgt Martin as No. 2 and Fg Off Georges

Waselet as No. 3. We cross the coast at St. Idesbald, fly low along the River Escaut to enter Holland at a few feet above ground level. The flat land runs under our wings. A few odd flak bursts pop up but it's nothing to worry about. Crossing the German border, we go round Venlo airfield but there is no activity. The area seems deserted. How is it possible to fly for an hour over enemy territory without meeting an interesting target? For our flying armada of nine Typhoons has a devastating total fire power of about 5000 20 mm shells, fired in less than one minute by 36 cannon.

After jettisoning our empty long-range tanks over open country, we turn round and start our return journey, still maintaining R/T silence. We fly a loose line abreast, with Pat leading slightly ahead. Flying to his left, I cover the port side, with Martin as extreme wingman. Navigation is Pat's business. But mentally I get my bearings every five minutes, just in case we get separated. Foreseeing such an occurrence is a normal precaution, for one never knows what may happen. A quick glance at the compass, a routine look at the watch, then a rapid check on the map lying on my left knee. A factory flies past my left wing. Good God, it's the Philips works near Louvain! I clearly see a German sentry, surprised, shouting over his shoulder as we disappear across the countryside. He does not have time to run before we are gone, following a railway line that leads to the north-west. Just time to think, then we see Brussels dead ahead.

'Beauty leader, here comes Brussels!'

Just in case Pat has missed it (which I doubt) I tell him the obvious as we skim the roofs of the capital. This was not exactly as planned, for it can be very unhealthy to provoke Jerry in a well-defended lair, and I see Pat, his head turned towards me with a grin on his face.

'Quite a big place, isn't it Charlie?'

I am at that very moment at the height of the second floor of the Bon Marché department store, on the Boulevard Botanique. Just by the Palace of Justice there is a fast-moving black spot at roof-top height — a Hun! Martin, on my left, has seen him too. Both of us fly at full boost towards our prey, about 500 yards away. Normal procedure and proper discipline require us to warn our leader first, and ask his permission to go poaching. But, as reflex is faster than thought and keenness is greater than respect, Martin and I have reacted long before the others — to snatch a kill before them, shooting down that Hun obviously unaware of our presence. My wing-man is dangerously near me, and makes no secret of the fact that he has decided to get the Jerry first. He opens fire just as I am quietly aiming at the Messerschmitt flying towards the Altitude Cent. For a moment, I am enraged to see Martin poaching on my ground, but at the same time I remember that he saved my life in the Channel. So I fire a long burst without saying a word, and concentrate on the enemy plane.

My shells or his — most probably both — hit the fuselage squarely.

The Messerschmitt is a ball of fire and crashes beneath us by the Alsemberg road. There is neither time nor space to take avoiding action. I am hemmed in by Martin on my left and the others on my right who are now coming fast to join the party. So at 20 feet, I fly straight through the explosion as the plane crashes into a house. There is a dull thud on my left wing. Hit? Everything seems normal. The instrument panel is O.K. and the Typhoon flies normally. Must have been the shock of the air in the explosion.

In my earphones, I can hear Martin's cries of joy while the others curse their bad luck, then Pat's voice comes over, trying to re-establish some kind of order.

'That's enough boys. Keep a sharp look-out — we're not home yet!'

Agreed boss. Another 35 minutes to fly, with twenty of them over enemy territory, before we see Dover and its white cliffs and then our lair in Lympne. I think of my friend Martin who sticks with me like a twin and whose smile can be seen even under his oxygen mask. It's his first victory. He fired first. It's the most fantastic day in the life of that Australian as courageous as a lion.

Without him, I would be at the bottom of the Channel, for he was responsible for my rescue last month. So? So I have decided: no combat report for me. I will just witness his kill and it will be his, his alone. After all, I owe him that; and anyway, I am sure that he really did score.

Lympne is there, in front of us. We land in close formation, and the ground crews wave at us.

Dispersal; engine off. The pilots gather around the CO, and Ziggy tries to get information. Martin is in the limelight, and everybody fusses around him. I am happy to see his joy, then I sneak under the wing of my Typhoon to remove the film that my camera took automatically when I fired my guns.

My rigger watches me unscrewing the cover of the camera, then calls me to his side. I join him under the left wing and my eye follows his hand to a ten-inch hole. Out comes some earth then a rectangular Belgian cobblestone, grey-blue in colour.

'Look, Sir. Are the Huns throwing stones at you now?'

So that was it! The shock I felt when the Messerschmitt exploded was a Brussels street cobblestone! Just as well it went in the wing. Had it gone into the radiator, I would never have got back.

Several years after the war, at home, I was listening to my wife telling friends that, at the end of 1943, she had been scared to death while returning from school. Waiting at Place Albert for a tram she had seen a German plane crashing two hundred yards away, followed by two British fighters. The empty cannon shells had fallen all around her. Quietly, I looked up my logbook. The date was the same, and the time too. The day of the Brussels cobblestone . . .

Chapter 13
Sink the Musterland!

The death of Pat Thornton-Brown left a big hole in 609. It happened two days before Christmas '43, when with seven other Typhoons he was escorting some B24s over Rouen. As the bombers turned for home over the target, some American Thunderbolts had mistaken the Typhoons for Fw190s.

In spite of signals from the 609 pilots, the Yanks had made several attacks at close range and unopposed, shooting down two Typhoons and damaging a third. This terrible mistake was made by an American squadron newly arrived from the States and on operations for the first time. It was the last too, for the American CO was sent back to the States the next day.

When a CO is killed, the whole squadron family feels like orphans. And when a leader fulfils his task with such physical and moral courage, as Pat did, finding a successor is very difficult. But war goes on, and two days later, a former leader of B Flight, Johnny Wells, returned to the squadron as Commanding Officer. Johnny did what he could to keep our spirits up and cement a team around him. Unfortunately the weather was foul, the Hun was rarely seen and results were meagre.

Stationed once again at Manston, we screen the Friesian islands, the Ostend coast, we even go as far as Antwerp and Liège, but without luck. Hard to believe, but Belgium seems devoid of Germans. On 10 January we try again to provoke the German fighters. After crossing the coast as usual in cloud, we hit the deck and sweep between Ghent and Antwerp. 'Poupa' Jaspis is lagging behind for some reason of his own when we hit a barrage of flak in open country. When we take avoiding action at roof level, Poupa loses sight of us. With the enforced R/T silence, Fg Off Jaspis decides to go it alone.

Regrouped, the remaining seven Typhoons reach Antwerp — where I find in front of me a German patrol-boat, quietly sailing on the River Escaut. A long squirt and the Jerries tumble down on the deck like dummies. Only a four-second burst but more than a hundred shells struck the upper deck and black smoke poured from the funnel. I disappear towards the town. The local flak is alert but rather wild, squirting their balls of fire well away from us. Then we turn slightly right and visit Venlo — without luck — so another turn and Liège comes in sight. At Bierset we are greeted by the usual fireworks but it's not very impressive. And after almost two hours we land back after an uneventful trip.

As we taxi to dispersal, I see with relief that Jaspis' Typhoon is already parked in its bay, so he managed to get home safely after losing us near Ghent. Parachutes on our shoulders, we enter the pilots' hut where Poupa Jaspis is waiting for us, a large smile on his face while he tells Ziggy how he shot down a Junkers 188 near Beauvechain airfield. What's that? Georges got a 188? We can hardly believe it, but the grin on his face tells the tale. Lucky bastard! Then comes the combat report, as told by Jaspis with wild gesticulations and in heavily accented English amid a torrent of laughter.

'I lose the formation near Ghent because I have finger in! Then I say to myself, "Bad Show, Georges!" and I am all alone — I decide to go and see my mama. So I get to my village, Pietrebais. I fly over my house — with a lot of noise. My mother she comes in the street. A Junkers 188 also. He flies in front of me and doesn't see me.'

'Then I leave my mother, I follow the big Jerry and pouff, I shoot — bang — he explodes. I take snap of the Boche, then I take snap of my mother — of my fiancée also, because she lives there with my mother. And the Boche he fries, and I come back quickly to Manston!'

Good old Georges! He has just got the 223rd victory of the squadron and his second personal kill. With his solid common sense, his cunning, matter-of-fact, country way of life, he picks off a Jerry next to his home like a poacher shooting a hare in a cornfield.

This exploit is of course celebrated in the mess, as it should be. The rest of us are maybe a little envious but comradeship is growing stronger every day in our family.

On 20 January, we are invited to a party. In preparation our Typhoons are loaded with eight high-explosive rockets under the wings and we gather round Johnny Wells while 'Spy' Ziggy briefs us: 'Right, boys. A German cargo ship of about 8000 tons, the *Musterland* has evaded our blockade all the way from Japan. She is loaded with rubber that's absolutely vital to the German war industry. The ship sneaks in and out of French harbours along the coast, hoping to reach Germany. So far, she has escaped our attacks all the way from Cherbourg, but last night she was hit and damaged by the long-range guns at Dover on sneaking out of Boulogne harbour. She now lies off Cap Gris Nez, and the Kriegsmarine will do everything it can to get the cargo safely to a nearby port. Some Spitfires from Biggin Hill will act as cover for you, but you are to sink the blighter.'

Scraping together every serviceable aircraft at such short notice, we can put about twelve Typhoons in the air. This means about a hundred rockets to send the blockade runner to the bottom. The very fact that she has escaped being caught on a journey almost half way round the world, and to be so near home only to be stopped rather unluckily by naval coastal guns, proves — if proof is necessary — how in wartime luck can last a long time and then suddenly turn aside.

But we shall need our quota of luck . . . For, by dawn, the Germans will have stacked the cliffs of Cap Gris Nez with hundreds of flak batteries, and the damaged ship lies only about 700 yards from the coast, waiting for a large tug to come and tow it to safety. And for sure, the yellow nosed Fw190s from St. Omer will be standing watch over the area. With our rockets, we will have our hands full and it will be the Spitfire boys' problem to deal with the German fighters. Our escort is already famous and includes the Free French Squadron with René Mouchotte as leader and my friend Pierre Clostermann — a future ace. As for us, our tactics, the only ones possible, will be to fly straight at the ship — and straight into the enemy fire!

Our propellers whine. The Spitfire escort flies low over Manston, exactly on time as we take off. Grey skies, low ceiling, choppy seas — typical January Channel weather. We are flying in two sections of six aircraft, at wave-top height. Course 180 degrees — the Spits are following, slightly to the left, in order to intercept the 190s in a right-hand turn. They have to keep below the low clouds, so the surprise will last only a few seconds. Whoever sees the other first will have the advantage. Then it will be every man for himself — and God for some.

I am in charge of Red section, to the right of Johnny Wells. Polo Cooreman flies as No. 2 and Charles Detal as No. 3. With that team, no problem. They will press their attack home and rockets won't be wasted from a range of 200 yards. But as we pull away there is bound to be a shambles. With such a steep turn after clearing the ship at mast height, and with the cliffs right in front stuffed with guns firing at point-blank range, evasive action by twelve aircraft at 350 mph is not going to be a piece of cake. There will be considerable danger of collision.

I can sense that everyone is concentrating on keeping in tight formation but with a determination to see the job through. The *Musterland* has been sentenced to death. And we are looking forward to the kill.

Suddenly the *Musterland* is there, right ahead, in a light haze. At once, the cliffs light up. Thousands of fireworks are thrown at us above the ship, which also lets loose with everything she's got. It's a barrage with its own cruel and savage beauty. I know these dangerous fireworks well and yet, each time, I cannot stop myself admiring the spectacle, at the same time as I feel a knot in my tummy.

Action! Action drives us into top gear. Push the revs up — throttle right through the gate — then aim calmly, be a professional, until the bull's eye is covering the hull.

Two hundred yards, then a hundred. I manage to take a quick glance to my right: Polo and Charles are there, a few yards away, concentrating on the target. Good God, how close they are — it's like being one of a covey of partridges!

We fire our rockets in a single salvo, fuses set for explosion on impact. I hope the ship won't blow up in our faces. No, loaded with rubber it will sink slowly. Ridiculous to have such thoughts a hundred yards away from the target but one can't help it.

Fire!

The rockets flash away with a whistling noise and we turn steeply away. The sky is full of planes and gunfire. I turn like a dingbat, stick pulled hard in to my belly. The G force pushes me down in my seat. My vision dims a little and my body weighs a ton. As my vision clears I am still in a steep turn about thirty feet above the sea. A quick glance to left and right: Polo and Charlie are there, just as though it were a training exercise — the others are spread ahead of us, and the Spitfires must be around somewhere, but I cannot see them.

A long look behind, no Fw190s on our tails! Good! Course 350 degrees, towards England, ease back the throttle and reform around the leader.

I am sure we hit the *Musterland*. I had a split-second view of the rockets hitting just above the waterline — and the others must have hit it too. I hope the blighter will sink, otherwise we shall have to do it all over again later in the day. It's funny, but I can feel my engine is happy, as though it's sniffing its stable. Maybe it's just in my head — an after-combat reaction — but it is sweet music to my ears. I seem to hear it with my heart, just as I feel that these men around me are of the same blood — belonging to the same clan. A measure of restraint prevents us admitting those bonds; and sometimes even a kind of harshness, a clumsy roughness, comes over our relationship — just like that, just for a moment. But deep inside, we are linked. And God help the odd man who does not integrate for he is left outside the circle and the family rejects him little by little until, one day, he finds himself posted. In 609, it happened very seldom, probably because the pilots who came to the squadron were carefully screened, maybe also because the strong succeed while the weak quickly fail.

Around the fire in the dispersal hut, ready to go back to Gris Nez if the operation was not successful, we sit waiting for Intelligence to give us the results. One hour, then two go by. I am sure we got over a dozen hits, but will it be enough to sink the ruddy ship?

Suddenly the phone rings.

The Controller says that a photo-recce Spitfire has returned with pictures. The pilot's report is definite: the *Musterland* is sinking; three-quarters of the deck is under water, and soon the sea will claim another victim.

Red Indian war cries, a mad roar, slaps on the back — a bunch of college boys after a football match. More! Section tells us that the squadron is released for the rest of the day. Whoopee! Now we are off to meet some English girls!

In Margate, the 'Old Charles' is our favourite pub. The bar is full of our stories, everyone in turn 'shooting a line'.

For these brief encounters, we wear our best blue, for it seems that the whole of England, from 16 to 66, is in uniform. We fraternise with our WAAFs, in blue like us, but we also appreciate WRENs for they seem to fall for our wings, even if the sailors take a dim view. The ATS usually come second in the beauty contests.

When 11 o'clock comes, the time-honoured British tradition closes the pub: the landlord intones the ritual 'Time Gentlemen, please'. But for us, an exception is made: 609 pilots go out by the front door . . . and quickly return by the back door with their latest conquests, while the lights are dimmed by the landlord, our accomplice. The 'Old Charles' always had a soft spot for us, as well as a warm welcome.

Chapter 14
Tourism Round the Eiffel Tower

16 January 1944. News travels fast: we are to go on a special op. Equipped with our long-range tanks, we shall land at Coltishall, an East Anglian airfield, and after refuelling we are to escort, at low level, 24 Beaufighters carrying torpedoes. Target: Heligoland and the German convoys to and from Norway.

A quick glance at the map. Over 600 miles of North Sea, near the enemy coast, all the way at wave height, and at 180 mph, the cruising speed of the Beaufighters. We shall even have to fly with flaps down to maintain that speed.

The op is not exactly popular with us, even if the Wing Commander in charge of the Beaufighters seems pleased to have us as an escort. To us, it looks like sheer stupidity, bordering on collective suicide, and the results are bound to be disappointing. It's a risky business, gratuitously ordered by a desk-bound official, that just goes to show that even in the RAF a mistake can be made from time to time.

A second thing to make one wonder if people are in their right minds is that our own CO seems incapable of convincing the lunatics of the insanity of such an op. This lack of firm disapproval by Johnny Wells is a matter for disquiet, for the consequences could be grave. At best, the Typhoon can fly for 3 hours and 20 minutes with long-range tanks, on condition we use a weak mixture and without using the supercharger at any time. This means we will be sitting birds if attacked, since we shall start a good 120 mph slower than the enemy fighters. Finally, to navigate for 600 miles at sea level over the North Sea really needs a crew with a trained navigator and a type of wireless set that we do not have. If there is a dogfight, planes will be scattered all over the sea, and any Typhoons separated from the Beaufighters may be unable to find their way back to England. Added to all this, the Typhoon has only one engine, and crossing as much sea as that in a single-engined aircraft is no joyride. The possibility of a prolonged bath in salt water at a temperature of 5 degrees centrigrade does not exactly fill us with enthusiasm.

But orders are orders, so we start grim-faced for Coltishall, where we are greeted with an air of commiseration. A charming atmosphere! The Officers' Mess seems totally impersonal. At the briefing, the form remains vague. None of this augurs well and our morale is not at its best.

'We will rendezvous at 11.15 hours over the airfield. Synchronise your watches now. Typhoons take-off at once. One circuit only and set course for Heligoland. Six Tiffies will fly to port of the first 12 Beaufighters, the other six Tiffies behind the second group. Button B on the radio for liaison with the Beaus. Mayday is on Channel D. A Walrus is standing by for air-sea rescue. On no account — repeat, on no account — will the Typhoons strike at shipping. Their task is to protect the Beaufighters from enemy fighters. That's all! Good luck!'

To be on the safe side I tuck a flask of whisky in my flying boot.

We take off on the dot as the Beaufighters fly over the field — like big silly maybugs. With 15 degrees of flap, we hover at a mere 175 mph. The slightest loss of speed and we will stall into the foamy grey sea twenty feet below. Whoever ordered this must be completely round the bend — and whoever allowed it is totally unthinking. Sheer madness that is to last for over three hours!

With my numbers two and three, I cover the rear of the formation. In order to keep a good look-out both ahead and behind, we are twisting our necks all the time. We also avoid as best we can the slipstream of the big boys, praying that no turbulence will flip us over on our backs. And we skid gently from left to right and right to left, zigzagging like sheep-dogs so as not to overtake our flock.

After almost an hour of this game, radio silence is broken by the Beaufighter leader who tells us that we have drifted to port, missing Heligoland, and that we are going to turn back. He then proceeds to make a wide turn to port to go home.

Drama comes suddenly! Two Beaus collide and fall in the sea, before anyone can get out. The tossing waters close over the planes, which sink like stones.

Poor devils! I feel the cold in my bones. The formation flies on, for we can do nothing for them. When we get home after about three hours' flying, we land in formation since we are so short of fuel there is no time for another circuit.

No one seems to have learned the lesson for, two days later, we are to do it all over again — same place and same actors. This time I am to cover the first wave with Polo Cooreman and Henrion, newly commissioned.

At take-off, a new British pilot, Fg Off Grant, has trouble starting his engine and misses the scramble; only eleven of us now to keep watch on the flock.

As we plough along, the weather goes from bad to worse and visibility becomes virtually nil. So, after about an hour, the show is scrubbed and we turn back. Since this time we are not short of fuel, I signal to my wingmen to stay close to me and I increase speed to about 230 mph making gentle turns to keep pace with our boys. This time, the journey back is uneventful.

But again this abortive operation could have ended in catastrophe. Our friend Fg Off Grant, after trying to start his engine for a good five minutes, finally succeeded and took off, trying to catch up with us. Following the given course at high speed, he flew for 15 minutes at sea level and joined a flock of 12 aircraft flying in bad weather on a northerly course. It didn't strike him that their path was across his line of flight rather than parallel to it.

Without any hesitation he proceeded to join the formation, still convinced that he was catching up with us. He discovered with a shock that he was flying alongside a squadron of Messerschmitt 109s adorned with large black crosses. The Germans must have been as surprised as he was but were slow to react, so our Fg Off Prune took his life in his hands. Without taking time to aim, he sprayed the centre flight with his four cannon, creating havoc in the whole wolf-pack. The leader exploded while the No. 2 finished his steep turn by hitting No. 3, both aircraft crashing as a result.

Three Jerries in one single burst! Our friend Grant must have prepared for war with a prayer wheel. But discretion can be the better part of valour in a case like this, so he declined the further honour of measuring himself against the remaining nine and, pushing his throttle through the emergency gate, he flew back to Coltishall like a dingbat to tell his fairy story. It was a happy, though still slightly bewildered, young pilot who was waiting for us on the tarmac when we came home.

After some thought, it was easy to visualise what had happened. The German radars must have detected the big Beaufighter formation and immediately scrambled a Dutch-based fighter squadron to intercept. The Me 109s most probably missed us by only a few minutes and were mistaken by Grant as friendly until he got amongst them. Their course and his happened to cross each other at the very moment the twelfth Typhoon was catching us up.

We may have been happy for Grant, but we were surely not overjoyed at being made fools of on those North Sea expeditions. The only good result from these outings was that the crazy idea was dropped, and so we left East Anglia — without regret — to return to our beloved Manston.

29th January 1944. Another special op for us over Holland: nine Typhoons to sweep the airfields around Eindhoven and Venlo at low level.

The weather as usual is clamped-in at this time of the year, and we meet with no joy: not a sausage to be found; all the German aircraft must be hidden deep in the woods. So we cross the coast in cloud on our way back, escorted by light flak, holding close formation around Flt Lt Smith, who is leading the squadron today. When we come out of cloud above the sea, no one notices that there is a Typhoon missing, Plt Off Henrion, who flew with me as No. 3 two days ago, fails to return. Not a call on the radio, no trace of him anywhere. He was flying arse-end Charlie in another section than mine, and no one saw or heard anything. We go back to patrol the sea, not even knowing where to look for him. So another friend has gone; another name is removed from the blackboard — to be added to the long list of 'Missing — presumed killed.'

Definitely, 1944 has not started well. With the exceptions of Jaspis' lucky shot, the amazing luck of Fg Off Grant at Coltishall, and the *Musterland* sunk in the Channel, I can only record in my logbook: 'A very dull January.'

But sometimes things happen when you least expect it. On 31 January there was nothing to suggest a field day. The weather was as usual cold and damp, with an overcast of loose cloud promising snow. At Manston, we had two Typhoon squadrons:— No. 198, under the command of Johnny Baldwin, ex-609, and of course 609 Squadron, which still had a few veterans left: the CO Johnny Wells, Smithy, Manu Geerts, Charles Detal and myself. Probably to boost morale, Johnny Wells and Johnny Baldwin decided to make a mass Ranger with 12 aircraft, six from each squadron. Our target will be Paris and, more especially, the German airfields around the French capital and to the north. Surely we are bound to shake them up, and surely they should accept battle on their own ground? Such a deep penetration into enemy territory cannot pass unnoticed and a reaction, maybe a massive one at that, is expected.

Seats are scarce for this show and there is a lot of pushing around the blackboard to get a ticket. Only six out of thirty pilots will be selected, which means five names plus the CO.

'I'll take Smithy, Johnny, Windmill Charlie, Starky and Detal. Take-off in twenty minutes. Thank you, gentlemen.'

Johnny Wells never was talkative. He just chose the old hands and he was right; a trip to the Champs Elysées is bound to be no joy ride, and each of us must be able to get back alone.

Leaving the Kent coast at nought feet, around 2 o'clock, with the six other Typhoons of No. 198 tailing us, we stick to the water in order to retain the element of surprise for as long as possible. We are old hands at this trade, which has become our speciality. As usual we will avoid the German flak by flying fast at ground level.

So we are deployed at 100 metre intervals, with Charles Detal on the far left and Starky on my right; the CO and his section are further to my right, while the 198 boys are behind and even further to starboard. Flying on a mile-wide front, we swiftly cross the coast at over 330 mph. The CO leads in silence but every pilot knows his true position within a few miles. Familiar pinpoints such as a cathedral or a railway junction have been listed and learned during the briefing.

Without warning, directly in front, an airfield looms out of the haze. We are at Roye, base for German twin-engined bombers. As I fly along the runway I spray a bunch of ground crew who dive for cover around their dispersal. From the corner of my eye I see Charles Detal dive on a Junkers 88 surrounded by mechanics. The 88 goes up in flames, the undercart collapses at the same time as the mechanics. Not a shot is fired at us. Surprise is total and we are already a long way away. The other Tiffies missed the airfield because they flew to the right of it — and they did not even see it.

Charles Detal cannot resist that kind of entertainment. Instead of following us, he spends his time playing havoc with that airfield, making no less than seven different attacks on different targets. After using up all his ammunition, bagging two more bombers on the ground and destroying the control tower, he then decides to record the damage with the special 35 mm camera fitted to his aircraft. So, amidst some very lively flak, now fully awake, he made another three passes to get perfect pictures of the devastation. There are days when gallantry overlaps lunacy. But Charles was made that way.

During this time, our remaining eleven Typhoons are approaching Paris by the North East. As we fly above the Forest of Compiègne the Eiffel Tower is just visible. Le Bourget airfield is not far off when, flying at tree-top height, we suddenly find ourselves head-on to about 40 Fw190s.

Why there was no collision I shall never know. But the combined speed of more than 600 mph explains why neither they nor we had the time — or the reflexes — to fire our guns. There was no time to waste: I steadied my Typhoon, ready to chase the flock that just flew through our formation.

Full steep turn to the left, throttle wide open and at maximum revs. Stick in the belly — my vision goes hazy for a second but I have time to notice three bluish Fw190s running away. Already I am on the tail of the last one; a quick look behind — all clear. Tallyho! I must have yelled on the R/T. But the gap is narrowing with the last one. At 300 yards, I hold my breath, still pushing my Typhoon to its limit, as the red dot meets the growing fuselage. At 200 yards, no deflection needed, I fire a three-second burst from dead astern. It's slaughter — just like shooting a sitting bird. Must have been a beginner for he never looked back, and if he did, he staked his life on running away, thinking that his salvation lay in escape. His plane disintegrated not far from Johnny Wells who was busying himself with the second Fw190 of the trio I was chasing. I now go for the No. 1. who had fled while his friends met their doom. But I still had him in sight and my Typhoon catches up nicely on him. Even better — he makes a bad mistake in turning to starboard.

I cut the corner, so he decides to fly straight on, but I have gained a lot of ground and I am on his tail at 400 yards. As I have used more than half of my ammo, I decide to get closer and fire only at 100 yards. I don't want to take any chance of missing him.

Seconds go by and I get nearer, yard by yard. Already the wingspan of the 190 is fully spread across the circle of my gunsight: 200 yards range. A little more patience: 150 yards. My aircraft and my body are one. I am a winged hunter, and I aim my rifle at the bird that fills my sights. I want it, it's the only thing I really want at this moment. I am like a God who manipulates thunder; I am Vulcan; I am the executioner of justice, and I take my time in erasing from the earth this bird of prey decorated with black crosses, who brought death and desolation to my country.

Nothing matters but to crush this viper, and I am filled with a terrible strength that makes me act with cool determination.

One hundred yards. Red dot right on his cockpit. Fire! A short burst — my shells hit the left wing and the rudder. The German turns sharply to the left and white trails appear at the wing tips as he tightens his rate of turn. He's on the verge of stalling. I can see his head turned backwards towards me — I am firmly positioned 75 yards behind him and turning inside him!

We are flying in ever-decreasing circles, twenty feet from the ground, near a little wood and over open countryside — playing a deadly cat and mouse game. I just have to wait till he makes a mistake, either stopping his turn or trying to climb away. I know my Typhoon and I know that it will out-turn the Fw190 if he chooses to go on turning.

Second by second, inch by inch, my gunsight creeps along the fuselage, then covers the cockpit, slowly to gain, reach and then move ahead of the engine cowling. I now have enough deflection to be sure that my guns will fully bear — when I aim ahead of him. There it is; steady: a short burst — my aircraft vibrates, my engine is screaming. My limbs are painful and heavy, and I feel the skin of my cheeks pulled downwards.

The engine cowlings of the 190 are ripped away as the fire starts; slowly at first, then with bright reddish flames. I just have time to see his head turned my way and to meet his distant look behind the goggles. How can I forget that look? I am about 40 yards away and I know the end is near. Another effort to tighten rate of turn and I will have him by the throat. One — at most two — more rounds of this deadly merry-go-round and it will be time for the *coup de grâce*. He must not escape, at any cost. I out-turn him easily, my aim is perfect: a long burst to finish. Sparks fly off the cockpit as my shells go into it. The Fw suddenly turns over and, with a last jerk, offers its grey-blue belly to the sky, then crashes to earth and explodes.

It's over. I circle the wreck to film the burning remains, black smoke billowing in the crisp air.

As I aim my camera at it, I see a French farmer with his great horse working in a nearby field. He throws his hat in the air to salute me. I waggle my wings, fly over to him at ground level and return his salute with my gloved hand: I salute at the same time a friend and a vanquished enemy.

The sky is empty. I must return home. But the road is going to be long. How long did the dogfight last? The first kill took me only thirty seconds. But the second? Was it two, or three, or ten minutes? It seemed long, very long, and suddenly I feel tired. Exhausted. After the concentration required for the fight, after the excitement of the duel and the euphoria of victory. I am seized by a strange sensation. For the first time, I have killed a man face to face. I have killed often and many, but it has always been impersonal, mechanical. Because I had to, it was my duty, because it was war, because there was no option. But this time, it's a different thing.

When shooting down the first 190, I thought of nothing else. Or rather, yes; I was already busy thinking of *the other one,* the one that ran away. Then for minutes — with open sights, almost near enough to touch him — I had a fight to the death with a man. Now that he is dead, the notion of enemy disappears, and there remains only the picture of the man I killed. A man I did not know, a man who had chosen to run away. Just like me, he must have a father, a mother, maybe a wife, or a girlfriend . . .

I am flying home. No more shells left. Just my homing-pigeon sense of direction, my petrol, and my speed. I'll have to play it cool to cross 200 miles of hostile land before I reach the relative safety of the Channel. That will require all my attention, my talent, my skill. And yet the satisfaction of those two victories does not erase the image of the man who saw death coming. I think I never hated war as much as at that moment.

Suddenly, I see a plane to my left, still far away. Gosh, a Typhoon! I quickly join him and recognise PR-O — It's my No. 2 Starky, and he is alone too. 'Hello, Starky. This is Charlie. Coming in from your right. Over.'

'O.K. Charlie. Welcome!'

The tone is matter of fact, as if I were visiting him of an afternoon — British humour, as usual.

'Did you have any luck, Pinky?'

'None at all, old boy. But I heard all about you, you lucky sod!'

I did not realise that I had talked so much during the fighting — unconsciously, I suppose.

We fly in loose formation, and suddenly come across a railway line with a stationary train. The convoy is a decoy, full of flak and obviously aware of our coming. As they let go at us with all their guns, I see the name of the station painted in white letters: Forges. My head seems to shrink into my shoulders for my own cannon are mute and I can only hope for the best while I fly through the fireworks. Pinky lets them have it but concentrating on his firing, does not see a large pine tree and hits it squarely. The pine tree is cut cleanly in two; the Typhoon flies on, but its speed is barely enough to keep it in the air.

'Charlie, I just hit a tree. My engine is rough and the propeller is bent. Could you have a look?'

The flak missed both of us, but his plane is in bad shape. As I fly in close formation with him to inspect the damage, I can hardly keep level with him. Our airspeed is around 150 mph. But it flies, and I concentrate on sizing up the visible damage.

It's not a pretty sight. The propeller hub is missing, and a 20 mm cannon is bent like a matchstick. One of the blades of the prop is turning at a kind of funny angle, obviously badly bent. And part of the trunk of the tree is stuck squarely in the radiator. Not much chance to get back to England with a cooling system damaged like that. And at that crawling speed it will take us an hour at least to get home — if we ever do — and with no shells left to fight our way out. But so far, Pinky is still airborne:

'Hello Pinky, not the prettiest sight there is! But at least it's flying, and if the temperature doesn't climb you've got a chance.'

'Temperature's O.K., Charlie, but the engine is growling like a skunk caught in a trap.'

'Don't worry, Pinky, I'll stay with you.' Flying alongside should give him a crumb of comfort. After all, if his kite packs up, he will have to force-land straight ahead, for he is too low to jump. The only chance is just to keep straight on; with the kind of luck that allows pilots to get home on a wing and a prayer, we should arrive at Manston only a little more than 40 minutes after the others have landed.

All the way across the sea, I keep talking to base on the R/T, telling them about Pinky, about the battle, about my two kills, so that Sector can get a good pinpoint if Pinky has to ditch. But not only does he succeed in making Manston but also manages to drop his wheels and land all in one piece. The people on the ground can't believe it when they see the Typhoon: on all sides, disbelieving aircrew admire the plucky PR-O standing firmly on its legs, although the damage is amazing. I bet no other aircraft in the world could have kept flying after such a collision!

On the airfield, everyone is in a festive mood, gesturing, laughing, and talking loudly. When I get to dispersal, I begin to get a clue: not only has Charles Detal come home safely with his film, but his camera reveals that he destroyed three aircraft on the ground and the control tower. But the remaining eleven Typhoons came home with a real collection of trophies! No less than 12 Fw190s are confirmed, three more damaged and a few ground targets added to the tally. All that at the cost of one Typhoon damaged.

The joy is overwhelming. But, as ever after an action, the mood quietens and then calm returns. Even if 198 Squadron got the lion's share with nine Huns shot down, 609 had no reason to be ashamed with three confirmed in the air, three damaged and three others destroyed on the ground by Charles Detal. It's virtually a draw between squadrons!

Next morning, the Press gave us the honour of the front page. The *Daily Express* headline was '12-0 victory won by the Typhoons', and it was followed by a lyrical article on 'The Tiffie Boys'.

In the evening, most of the pilots had a noisy party at the 'Old Charles' whilst I spent a quieter evening at the mess with Ziggy and Pinky. We sipped a few beers, quietly reviewing the day's emotions, the fear and the joy, still wondering at Pinky's miraculous return. But, the picture of that German pilot, who fought to the last, wouldn't get out of my head.

When we went to our rooms, Ziggy asked as he open his door,

'What's bugging you? You ought to be celebrating!'

'Yes, Ziggy, but I guess I celebrate my victories my own way. I think I forgot to tell you something in my report: killing a man is often necessary in wartime - but it's never a pretty business. Good night.'

Chapter 15
Dogfight

We returned from London rather tired, after a full day. It started at 11 a.m., on Croydon airfield, with a very official parade: Yvan du Monceau de Bergendael, Georges Jaspis, Charlie Delcourt and I were standing to attention in front of a distinguished company to receive awards. A single bugle and two drums opened the ceremony, then closed it after the reading of our citations. The Belgian Prime Minister, Hubert Pierlot, and Defence Minister, Camille Gutt, had reviewed the guard then pinned on our chests the Croix de Guerre. As the ministry car left so did everyone else, going through a barrier where a Belgian gendarme, still in his pre-war uniform, was waiting for us. The policeman came towards me as I was leaving and lifted his hand towards my chest. To my amazement, he removed the newly bestowed medal; then as he went to the next one, 'Missing, the hell are you doing?'

'Sorry, sir, I have orders to take them back. They have to be used for other officers!'

I couldn't believe my ears, and the gendarme, noting my amazement, volunteered: 'The medals are only now being made, and we haven't got enough for everyone yet!'

It was not the first time I'd appreciated the twisted sense of humour of our admin geniuses. Two weeks after my enforced bath in the Channel, the first cheque I wrote had bounced. Paying a call on the bank manager, I learned that I was officially 'Missing, presumed killed' — the kind of joke that really makes one happy. I soon learned that there were standing orders — a secret agreement between governments — which made my own government my next of kin. Anyone not having returned to base at the end of a patrol was reported missing and a confirming signal was sent to headquarters at Bentley Priory. This signal was re-transmitted to the Belgian Embassy by telex, and the admin department took over. Its first action was to freeze the missing airman's bank account, and transfer it to a special account under the control of the Air Attaché. It even came out that some of the seized money contributed to burial expenses at Brookwood cemetery where the Belgian forces had reserved a section.

That was not the end of it! Having visited the Belgian administration at 107 Eaton Square in Belgravia, I was — very politely — told to obtain a 'Life certificate' from the Ministry of the Interior so that I could be officially restored to the land of the living. Without this there was no official way of crediting my account with the blocked money — reserved for my burial! It took me another ten days to get the red tape undone — and to become solvent again.

When one thinks about it, it was the only opportunity for those gallant civil servants, stationed far from the front, to fight with distinction their own — paper — war!

We had other preoccupations: mostly to destroy the Nazi Number 1 secret weapon, the V1 launching ramps. Nicknamed doodle bugs the flying bombs were to be launched against London from 12 June 1944. But we had known about them since the autumn of 1943. Often we attacked the launching sites under construction in the Pas de Calais. Aerial photography told us about the completion of the work and the French Resistance kept London informed of the German progress in getting the weapons operational. In the beginning, we were equipped with two 250 lb bombs, later with two 500 pounders, and from an altitude of 10,000 feet we happily dive-bombed the targets, releasing our eggs at about 3000 feet.

It was a new job for us, and we had to devise an attack technique by trial and error. This consisted of a steep turn at altitude, turning almost upside down, then diving at up to 500 mph and, using a very primitive aiming device devised with the engineer officer's vivid imagination and ingenuity, we hoped that our bombs would create havoc among the V1 ramps. It was a new experience, and pulling out of the dive was a stressful manoeuvre. The 'black veil' was guaranteed, but on the plus side it served to blur our vision when the flak barrage was at its best.

Personally, I doubt that, against such targets, we were much use. How could we cause a lot of damage to concrete ramps, or even kill enemies when it was known that slave workers were used to build them? It would plainly require the big boys to lay down the kind of carpet bombing that was dear to the heart of the Flying Fortresses in order to score enough hits on those targets. But I admit that those ops were useful to train us in new tactics, and prepare us for invasion work. After all, once our bombs had gone we were fighters again and ready to take on an enemy who was becoming scarcer and scarcer. The German fighters now seldom accepted our challenge, leaving it all to their deadly and highly respected flak.

February 29th, 1944. An odd day in the year. Johnny Wells chooses it to visit our Jerry friends in Venlo. Ideal weather, with a cloud layer, not too thick, around 2000 feet making perfect cover in case of trouble. But with our superior armament, our top speed and our manoeuvrability, the Typhoons can penetrate confidently to the heart of the German defences. As usual, it's going to be a two-hour operation, and we fly with long-range tanks.

At Venlo we play hide and seek with local defence, but Jerry does not challenge us in the air. There are only two Dornier bombers on the ground, a petrol bowser and a few lorries on the airfield. My old pals Smithy and Jaspis dive towards them — catching me unawares, and preventing me from firing for fear of hitting them. It's so beautifully executed that although I swear at them I must admit that if I had been a little more alert I would have done the same, leaving them no chance to beat me to it!

At the last moment, I see another bomber in a corner of the field, with mechanics frantically dropping the engine covers to run for cover. A little rudder, nose down, and then a long burst: shells ripple from the foreground towards the plane, hit the cockpit and the undercart is whipped off as fire starts in a wing.

Full right rudder to miss a hangar and I join the rest of the pack flying away. The flak is wide awake, but have the Germans stopped at this height because they must shoot towards each other if they want their guns to bear? It's an interesting theory, but one that I don't really care to check on, so we take our leave and cross over into Belgium. A familiar way home, one that takes us towards Saint Trond, and we're keeping our eyes open for anything flying around there.

Nothing in sight. Ditto at Chièvres. At 14.05 hrs Johnny turns slightly left and leads us into France, hoping that around Beauvais airfield we will meet with better luck — and suddenly, we hit a snow storm. Very poor visibility, down to a few yards, compels us to fly in close formation. I stick to Smithy and Jaspis, while the other five Typhoons are with Johnny Wells to our left.

We fly at about 150 feet, and barely manage to keep together through the snow. Dark patches alternate with short clear spaces.

Suddenly, two shadows cross our path, just above us, and then disappear to our left into broken cloud. Not fast enough to prevent me from identifying two fat, juicy Ju188s, medium bombers sometimes used as night fighters.

The three of us, at great risk of collision, make a sharp turn after the shadows, without waiting for the other Typhoons to join-in-the-chase. It's free for all. Full throttle, screaming engine and fingers on the gun button, we go flat out after the Ju188s and within a few seconds come upon them in a clear patch of sky.

Fire! No waiting! My distinguished colleagues are not about to do me any favours — everyone's appetite is whetted.

In front of me, a multicoloured ribbon streams towards my Typhoon and I can see the rear gunner of the second bomber throwing tracer at me. A little rudder to correct and his turret becomes mute as the gunner crumples on his seat.

It's the moment chosen by the first bomber's rear gunner to bring us under cross-fire: the bullets pass over my cockpit. This is not cricket, pal, and a little rudder to left brings my long burst home. Streaks on the fuselage, left engine on fire — the ball is in full swing. But the place is getting rather crowded, with eight Typhoons now keen to join in the kill, with guns all firing at the same time. If this goes on much longer we are going to shoot each other down, because everyone wants a share. In fact, we are killing the dead, for the two Junkers are fully ablaze and tumbling down. Two seconds later, they explode on the ground, which we miss by a narrow margin.

The Typhoons reform above cloud to cross the nearby coast at Hardelot. Only seven of us. One Typhoon is missing. It's Shelton, Johnny Wells' No. 2. In the shambles, nobody saw what happened, and nobody heard a thing.

When we land at Manston the clock shows 2.27 p.m. on that 29th of February. Nothing will ever be heard about Mike Shelton, a charming fellow, whose loss is keenly felt. Our victories have a taste of blood, and we share the first 188 among three of us, while the second is credited to the other four. It was a collective effort, and everyone contributed willingly.

A few days later, another Junkers 188; this one, making a reconnaissance over the Thames Estuary, was shot down over England by a Spitfire patrol. The only survivor was the observer who baled out and was taken prisoner. The interrogating officer found a diary in his tunic pocket.

On the page for the 29th of February was written: 'Today our Gruppenfuhrer Major Furhkops was shot down near Beauvais by Typhoons, together with Werner Bahnof.'

Chapter 16
London Balloon Barrage

Our squadron has left Manston for firing practice at Fairwood Common, an airfield in Wales, part of Training Command. The aim is to spend a week practising target shooting over the sea with a new type of rocket.

As soon as we arrive we feel the difference between the usual warm welcome and absence of red tape on a front line airfield and the stiff discipline, the bullshit that one gets on the non-operational bases. We, survivors of so many operations, resent the indignity of being treated like wingless wonders — penguins.

So it's with very little good grace that we wear our ties instead of our colourful silk scarves, that we change from flying boots to polished shoes to enter the Officers' Mess. There are many long faces, and frowns too, when the station commander makes it quite clear that full discipline is to be restored; top tunic buttons are to be correctly buttoned, and carrying a gas mask is required when leaving base! This joker does not seem to know that leaving our button undone is a privilege that we shall never relinquish. Moreover, we fighter pilots, who always fly wearing oxygen masks, have ages ago forgotten everything about ugly gas masks!

But the biter can be bit. In place of gas masks we are going to wear our oxygen masks when leaving camp in our best blue! No sooner said than done. Accompanied by Jo Seguin, a Canadian Warrant Officer newly arrived in 609, I give it a try. We arrive at the guardroom so disguised, but the duty officer does not share the joke. He submits an official report, which is transformed into a charge by the witty station commander. He says disciplinary action is to be taken by 609 CO Johnny Wells, who has to decide on our punishment. Johnny has risen from the ranks and he too loathes stupidity, but he has to take some action. He decides that we will be grounded for two days, which means till the end of our stay at Fairwood Common. A very wise decision for, quite accidentally of course, one of our training rockets might easily have scored a direct hit on station headquarters! But, adding insult to injury, we are not returning to Manston in our Typhoons, but piloting the dead-beat Tiger Moth two-seater, used as a means of locomotion for weekends.

The punishment is almost a reward, except that winter flying in a slow open trainer is not exactly a joyride — especially as the weather has closed in. But I laugh it off and with an air of satisfaction I step in the cockpit with old Jo in the passenger seat. We take off at 9 a.m., without a second look at the inhospitable place.

I had planned to refuel near London, without having decided on any particular airfield, then to reach Manston in the early afternoon. But as soon as we are airborne a wall of cloud blocks our way.

With no radio I have no intention of blind flying, solely on instruments, so my only option is to fly low, blown about by a strong wind. A glance at the map tells me that we will have to cross some country with hills above 3000 feet, which is not good news with the cloud base down to 1500 feet. So, I'll not only have to stay below cloud but also to follow valleys which, obviously, will not all head in the right direction.

So, caught between the cloud base and the capricious valleys, I try to maintain a general course towards London, but time gallops past. As fuel becomes scarce, I busy myself with finding an airfield. On my map I select Wroughton, a nearby station. I now have to find it, which is not a piece of cake.

Behind me, Jo Seguin, probably freezing in the open rear seat, seems to be enjoying the ride. When I turn round, he waves at me with a smile and says something that the wind carries away. He must have a lot of confidence in me!

The minutes go by. When the fuel gauge indicates about only 30 minutes reserve I locate the airfield. Much relief on landing, especially as the weather is better, with a timid ray of sunlight to welcome us.

Refuelling is another problem: the bowsers are full of 100 octane petrol, and our glorious Tiger Moth needs feeding with 80 octane. So the fill-up has to be done with jerricans, and it takes a lot of time. Having had no time to feed ourselves, we take off around 2 p.m., still about 130 miles from London, and a good 250 from Manston. At a cruising speed of 70 mph it's going to be a close run thing to land before dusk. But, being an optimist . . .

All goes well for the first hour, then we hit a strong head wind, and I start worrying about our ETA. Further bad news: the weather changes and a front develops straight ahead, while a snow storm hits us at about 3.30 p.m. It's a safe bet that the London balloon barrage has been lowered below cloud base, but it will hang in front of us at our altitude. That means hundreds of sharp-edged cables hanging in our path, with no possibility of seeing them in time to take evasive action. I am now flying practically blind, at 100 feet, sometimes catching a glimpse of the ground through the snow.

A quick glance at Jo in the back; he's still got that stupid smile on his face! I want to shout at him, for we'll have to think of baling out if I don't find a landing ground soon. But he seems to enjoy the snow as a fish enjoys water. It must be his Canadian origin! Anyway, I am too busy to indulge in speculation; my watch indicates 4.20 p.m. with darkness falling fast in an already dark sky: I will have to land fast and, I hope, in one piece. I must also keep calm, for anxiety impairs judgement. From my course, even allowing that I did deviate grossly, I had to be somewhere in the vicinity of Croydon airfield. But circling around I can find no trace of it. Around me are grey roofs, small houses, green spaces, but nothing that will let me land my little plane.

All at once I see a searchlight battery. The soldiers wave at me with their helmets and even their khaki scarves. I circle them with relief, sure that they will understand my predicament and soon show me the way to Croydon by giving me a flat beam in that direction. That's normal procedure. In the coming darkness it should be easy to follow the beam. We have at most ten minutes dusk left.

But it's not my day! I skim their heads, I simulate a landing on their battery, and those thick-heads laugh and toss their helmets, clap their hands, as if they are enjoying my show. Never seen such stupid asses! Pongos, obviously; which accounts for it. But still hard to believe! They will never light their searchlight. No time left for philosophy. I'll fly a mile south, then I will have two possibilities: either climb and bale out if I find no open ground, or, if a space is available, land straight ahead and hope for the best. There we are! Some grass fields ahead. Oh, nothing to brag about — the size of a big handkerchief seen from here. At most, a hundred yards, but with a hedge to clear on the way in.

My mind is made up. In we go — almost at stalling speed — then cut the engine, pull the stick back, and wait a long second till the plane touches down. The Tiger Moth meets the grass without losing its fixed undercart, rolls for a while, then slows down to come to a stop 10 yards away from some trees. The kite is undamaged — and so are we. Climbing out of our plane, we sink onto beautifully kept grass, as a swarm of babbling blue-clad females greet us with huge smiles. They are nurses from Croydon Hospital — and we have landed in the garden of the Nurses' Home! Hugged and kissed by our chattering lovely hostesses, we are invited to tea, and reach their Home with our chutes on our shoulders.

We hardly have time to ring up Croydon airport to get a guard for our plane before we are being filled with cakes, sandwiches, jam with bread and butter — very welcome, because I feel pretty hungry after a long day. We are treated like heroes, but certainly neither of us feels like one.

While Jo is thoroughly enjoying himself, I begin to wonder what kind of reception I will get when I return to Manston. I had better phone the squadron, talk to the CO and tell him what has happened.

It must be 5.30 p.m. before I get Manston on the phone, but the CO is not there. That's good news. Smithy, B Flight commander comes on the line: 'Hello Smithy, Charles here. We have had to force land in a field near Croydon. The kite is O.K. but no way to take off again. Better send a Queen Mary to load her on. But you will be overjoyed to hear that we are safe!'

'Is that so? That's wonderful news. But how did you manage not to break your pretty little neck?'

'That's just what I am asking myself. Just in case you are interested, we are in the expert hands of some Croydon nurses. When I last heard, the head nurse wanted to put us to bed after such a hard day!'

'You bastard! With your French accent and your smooth manners, I bet you'll land in the wrong bed — I know you!'

'Yes, Smithy, you know me too well! Anyway we're looking forward to a most pleasant evening . . . Bye, old boy.'

Good things never last long. A car from Croydon later fetches us to drive us all the way to Manston. When we arrive, everybody is asleep, which saves us from the jeers of our friends. The Tiger Moth will return later, after removing the wings and loading it on a trailer, to be reassembled the same day at Manston.

No ill effects for Jo or me . . . except that a few weeks later Jo finds himself engaged (but is it a bad thing?) to one of the pretty Croydon nurses.

Chapter 17
Test Pilot

Every day brings new signs of preparation for the invasion of Europe. Soon, we shall be integrated into the monstrous military machine that will breach the Atlantic wall and arrive somewhere in France. Our freedom of action in 609 is almost drawing to an end. No. 609 Squadron's days are numbered.

The other fighter squadrons of Fighter Command have already been transferred to a new command called No. 2 Allied Tactical Air Force (ATAF) divided into two Groups, Nos 83 and 84. Our airmen, the auxiliaries who have served in the West Riding of Yorkshire Squadron since 1937, are pooled with unknown other airmen and then posted to other units. To replace them we get nice little WAAFs in battle dress, who do the daily inspections, refuel and rearm our aircraft. More or less with success.

On 15 March I took off from Manston with my No. 2 to escort a convoy in the Channel. To fulfil my mission, I had to use up the petrol in my auxiliary tanks first, otherwise I'd have to shorten the patrol, leaving the convoy without our protection. I quickly fed the engine from my left long-range tank. Barely 30 seconds after I switched to that tank, my plane was shaken by a muted explosion and the engine cut dead. Flying about 10 feet above the sea, I switched back at once to the main tank, pushed frantically on the petrol pump and with relief heard my engine pick up after a few seconds that seemed like a century. My heart was beating like a drum. At that altitude, there was no question of ditching safely in a Typhoon.

I pulled myself together. I tried the right, full, auxiliary tank — and, sure enough, after thirty seconds, the same muted explosion and no engine. Even faster than before, I went back to main tanks, and the engine came back to life.

Enough of this, I signalled to my No. 2 to formate on me and off we went, to land at base. I was not in a good mood, to say the least; I was really worried because there was no explanation for those engine failures followed by recoveries. But at the back of my mind, there was a large question mark over the female mechanics looking after our planes. What could I do about it? I warned Sector about my problems, and told them that I was returning. Better talk this over with the engineer, Flt Lt Jackson.

As soon as I got back to dispersal, I went to him. His big red nose attested to his liking for alcohol, and seemed to focus my anger: 'Jackie, that blasted kite let me down twice in five minutes, I've had enough of these engines cutting out at sea. Now, you'd better shake up your bloody women . . .'

Jackson's nose grew even redder, his big round eyes rolled under the bushy eyebrows, but he chose not to answer. He went slowly towards my plane and started to inspect it with great care. I left him to it and went to my locker to store my chute and helmet. When he returned he looked sadly at a pilot who dared wrongly to criticise his little harem.

'Come and see what you did, clot, and you will understand why your engine cut! Look, you hit the water and your auxiliary tanks exploded. Next time, just learn to fly before you tear me off a strip!'

With disbelieving eyes, I saw that both auxiliary tanks were holed and obviously empty. And yet, I knew I had not hit the sea — or anything else. It was absolutely unbelievable.

Something told me that I was right. But I would have to prove it. So kneeling under the wing, I looked carefully over that metallic cylinder, five feet long and one foot in diameter, that we used as a long-range petrol tank. I could see the holes in the metal but, turning round, my eyes went to the blades of the propeller. The tips of the four blades were almost two feet lower than the tanks. Now, since the blade tips were undamaged it was quite clear that I could not have hit either ground or sea.

'Jackson, I bet you your monthly whisky ration that you are totally wrong!'

My assurance was such that the prospect of going on the wagon was painted on his panic-stricken face. He did not take the bet, but still tried to bluster: 'Well, where's your proof, genius?'

By his tone, I knew that he was no longer sure of himself. His eyes followed my finger pointing to the propeller.

'The proof is there — right in front of your eyes. How could I hit the sea with my tanks without bending the propeller tips?'

A look of understanding came into his big round eyes. He moved quickly under the wing and closely inspected the open undercarriage bay where the double air and petrol pipes were located. With an ashen face Jackson cried, 'The air-pipe tap is not open! That means that it was not an explosion, but an implosion. As the engine sucks in petrol, the pressure inside the tanks is lower than outside. If you don't vent air into the tanks as you use up the petrol they'll just burst! In this case the air couldn't get in because of that closed tap! Sheer stupidity that could have killed you! Trust me, this won't happen again, Charlie.'

Dear old Jackson! I knew that he had been hit hard when the old 609 erks were posted. He didn't really have confidence in those girls, who were turned into mechanics in just a few months. But, after all, mine was the neck being risked!

The incident was over — but I decided to check everything myself in future, and to warn the others to do the same.

Back to the mess, driving the Barouche. Just in time to learn that our stay in Manston has come to an end: we have to move to Tangmere — it's the end of an era. Back to square one; we are now just another squadron in the RAF, losing our identity, abandoning our privileges, and most certainly our own private personal way of making war.

As we soon find out, even Tangmere has lost the air of a front line airfield. It's overcrowded with several Typhoon squadrons, but most of the pilots' faces are unknown. Where are the old hands?

Barely a week after our arrival, we hear of a new move that makes our enthusiasm fade even more: 609 is to go to Acklington, to do some practice dive-bombing. We are to be relegated to the level of apprentices when in fact, a year ago, we were the first Tiffies to carry bombs — and even at night! But I suppose some of the new pilots need practice, and so on 22 March 1944 we take off, with very little enthusiasm for our 'bombing week'.

Next day, training starts. Armed with practice bombs, Typhoons take off in pairs at 20 minute intervals, and after a few minutes reach the target about half a mile from the coast. The form is to fly over the controller's hut, contact the man in charge by radio to get his O.K., then proceed to bomb the target in a 45 degrees dive. From his bunker on the cliffs, the controller records hits and misses, while our bombs splash harmlessly in the sea on or around the target.

This war game seems childish to us; we would much rather practice on Jerry than waste our time and petrol on dummies. Added to this, Acklington is not my cup of tea, and the local staff do not take easily to fighter pilots' ways.

On this first day, Polo Cooreman forms up with Charles Detal and the pair take off around mid-day. Once over the bombing range, they are told to orbit for 10 minutes till the target is clear. So Charles Detal challenges Polo to a mock dogfight at less than 1000 feet — so as to kill time and allay his impatience.

After a steep turn, Detal's Typhoon goes into a spin. Probably forgetting the increased wing-loading from the practice bombs was his fatal mistake. Watched by a disbelieving Polo, Detal succeeded in pulling out of the spin. Alas, he was too near the ground — and that magnificent pilot, credited with six victories and more than a hundred ops, crashed to his death on 23 March 1944. One of the best Typhoon pilots in the RAF, who so often had defied deadly flak and won his personal battles with German fighters, just killed himself in a stupid practice flight, far from the enemy.

Polo and I had the sad honour of escorting his coffin to London, where he would be buried at Brookwood Cemetery the next day. An RAF guard of honour fired a volley of blanks over the grave: blank cartridges, dummy bombs, a life wasted.

When we return to Acklington, Polo and I feel very lonesome. And, when we leave the airfield a few days later, morale is not good. The shadow of our lost friend seems to haunt the dispersal, and the pilots speak in low tones. The old hands are silent; everyone feels that the marvellous 609 spirit is dissolving in the moist air of the end of March.

The CO Johnny Wells seems invisible and B Flight Commander Smithy, to whom I am now deputy, says one morning: 'Something tells me, Charlie, our days here are numbered. For you and me, it's maybe the best thing we can hope for.'

'Yes, a little rest before the balloon goes up could be useful. We'll need to be on top form for D Day!'

'Agreed. I hate the way things are going in the squadron right now . . .'

Old Manu, A Flight Commander, is not very talkative. With his experience he has seen a lot of water under the bridge and his philosophy is solid. 'With the invasion, all that will change — and it can't be long now. Just in case "they" put us in the infantry, I'm going to practise pistol shooting . . .'

The joke falls flat. Maybe I am wrong, but since Pat Thornton-Brown got killed, we haven't had a *real* boss. Johnny lacks communication with his pilots, and further, he just has not got what it takes to be an undisputed leader, a real leader. Wells has not managed to restore the 609 spirit. So back in insipid Tangmere, we feel lost among the strange faces that crowd the airfield.

Now under the distant and impersonal rule of Group Captain Dennis Gillam, we old pilot boys have just lost our identity and are merely numbers. The 'groupie' is a real hero; way back in 1939 he fought in Hurricanes and then, as a regular officer, got promotion for his Typhoon exploits. But he is also a cold, calculating, ambitious man, with the warmth of an iceberg. As a result he is feared rather than loved. Between him and his pilots there is no spark. When, a few weeks later, Smithy and I have the honour of an interview with him, we hear almost with relief that we are to be posted for a rest, to 84 Group Support Unit at Aston Down.

The date is 6 April 1944; my logbook shows 509 flying hours, of which 199 were on ops with the Typhoon. That amounts to 121 operational sorties. My first tour of ops is over; I am alive.

When the interview is almost over, Gillam says to me, 'Both as an experienced pilot and deputy Flight Commander, you are now due for a rest, normally for six months, before you can come back to an operational squadron. But the balloon is going up in the not too distant future, Charlie, and we shall need pilots of your calibre to lead flights, or even a squadron, so your rest will be short. I hope you realise that my decision is right and don't feel sore about it.'

O.K. I guess he is right. I need some rest, to recharge the batteries, and to be in top form at the right time. But I suppose that we fighter pilots are sentimental and we can't leave the front line without a sense of loss, for being on ops is our normal way of life and, to some extent, our drug. Before I salute to take my leave, I try to probe the future.

'Can I hope, sir, that I'll be back in 609 when we start the invasion?'

'Of course. As I told you, you will be back with added responsibilities where you will be most needed — and if possible, in your squadron. That's all I can promise now. But don't worry, we shall need every one of you to win this war.'

So that's that! Smithy and I, with Bob Watts, are posted to the reserve pool of Typhoon pilots. The next day I leave for Aston Down, driving my own car with Smithy as passenger. Our route takes us through the prettiest countryside there is in the British Isles: the Cotswolds, full of green hills, wooded valleys, beautiful old houses, famous too for its old inns, the pubs where the beer is light and the friendship long. The villages seem still to be living in the Middle Ages, and the lanes are bordered by beautiful elm trees. By the time we arrive I am already in love with the landscape and I feel at home on this airfield near Stroud.

There is just one runway in use at Aston Down, and the few hangars cannot house the many aircraft lying about the field. There are many different types of single-engined fighters in the tactical reserve, and our job will be to test them, then ferry some of them to operational squadrons. One minute I am enjoying flying a Spitfire 9B, the next a P51 Mustang. The Mustang is used by the Americans to escort their bombers all the way to Berlin and back. It flies beautifully, much more comfortable for the pilot than most British fighters, which are of more spartan design. But the Spitfire XIVs are the kings at high altitude, and I love to do aerobatics with them. And, of course, we test both Typhoons and Tempests as they are ferried from the nearby factory in Gloucester. We also make the acquaintance of a small army co-operation plane called an Auster. With its gull wing, the four-seater takes off in about 20 yards and, properly handled, can land on a handkerchief. We use it for our weekend picnics, and the odd joyride with local beauties — this, of course, is strictly off the record. As is the return hospitality provided by our grateful guests.

Life in Gloucestershire at this stage of the war, when flowers are blossoming all over the countryside, is an enchanting experience. Mixing the professional life of test pilots with visits to the local beauty spots, both architectural and more humanly shaped, we are having the time of our lives. The hospitality in this county is really fantastic and soon we all have families who welcome us into their homes. Time flies by happily, as we wait to get back to the fighting. Not far from the airfield, the Gloucester Works produce the still secret Meteor, the first jet aircraft to operate in 1944. Smithy and I are authorised to go and see it on the production line as well as in a closed hangar. We also meet Jimmy Warren and Michael Daunt, both development test pilots. We see them often in the following weeks, for drinks in the evening.

One morning, just as we were about to take off, we heard a prolonged whining sound in the sky, followed by a loud explosion nearby. We jumped into my car and drove as fast as we could towards the Common outside Stroud. There, a hole about 50 feet wide, and not very deep, was covered with small bits of metal. As we searched the area, we found a scarf among what was left of the wreck. It was also all that was left of Jimmy Warren and his Meteor, which hit the ground at over 500 mph.

While the rescue team and the experts recovered the tell-tale bits of metal, trying to work out the causes of this crash, the medical orderlies filled with bloodstained sand and a torn scarf the coffin that would be buried by his family. Today, tourists who fly in jet aircraft don't even know the name of the test pilot who died in the first Meteor so that one day they could travel safely.

Chapter 18
Chance and Destiny

On top of our test pilot activities, we also have the responsibility of preparing the 'sprogs' just out of the flying schools for war. Most of them are young and unpolished, but they make up for this with their keenness to fight. Trawling for college boys is no longer the form. To cope with the ever-increasing demand, recruiting has been widened to include all kinds. Some are as good as before, some less so. Endlessly, we take charge of them and try to pass on all the tips, the basic rules of the fighting game. But our own experience, the result of many hardships, will not be sufficient to make up the difference and it is obvious to us that many of them will not live long.

Among those young ones there is a Pilot Officer, rather shy and very reserved, whom I decide to help personally. I want to shake him up enough to give him a chance of survival. This well-bred lad seems a bit lost in the tough world of warriors, being rather fragile, almost delicate.

Pushed against the wall one evening, with a pint in his hand, he goes as far as admitting he volunteered as a fighter pilot to prove to himself that he was a man. He also reluctantly confesses that he is sometimes afraid of his plane. What can I do? Save him by telling him to throw in the sponge, or try and give him enough self-confidence to make the grade?

Honestly, I don't have the heart to put in an adverse report that would take him away for ever from the fighting — have I got the right to settle a man's future? And yet, my duty is clearly to assess his capabilities, either opening for him a road to glory or stopping him ever getting a chance to fight. After a few moments' reflection, and a last glass of ale, I take the plunge: 'Listen, boy, either you get over your apprehension and you go on, or you apply for a posting. You've got to decide what you really want, and be honest enough with yourself to say if you've got the guts to do it.'

With what may have been a surge of pride or a touch of vanity, he replied, 'I'll try once more — if you will help me!'

Right, I will help him. Next morning, I sign him off on a Typhoon and, taking off together, we climb to 10,000 feet. I have decided to get him confident by flying first in very close formation, wingtip to wingtip, to give him the feel of mastering to an inch the brutal 2400 hp force at his finger tips. Then, when he has gained some confidence, we will do basic aerobatics in line astern, which can be a tricky business in a Typhoon. If he does well, he's bound to get rid of his fears and realise that he can do it. Having overcome his anxiety, he will be able to fly confidently on his own.

Everything went as planned. The sprog flew as though glued to me, was not shaken off during the aerobatics, and followed me closely in power dives that would have scared many. I even let him get on my tail to give him a boost, though it was a piece of cake to get on his tail unobserved. I am sure he will make the grade and that he has got over his fear, so we land perfectly in close formation and taxi to dispersal.

It's now time to exploit his newly gained self-confidence and send him off alone for another hour of circuits and bumps: 'O.K. As soon as the kite is refuelled, off you go again. Circuits and bumps just to polish off your landings. Best way to get the hang of this beast. You've done well, but now you must confirm it as soon as possible, to keep up your confidence in your own abilities. Understood?'

When he is about to go, with a kind of premonition I add quickly, 'Should you land too long, don't hesitate to push the throttle right through and go round again. There is no shame whatsoever in misjudging a landing — but make sure you decide while there is still time to go round again!'

A cup of tea at the NAAFI van and off he goes to his Typhoon, while I sit in dispersal and watch his take-off through the open window. From there, I can also talk to him directly on the radio.

Perfect take-off; fine landing; another take-off — all O.K. There he is, landing again — too high! Too fast — Good God, time to go round again! The bloody fool, he does nothing! I am an impotent witness; I can see he is already two-thirds of the way down the runway, still floating three feet high, trying to land with too little space left to stop before the end of the runway. And yet he doesn't open up and go round again. My cry dies in the radio, too late to save my young friend.

He does not react and flies into the stone wall at the end of the runway, loses his undercarriage, crosses the road skidding on his belly, collides with the next low stone wall and finishes his mad run in a nearby field. The aircraft goes up in flames as soon as it comes to rest. The poor fool must have forgotten to switch off as he crashed.

Jumping in the car, we go at full speed towards the scene. The crash wagon, the ambulance, the firemen race across the airfield to find the plane in one piece, though badly damaged, lying flat on the ground, the pilot upright in his seat but with his closed hood perfectly intact.

The flames spring high from the engine cowlings, and the intense heat pushes us back. We are just two yards away, going towards the cockpit to help, when the heat beats us, and even the firemen spraying the fire with foam have to retreat. Another fireman tries to open the hood with an axe. I can see him sweating under his asbestos clothing, but the fire spreads quickly, licking the crash crew who also retreat.

During those long seconds we can all see the pilot seated in the cockpit, most probably unhurt, but shaken, sitting with frozen hands, immobile as a statue. Perhaps he was not badly hurt — maybe just knocked out, unconscious?

The fire rages on, an inferno that halts all attempts to get near it.

It takes ten minutes to put out the fire completely. Then the burning metal is attacked with axes, until finally the cockpit yields and the hood is removed — but the pilot is dead. His body, still strapped in, disintegrates into ashes that fly in the light May wind.

That evening in the mess, people avoid each other's eyes. Some pilots pretend to read their newspapers. Others busy themselves listening to the news. But I can't deceive myself, pretend that nothing has happened, so I go out. I shall go to a pub, alone, to drink a pint — to drink many pints — to find out from the bottom of a glass why the hell I allowed that poor fellow to fly to his death, to put an end to his dream?

I am responsible for his death — by taking the wrong decision, by weakness of character, for not having the guts to tell him harshly, finally, that he was the wrong man in the wrong place! I did not understand what he was trying to tell me. I did not see that all he wanted was someone like me to tell him he was not cut out to do the job. He cried for help, for someone stronger to take the decision. Lack of judgement, of perception on my part — and yet, up to what point can one decide for someone else? Has not everyone the right to make his own mistakes?

As I sink into my drunken melancholy the door of the lounge opens and in comes my friend Squadron Leader Walter Drink.

'So you get drunk alone now, Charlie?'

'No, Walter I just can't get drunk. I can't stop thinking about that poor bloke. Did you see how he was cremated in his plane?'

'Yes, I did — but one way or another, when your time is up, there's nothing you can do about it. You know, Charlie boy, I've given a lot of thought to life and death, luck and fate — but I only know one thing: we are born naked and alone, and we die naked, for nothing goes with you. We die alone, and those who remain are the ones to be pitied.'

My friend Walter is a very calm, stocky man, formerly a rich farmer and very well bred, who fights his war quietly and without fuss. I like him a lot, even though we met only a few months ago. Until now, he has never opened his heart; natural modesty, I guess, or more probably plain shyness. That typical British restraint, which teaches that it is not good form to talk about personal things, or about oneself. But I feel tonight that he is in the mood — a rare thing with him — probably without saying it he also feels the strain and sorrow resulting from this death.

'Listen, Walter, you are right when you say that we are alone at birth and alone in death. But between birth and death, we need company, we need affection, we seek love. It's our way of proving ourselves and of reassuring others. Human beings are essentially gregarious.'

'Of course they are. It's because of man's essential weakness. Look at it this way Charlie — we men, we have the self-conceit to believe that *we* choose our love affairs, our feminine conquests. How wrong can we be!

It's the women who do the choosing! For women trap us; they let us believe that we choose them, but, in the final analysis, they are in charge.'

'So what? Our brief encounters are not important as far as the future is concerned . . .'

'Fiddlesticks Charlie! Nonsense to all that! Our girl friends also like a spot of adventure, but what they basically seek is to feel secure. Man is a hunter, a predator, but he falls into their trap all the time!'

'Walter, you are a fatalist — but I've got a theory on that subject too. I believe that everything in life is a succession of human choices that generate predetermined consequences, which most people call fate. The fact that you were born was fate for you — you could do nothing about it — but it was the result of the exercise of human choice by your parents who decided to give you life!'

'Don't you believe in fate Charlie?'

'As I just said: fate is the result of free decision — whose consequences belong to fate, in as much as we cannot change them. But I still maintain that man has choice and, once he has chosen a course of action, only then do the consequences of that choice (whatever they may be) become fate. In fact, everyone has his fate in his hands, but not everyone realises that it may be the result of a decision taken freely long ago! To say, for example, that "It was written from the beginning that flak will spare us" is too easy! It negates the very important part played by our personal ability, our superior training, our intelligence, and our luck.'

'That's the word I was waiting for — luck. What is luck, Charlie?'

I have to admit that I am taken aback; we use that magic word every day — good luck or bad luck — to describe something that seems beyond reason. However, I take the plunge:

'Luck? It's one of the elements of life like water, salt, want or shame. It's a fortunate arrangement, a providential conjunction that crosses our path, and just like a pretty girl, favours only those who can court it in the right way. Everybody has luck, but only few recognise it and take advantage of it!'

I said it just as it came into my mind — without thinking, partly because it was the first time I had tried to put into words what I had felt, confusedly, for years.

'So, when you go through flak, you are grabbing your luck?'

'Listen, Walter, I know just like you that luck is blind. But those who help luck, who can take it, have better — God, I was going to say luck — let's say a better opportunity to be on the right side than those who do nothing about it. When action is necessary, for example, to consider action as unnecessary would be tempting death.

'Maybe it's the right way to look at things — but our young friend who killed himself today was unlucky!'

'No, Walter. He didn't *recognise* his luck while there was still time to go round again. And maybe long ago he made the wrong choice when he freely decided to be a pilot?'

Part Three
The Longest Days

Chapter 19
D-Day

June 1944. Although still confined to the reserve pool at 84 Group Support Unit I am enjoying the testing of all types of single-engined aircraft stored at Aston Down after they leave the production line. In fact, I fly a whole range of fighters, from the Spitfire IX to the Mustang P51, and including the Spitfire XIV, the Tempest and the newly modified Typhoon — this last one coming out, unfortunately, at a very slow rate from the nearby factory. My job includes delivery of some of these reserve aircraft to squadrons, as they need them, and, while doing so, I see the last preparations for the invasion. As I often deliver the aircraft in the South of England, it is soon clear that D-day is only a matter of weeks if not days away. Virtually all of the South of England has become a restricted area full of troops and equipment. Landing barges are spread right along the coast and around the harbours.

I am waiting — and also speculating on my chances of being posted back any day now to an operational squadron, before the start of the greatest battle of the war. At the same time, I know that I will not be called back unless a pilot is killed or missing. I would prefer to go back to 609 Squadron, but the chances are remote because the Tactical Air Force, to which I belong, has no less than 23 squadrons equipped with Typhoons, which reduces the odds to about one in four. On the other hand, with the general shuffle that occurred a few weeks ago, many familiar faces have gone, and therefore, here or there . . . I try to convince myself that where I am posted is of little importance, but I must admit that I am deeply attached to my old squadron. Insh-Allah!

On the morning of 6 June the news reached us in the Officers' Mess at breakfast time: our troops landed in France at 5 a.m. near Bayeux. It comes as no surprise, for all night the drone of heavy bombers has been heard over the airfield.

I run to dispersal, read the daily orders, and find that there is a request for reinforcement from Tangmere: A Spitfire XIV is required. It takes me only five minutes to sign the Form 700 that certifies the plane is serviceable, fuelled and armed, before I take off towards the south.

Landing at Tangmere, I find myself among exuberant pilots, as keen as can be, who have just returned from their second operation of the morning. Within half an hour, they will take off again and they say that the landing is taking place successfully, though faced by strong German resistance on the beaches.

A crazy idea goes through my head. I don't want to miss this; maybe could I fly this op with them? It would have to be 'arranged', but it is my lucky day for I find that the CO of the squadron is an Australian who

can close his eyes to what one might call something 'not in the book' —
so I can join in as arse-end Charlie. For one hour we fly as top cover over
the beachhead at about 20,000 feet. It is a fantastic sight: ships of all
sizes between England and Normandy, from battleships to landing
barges, seem to join the two coasts by a long mobile chain. There are
also tugs that trail behind them the big square concrete caissons that will
become artificial harbours. Convoy after convoy fills the rough sea,
with their sheep-dogs — destroyers and frigates guarding their flanks.
Meanwhile minesweepers plough along in front to clear a path through
the heaving water.

On the ground, explosions mark the fighting. It's difficult to see
what's going on, but smoke inland seems to indicate that our troops
have advanced from the beaches. There's not much time to admire the
landscape for more than 10,000 planes, at one time or another, fill the
sky, to us the greatest danger seems to be collision. No German fighters
anywhere and the flak is intermittent, kept busy I guess by the low-level
Typhoons. So my part in the invasion turns out to be a doddle, a patrol
high above the gigantic battle, with no opportunity to fire my guns in
anger.

Our return to base at lunchtime goes smoothly. When I climb aboard
the liaison Anson that will take me back to Aston Down, I am deep in
thought: in a few days, I will be back on operations. I will be one of the
first to land in France: with a bit of luck, I may even live long enough to
return to Belgium . . .

I have another week at Aston Down before I am posted to 183
Squadron as Deputy Flight Commander. Chance has it that 183
Squadron is part of 123 Wing, and 198, 164 and 609 are sister units. So I
find a few old hands like Manu Geerts (now CO of 609) Poupa Jaspis,
Polo Cooreman and 'Men' Blanco. Some young pilots have also come
from training, including many Belgians: Crikellie, De Bruyn, De
Bueger, Deschamps, Jacquemin, La Force, Matthys and Watthieu. I
will get to know them better in a few months when I take over command
of 609, but I am very happy for the moment to be in 183, for 123 Wing is
commanded by my old friend, Group Captain Scott, DSO, DFC and
Bar, a huge New Zealander and an exceptional pilot, while the Wingco
Flying is Walter Drink, with whom I spent the last wonderful weeks at
Aston Down. But I also mourn several friends killed in 609 since I left
the squadron. One of these, Flying Officer Pierre Soesman, brings me a
special grief; not only was he a friend, but in 1943 he flew his first ops as
my No. 2. I learned that, returning from a sweep over France, he was hit
by flak and baled out over the sea; he was just 22. Although the
Typhoons went back to search, and Air Sea Rescue tried hard, he was
never seen again.

Our base is now Hurn Bay, not far from Portsmouth. From there we
operate daily over the bridgehead. It takes us 20 minutes to reach the
front line; and every day our job is to destroy panzers and clear a path
for our own tanks.

As the bridgehead spreads, the field engineers build small airfields in the Normandy countryside, some of them only a couple of miles from the enemy lines. Those roughly built airfields have only one short and narrow runway, about 800 yards long, made of pierced-steel planks fixed together by hinges, like a giant Meccano.

At the beginning of July we move to France, to B8 near Bayeux. Every night, and sometimes even in daytime, the German batteries positioned around the Carpiquet airfield shell us, damaging our planes, killing some of the ground crew, and forcing us to leave our tents and dive into slit trenches. Although I am used to flak in the sky, and have to live with it, I hate being shelled on the ground without being able to retaliate. After a few days of this treatment, I refuse to degrade myself by giving up the relative comfort of a camp bed so I decide to stay in my tent, tucked in my sack, and I sleep with my tin helmet over what is known in colloquial French as the 'family jewels'. If a shell falls smack on the trench or the tent, that's just my bad luck . . .

But HQ has another problem to worry about as well. The dust and dirt raised by our propellers gets into the radiators, clogging them and producing overheating. Quite a few pilots have had engine failure on take-off and some have been killed. The shelling and the dust problem force a decision to send us back to England every night — returning to Normandy every morning — so that pilots can sleep quietly and the planes can be maintained overnight without enemy interference.

On 12 July, 183 attacks enemy positions near Cap d'Antifer and our commanding officer Sqn Ldr F. Scarlett is killed during the fighting. I regroup the remaining Typhoons and we put down at landing-ground B7 — Vaussieux — an airfield we use for diversions. The flak scored a direct hit on the CO's plane when he was leading us into a 500 mph diving attack. His Typhoon disintegrated in mid-air and crashed near the target. I went through the barrage without a scratch, but three more planes were damaged.

A few hours later, we take off again to attack Esquay with four replacement Typhoons and a determination to avenge our CO. Our rockets start explosions in a forest where an armoured division is hiding. The flak defences in the wood fire from all directions, and the tops of the trees look like candlesticks but, like angry wasps, the Tiffies dive at the target with all guns blazing and starting fires in several places.

As I'm regrouping the squadron again, I feel my plane judder and the engine vibrates. My radio is silent and there is a big hole with the wind whistling through the fuselage, just behind my seat: things are going to go from bad to worse . . .

Instinctively, I climb towards our lines not very far from the target, and I watch my temperature gauge climbing towards the red danger zone. I won't make base. Surprisingly calmly, I nurse my wounded plane towards the safety of our lines before I have to abandon her. Near

Caen, the flames start melting the engine cowlings and the acrid smell of black smoke fills the cockpit. It's time to go: canopy jettisoned, straps undone and stick in the belly — barrel roll and exit . . .

A sharp blow on my shoulders, a white mushroom above my head and I land quite peacefully in an orchard, narrowly missing an apple tree. All in one piece, and already surrounded by Scottish tank crews who seem to want to throw a party. They say that they like us a lot, and often see our attacks in support of their units. I feel positively welcome at their command post where a Major with a ginger moustache insists on quenching my thirst with a splendid whisky. But they gave me the fright of my life when I was taken back to base in a jeep driven by a lunatic who wanted to show me how good he was. I was so scared that I clean forgot my earlier escape.

Walter Drink welcomes me back. Teasingly he tells me that it's a pity to lose a Typhoon when we are so short of them — as if I had done it on purpose! But it is just his sense of fun, forgiven instantly when he says I can go to Aston Down, spend the weekend there and bring back a new Typhoon. Then, he goes away with a twinkle in his eye, hinting that someone around Stroud will be pleased to see me.

When I return with my brand-new aircraft, I am told to take my flight to Eastchurch for a whole week of practice rocket firing. They are sending us to play about on imitation targets when there are plenty of real ones to be destroyed in the front line! Although I am fed up playing nurse to a bunch of newcomers, maybe it is the safest way to train them; we lost about a quarter of our squadron during those few weeks. The sprogs leave training with only two to four hours' practice on the Tiffie; obviously losses would be reduced if the reinforcement pilots had more practice on the aircraft. But my inner feeling is that a fighter pilot does not become operational after just a few hours of rocket practice: at best, he will buy time before the real thing, which will always be the best proving ground for anybody.

The week was spent without major problems and I managed to give every young pilot about ten hours of practice. Direct hits weren't common, but at least they managed not to crash. So, back to the front line, where the general situation is far from trouble-free. At landing-ground B7, Vaussieux, we are back in our tents in the orchard and food is restricted to tea, spam, bully beef and dry biscuits.

As the convoys seem only to bring in men and equipment, we brought back from England in our empty gun bays lots of white bread, bags of coffee, cigarettes and soap. I also discovered that in the nearby village, about a mile from the airfield, there was an inn, closed down for lack of clients. The owner was the farmer upon whose wheat field the airfield had been built. Relations between the farmer and the 'invaders' were somewhat strained and were rapidly deteriorating. The soured farmer declared he was being ruined by the very people who had come to restore his freedom! When I asked him about his feelings, he explained that in four years there had been no damage done by the Germans but that in the last four weeks he had lost crops, apple trees and a year's harvest, not to mention cows killed in the fighting. One had to see his point. We improved matters a bit by convincing him that we could repay him in part with coffee, cigarettes and soap — all black market and expensive items in occupied Europe — later we added some bicycle tyres. I managed to re-establish a strong and business-like *entente cordiale* based upon a simple and highly efficient barter system. He would open the inn for the exclusive use of my squadron's pilots, providing delicious fresh meat, fresh garden vegetables (french fried potatoes were very favoured), Camembert of the finest quality and lovely French wines. Finally, to go with our own coffee, a generous shot of that fiery French spirit, Calvados. Fresh cream was always on the menu, cider was very popular, and oysters (out of season), for oyster beds were nearby — all this was quite a change from our rations. When we needed new Typhoon replacements each pilot in turn got 48 hours' leave in England. He, personally, had to contribute to our operational mess by bringing back two kilos of coffee, 200 NAAFI cigarettes, one kilo of soap and two bicycle tyres. This was the agreed tithe to the farmer for lavishly feeding the whole bunch of pilots every day. Any bartering beyond that was entirely up to the individual!

This scheme, if outside King's Regulations, worked beautifully until the fame of the revived inn became too well known along the beachhead; so widespread indeed that customers from outside our squadron began to invite themselves at short notice. In fact, several aircraft daily, belonging to other units, found it convenient to land at B7. They had spontaneous engine trouble, strange shortages of petrol, all coupled with the most odd kind of radio failure that prevented them from asking permission to land. Being popular can become dangerous, and trouble came with Air Vice-Marshal Brown, in charge of 84 Group. He visited us without warning and, having lunched in 'my' inn, uncovered the whole thing. Apparently showing no gratitude for his full belly, he took me aside and said that a sign 'Out of Bounds to all ranks' would have to be displayed on the front door as from that very moment. As he got ready to leave, he added with a smile and with typical British humour that — for 183 pilots only — the back door could be quietly used. Alas, a few days later, as the bridgehead was widened, we left for Sommerville and kissed our lovely old French inn goodbye.

July came to an end with a ferocious tank battle around Caen, while our American friends cleaned up the Cherbourg Peninsula and progressed towards the south. General Montgomery lured most of the German forces to the Orne Canal area. Then, all together, the British, Canadian and Americans could strike at the Falaise bottleneck.

Each evening, dog-tired and covered in dust, I sank onto my camp bed after swallowing gallons of tea. General Eisenhower and some of his staff visited our airfield. I had the honour of talking freely to him for a few minutes. I was fascinated by his quiet demeanour and the air of efficiency and strength that radiated from the Supreme Commander. Ike told us how important our work was and congratulated us on our keenness, going as far as to declare that the path to victory would be opened by us in the present decisive battles.

During these last few weeks we suffered heavy losses, most of them newly arrived pilots; more than ever, the problem is to keep going, to remain alive.

The glory attached to big aerial battles has been replaced by hard, strenuous, sapping action, sometimes obscure, often thankless: in the great struggle for the conquest of the European fortress, we are now the German tank-busters.

Chapter 20
Riveted to the Controls

The countryside has an air of holiday about it. The front line is calm, as if, on either side, the adversaries are observing a lull, a moment of truce tacitly accepted by the belligerents. We take advantage of it to send newcomers off to fly their first ops. These young pilots fresh out of the operational training unit (OTU) are keen to prove their skill. We, the old hands, know that it takes more than enthusiasm, or keenness. What is needed is experience, and the ability to court Lady Luck. At briefing, Rex Mulliner, the CO, takes me aside to tell me to keep a special eye on the new boys in my Blue section, and to assess their airmanship.

Two other Typhoon squadrons, 164 and 609, have taken off shortly before us to make an armed recce up to Rouen, where the Germans have been trying to cross the river on a pontoon bridge — demolished each day and rebuilt each night. In brilliant sunshine Eric Harbutt takes Red section up in a cloud of dust that threatens our big radiators. As the sandstorm drifts away, I taxi down the runway with my youngsters, easing the stick forward with just enough throttle to make the formation take-off easy.

My 'P/O Prune' has been so busy that he clean forgot to retract his undercart after getting airborne. 'O.K. Blue Two — get your wheels up gently, and keep close to me. Like that — well done!' This is not a good omen but tearing a strip off him now won't help. On the contrary, it might take away what little confidence he has and make him feel panicky.

After a wide left turn, we climb to 3000 feet in about 40 seconds and adopt a wide formation, almost line abreast, in order to protect each other from enemy fighters. At that height we are obviously more exposed to flak but it's the best altitude to see every detail on the ground. From time to time, we hear faint voices on the radio, coming from other formations operating in the area.

Eric Harbutt and his Red section are on the left of our formation, slightly in front, when suddenly black spots stain the horizon far ahead of us, showing the marks of the ugly 88 mm shells as they explode. At the same time, a pilot's voice can be heard, slightly weakened by distance:

'Red One, Pee Wee calling — I've been hit.'

'Pee Wee, Red One — how bad is it?'

A strangely calm voice comes back on the air, then the words hit me. My blood freezes in my veins, so detached is the tone.

'Red One, this is Pee Wee. I can't hear you any more — my radio is stuck on transmit. I can't move my hands or my legs — I'm paralysed. No use calling me, I can't receive you — got a splinter in the spine — my plane is flying on the trim, but I can't pilot it now.'

A horrible silence, then the voice of Red One bites the air, more for the sake of the others than for Red Four, who obviously can't hear him.

'Pee Wee, for God's sake jump — you have *got* to jump! Try to jump, Pee Wee!'

We can hear his words are a cry, an order, and a shout of anger against the inevitable — the impossibility of helping a friend.

'Listen pals, it's Pee Wee. I have had it — there's nothing to be done about it — it's the end. I'll just talk to you all the way . . . it'll make it easier . . .'

Dreadful seconds go by, marking the slow agony of Pee Wee, the 609 Squadron sergeant pilot whom I had known for over a year. He got his nickname because he was so small and always smiling — one of those fellows who never make the hit parade but always do everything asked of them.

Hardened though I am, I can visualise with horror that plane flying on a fixed course, at a fixed altitude, taking with it the paralysed pilot — all the way to death. The situation is made worse by the feeling of 'slow motion', in which everything happens almost imperceptibly, causing the end to be more cruel, slower to kill, but pitiless and ineluctable all the same.

Nobody can do a thing, not even get him to hear a soothing word: just fly along with him as long as possible on that trip without return.

The radio crackles in my ears: 'There we go pals — one wing is dropping steadily, and the Tiffie is skidding. I don't feel anything — it's not even painful. But time is getting short and my sun has gone. I am now below 2000 feet over lovely countryside.'

Silence. A silence that seems to last a century and I can hear my heart beating. My eyes moisten. I am listening to a man telling us of his slow agony, looking at death with open eyes for long seconds. We all fly without a word, conscious of the weakness of a human being faced with destiny. The air is filled by a long agonising cry, followed by a loud explosion. Then silence falls upon our sky and the Norman countryside.

I have to break the silence that has fallen upon those who are still alive — for the time being?

'Beaver aircraft — keep your eyes open. Target straight ahead!'

I speak the words — I would have said anything — to re-establish the current that had been short-circuited for a while. It won't help us to cry over spilt milk when we need all our energy to survive. On our left, the flak is already reminding us of our normal problems. It fills the sky, a mixture of big black puffs made by ugly 88 mm shells that make the air feel bumpy as they explode, and the beads of 20 mm tracer that stripe the azure vault before they fall away in strange arabesques.

Eric has located the enemy gun positions and falls upon them with his section, diving at an angle of 45 degrees. I follow them by sight while I get my own section in echelon starboard, spaced 50 yards apart so as not to lose sight of me during the dive.

A little pause before we go down, just a few seconds to allow the first section to get clear of the target before we go for it at 500 mph.

A few quick words to grab the new boys' attention: 'Each select your target and don't waste shells. Fire your rockets in salvos — and pull out in time. Don't lose sight of me — a lonely plane is a defenceless bird. Let's go!' and I fall like a stone on the German guns.

Every man for himself. Now I can do no more for my chickens, just guide them down the muzzles of those guns and give them the best possible aim.

Five hundred yards. The target fills the gunsight. I choose a four-barrel gun that is firing at me and let them have the full salvo of my rockets and, at the same time, a long burst of cannon. The gunners fall around their guns like dummies.

Explosions on the ground — others in the sky. Smoke hides the scenery while I pull the stick back and climb towards the sky.

Bang! Bang! Bang! A thump — the engine chokes, roars, chokes again, then recovers its steady noisy song. I know I have been hit — it's becoming a (bad) habit, but one gets used to anything, even to being a clay-pigeon when bullets hit the fuselage with the noise of broken glass.

A quick glance in the mirror. Three black dots are following me, the last one some distance away. All is well, here are three of them who have gone, unhurt, through their baptism of fire.

Set course for base. It has not been a happy day.

Main thing now is to get the new boys operational as soon as possible, so that they get a chance to be old boys — if their luck holds.

Once over the front line, we get on to the B8 circuit and land in a dust storm that follows us up to dispersal. There, sad news awaits. Not only did 609 lose Pee Wee, but two aircraft of Eric Harbutt's section did not return. They were shot down during their second attack on the gun positions.

Eric himself was hit but managed to creep back. My number 2 looks at a big hole in his left wing, which will confer on him a sort of seniority and be something to write home about.

I turn towards Chiefy Hanson who is busying himself with my plane. 'Look, sir, could you possibly pick some more peaceful targets? We are overworked with repairs, and your wingmen seem to copy your bad habits, getting holed all over . . .'

Good old Chiefy! He goes around 'his' planes and nurses 'his' pilots like a mother hen, hiding his emotions beneath traditional British understatement. The sight *is* rather impressive: two starred holes in the wing, a dozen bullet holes in the fuselage between cockpit and tail — but nothing really bad enough to prevent my Typhoon from flying next day . . .

Chapter 21
The Panzer Division

30 July, 1944. My plane looks like a convalescent wearing bandages. The riggers have managed to patch the holes with sticky tape, but they are short of grey-blue paint to camouflage the damage. They have covered the patches with blood-red anti rust mixture that gives a funny look like a wounded out-patient . . .

I take advantage of the sun to lay out my large-scale map on the wing and study a point circled in red. It's a wood on the side of a country road that leads to Vire, a charming little town in Normandy.

According to the Intelligence Officer, there is an old mansion hidden in that wood, which is the hideout HQ of an armoured division. The Resistance got the gen through to us this very morning and Group Captain Scott has decided to go hunting Nazi Generals. It's a free op. Each squadron will send up eight aircraft at 15 minute intervals to cover the Caumont-Vire area. Good luck to the first to find its prey!

In 183, Rex Mulliner briefs us to fly high to Vire, then descend behind the town in order to come low over the marked wood and hope to get the advantage of surprise.

No green pilots today, it's a free-for-all reserved for old hands. Well, let's say for seasoned ones; out of 28 pilots, there are only five veterans still around.

Airborne, I sort out the housekeeping chores: align the red dot on the aiming sight, take off the safety catch of the gun button, adjust my seat in the high position, select 'pairs' on the rocket-firing system and check my Smith & Wesson P.38 is firmly secure in my left boot. These automatic actions keep me busy for the first few minutes of my flight.

Now, I concentrate my attention on the sky — but without neglecting the Normandy countryside that passes under my wings.

The map open on my left knee, the left gloved hand going to and fro between the throttle and the route traced on the map, we go over the bomb line — that moving, abstract, edge of 'no man's land', theoretically marked with orange smoke to allow pilots to attack freely any target beyond it.

We dive to ground level just beyond Vire. Rex takes us over fields like schoolboys on holiday, jumping over hedges, flitting past tall poplar trees,— skimming grass fields and making cattle, frightened by our monstrous cavalcade, run in all directions.

The wood is there, suddenly, to starboard. Grey-clad little men run for cover and tank gun barrels stick out of the trees. The rats are caught in their lair so the ball can start.

Free for all — to each his own.

No flak whatever — a pleasant change to achieve total surprise. I turn steeply, without losing sight of my Huns, to get my guns to bear on the little wood.

My number two is glued to me like a leech, ready to dive at my side, when suddenly, out of a side lane, rolling quietly towards us, come a dozen staff cars, wearing the insignia of their HQ, and driving a little apart from each other.

In a split second, I realise what's happening and forget all about the tanks to concentrate on this unexpected gift: I have in front of my eyes the General Staff of an entire Nazi armoured division!

'Rex, north of the grove: staff cars — bring in the boys. Tallyho!'

I don't wait for an answer. With Teddy, I open fire with my 20 mm and let loose the rockets, pair after pair, at one-second intervals just like in practice.

A car explodes. A motorcyclist slides under the wheels of the next car as my shells cut it wide open. Another car collides with the one in front. It's hell down on that road. Already I am past the convoy, or what's left of it. The other Tiffies dive, fire, pull up, climb and dive again. Fire, explosions, black smoke — the whole countryside seems to change into a torch that spreads to the neighbouring wood.

And still no flak. The massacre goes on for several minutes, until we have expended all our ammo.

Now we reform around our leader while we climb to observe the damage. Not a staff car was spared. All around the thicket, and in some spots inside the wood, big fires and explosions are raging — total carnage.

A few days later, as our armoured divisions penetrate in front of Vire, they find a lonely wooden cross in the country lane next to the little wood, with these black letters on it: 'Major-General Ritter von Alber con Dawans — 30th July 1944'. A few yards away, there are other black crosses by some shallow shell holes. The list includes two Majors, two Captains, together with 14 other officers and non-coms.

A Nazi Panzer division had lost all its General Staff.

Chapter 22
Polo Cooreman's Gremlin

I should have told you about them long ago — admit to their existence, allow that we lived daily in their company, that we felt affection for them, feared or venerated them, all at the same time. But then — who would take fighter pilots seriously if they believed in Gremlins?

And yet, we do believe in them!

Half midgets, half elves, the Gremlins were in fact fairies, little jumping gnomes that haunted us, shared our joys and sorrows, and flew with us. Each of us had his own personal Gremlin, either guardian angel or little devil according to its fancy, its mood, or, more likely, as a result of one's own attitude towards it. Sometimes a bunch of Gremlins would get together, dancing a mad saraband in the cockpit, or ballet dancing over the engine cowlings, or on our wings.

Agile as cats and clever as monkeys, they loved to pull a fast one, sometimes in poor taste, or mischievously take us for a ride — such as pressing button B when the radio channel in use was supposed to be on button C, or shutting off the petrol tap in flight, or retracting the undercart during landing. All these little jokes were part of their repertoire that our superiors — quite rightly — punished, holding us responsible for our Gremlins. Just try to prove it was a malign little fairy that pressed the firing button of your cannon in the middle of the dispersal area, spraying the whole place with shells without warning, when, in your single-seater, you *know* that your finger never went anywhere near the firing button!

But if a pilot was on good terms with the Gremlins, then they would oblige in many ways. For example, making you look round without reason if a Jerry was creeping up on your tail, or making you suddenly see the Hun sitting up-sun. All RAF pilots, after two or three pints, will tell you that they live happily in symbiosis with the Gremlins, although they are quite invisible to the uninitiated. This results in complete incredulity on the part of pongos or naval types, who are not honoured by the Gremlins' attention.

Take for example, the evening of 3 August 1944 at B7, the airfield near Bayeux. We had already flown several ops that day, at the request of the Canadians moving around Vire. It must have been close to 8 o'clock when the four Typhoons at readiness on the runway took off under the command of Flt Lt Polo Cooreman, DFC, to answer a last request.

A few clouds in a sunny summer sky were losing themselves in an ocean of tired blue. The dust lifted by the take-off slowly settled on our tents in the orchard.

'Hello, Control — Blue section airborne.'

'Hello, Blue leader — climb to angels 3, in square D4.'

A quick glance at the map spread on the left knee, while the wingmen closed in, on each side of the leader. D4 was Vire again, on the road leading to Falaise where the SS Lehr Division's armour was barring access to the valley for the Canadians of the 8th Brigade. Tiger tanks were concealed in the woods, blending with the landscape, and around them was deployed a formidable umbrella of motorised light and heavy flak, which revealed themselves only when you started diving at them.

'O.K., Control — send up the markers.'

Polo has pinpointed D4 and has reached 3000 feet as ordered, — which is the most effective height for all types of anti-aircraft fire. Now he waits for the forward troops to fire their mortars with special smoke shells to mark the target.

'Blue section keep orbiting D4 for the moment.'

Section gives the orders, but parading around there at that height, waiting for the smoke markers and in full view of the Germans, is not a healthy pastime.

'Blue section, starboard echelon — go!'

The Typhoons stack up to the right, and space themselves so as to offer a less concentrated target to the silent but certainly waiting flak gunners.

'Bloody pongoes again.' Poupa Jaspis expresses his opinion of the army chaps who are late in putting down their smoke markers, and Pedro Hue who is flying No. 4 adds, 'Finger trouble, as usual.'

'Shut up!' This time it's Polo — for the last few minutes he has been trying hard to discover the hidden Tigers in the landscape dimming in the fading light.

Bang! A noise like a whiplash, and the plane shudders. At the same time, a volley of tracer shells, an acrid smell of cordite and the engine splutters. The barrage has opened up all at once, setting the sky ablaze.

Polo turns towards our lines just by instinct, knowing that with an engine on fire, he won't get far. No time to think twice: hood jettisoned, helmet removed and straps undone, he jumps and quickly opens his chute. Two, three somersaults, the harness cuts his shoulders and crutch, then the white umbrella is fully deployed. Under his feet, an orchard full of shell holes: the battle has been raging in this corner. Quick, feet together and bend the knees: a thump followed by a roll and the silk cascades softly into the branches of an apple tree.

Entangled in the cords, Polo manages to get free while the other Typhoons do a last beat-up above his head. A wave of the hand, and suddenly loneliness. Alone, but alive. Nothing broken. Within seconds, repeated whining cat-like noises bring him back to reality. Somebody is shooting at him! No time to find out where it's coming from — the large white landmark of the open parachute is too good a target. Diving into a shell hole, he realises that he has come down in no man's land, somewhere between the lines. Got to run for it before the Jerries come along. Towards the west — but where is west? The sun has gone down somewhere behind that thicket. Ping! — Another ricochet, like a furious wasp. Let's go! A hazardous zigzag run for a hundred yards towards a thin grove.

The sods! Shooting at a plane, that's normal. But shooting at a pilot who has jumped, that's shocking. Simply not done — not fair play. But how can you explain the rules of a game to bastards who have never played cricket? Better add some distance between those barbarians and you. Polo heads into the twilight. In the darkest part of the little wood, he stops to get his breath, still undecided as to which direction to choose. Run he must — but where to?

This is not the first time that Polo has escaped the Germans. Four years ago, he was a reserve lieutenant in the First Regiment of Guides during the 18-day Belgian campaign. Grandson of Gérard Cooreman, Minister of State and former Prime Minister during World War I in May 1918, son of a patrician Ghent family, he had been sent to prison camp in Germany for several months. He had even become acquainted with the amenities of Colditz. Then came the German propaganda: Flemish-speaking Belgians could go home, while the French educated ones were to be kept prisoner. So this French-speaking officer used Flemish to get repatriated — and then took French leave, together with Paul Giroux and Bob Meus.

After a brief stop to say hello to his family they started on the long escape route to England to fight again. They crossed the border into France, where the Count of Alcantara, at great risk, helped them to go through the restricted area round Amiens. Safely in Libourne, the trio took refuge with Mr. van den Boogaerde, brother of the Governor of oriental Flanders. This Belgian gentleman living in France was the head of a very prosperous wine business, and the unwilling host of an undesirable guest: the German officer heading the local Kommandatur. Right under the nose of that thick-headed German the two beautiful daughters of Mr. van den Boogaerde smuggled the three young Belgians into the unoccupied French zone. After crossing the Pyrenees, they enjoyed the hospitality of a Spanish prison at Miranda for another three months, until the British Embassy managed to get them to Gibraltar.

Polo had contracted typhus in prison and missed dying by hours, thanks to a young M.O. But when he reached London the summer of 1941 was still young and he learned that he was to be posted back to Portugal as a diplomat. Polo would have none of it, letting the Belgian Government in London know he had come all the way from Belgium to be a pilot and to fight — not to bow and kiss hands at diplomatic parties. So, in 1943 he was posted to 609 Squadron as a fighter pilot, where he was to fly more than a hundred Typhoon missions and become a flight commander in Normandy.

All those achievements are behind him. He's going round in circles, lost somewhere between Caen and Falaise, in the twilight and under a starless sky that hides the small trees which keep tripping him up. In the gathering darkness, he gropes his way towards a clearer patch. There's a farm on the edge of the wood. A farm with no sign of life, no light visible. It's a jumble of buildings, surrounded by a low dry-stone wall. Nothing moves — the place looks derelict, abandoned. He's thirsty. He must have a drink, and eat too if possible. Carefully, he climbs over the wall and finds his way to the barn, passing through a meadow whose fence is lying on the ground. Just as he gets to the corner of the barn the earth shakes, freezing him to the spot — he's in the middle of a herd of cows that surround him and let loose a chorus of desperate moos. The nearest ones push their heavy flanks against him and the most loving ones start to lick his face. The raucous bellowing makes as much noise as the trumpets of Jericho: enough to alert the whole Wehrmacht, if they are lying nearby.

After a cautious retreat, Polo returns to the thicket and runs as fast as he dares in the opposite direction, still chased by the cattle whose heavy udders show why they need so badly to give their long overdue milk.

After wandering hither and yon, meeting all the hidden traps of the undergrowth, Polo hits a country lane bordering an open field. Too dangerous to move in the open, so he turns back and goes into a thicker patch of woodland to wait the dawn. The July night is warm, but the ground is damp. Lying on the moss Polo shivers nervously as time passes slowly, disturbed only by ordinary night noises.

In his hand, he has a comb. Just a comb; one that would look absolutely normal to the inexperienced eye. Yet, inside the back of the comb, he knows there is a wire magnet. It's one of those gadgets given to pilots to help them to escape — it's a compass, and the thin side turns to point north. Polo tries everything he can think of — twiddling the comb a hundred times — it's no good, he doesn't know how to use it!

Branches crack. Heavy boots crush dead wood. Guttural voices are getting nearer, calling to each other from time to time.

'*Walter, wo sind Sie?*'

Another voice, away in the distance: '*Hier, mit der Gefreiter. Wir konnen nichts sehen.*'

A few feet to Polo's left, a shadow appears, treads by heavily, then stops at the edge of the thicket. Looking at the open field the German shelters a lit cigarette in the palm of his hand. In his hide-out, Polo shrinks. He holds his breath and his leg aches under him. At the slightest move, a burst from a Schmeisser will echo. No chance to run, just wait and hope.

After two minutes that seem like a century, the soldierman puts out his cigarette against a tree trunk, pauses for a moment, then rejoins his patrol along the road. The noise of boots goes away and the silence of the night closes in.

Safe, Polo breathes again quietly. Circulation returns to his frozen body. He can only wait till daybreak.

Dawn comes slowly, hesitantly, like a cold morning after a sleepless night. On the country lane, spaced at 20 yard intervals in Indian file, four men advance at an even pace. The British army's pace. The officer leading the patrol balances a Sten gun on his arm, finger on the trigger, and the men following cover him, hand grenades hanging from their belts.

The joy of seeing friends coming gives way to the fear of being shot before being identified — let's face it, in the pale light of morning RAF battledress is not all that different from the Luftwaffe uniform. Hidden a few yards from the road, Polo waits until the officer has passed by, then comes out between the leader and his men, crying 'Friend! I am a Typhoon pilot.'

The lieutenant has turned round with his Sten gun ready. But a shot is not fired. Self-control — and luck.

'Advance friend, and be recognised.'

It's the standard procedure, just like on manoeuvres. Polo advances with his hands up. The four men surround him, guns at the ready: 'Name, rank, number and unit?'

'Cooreman, Flight Lieutenant, 139825 — 609 Squadron RAF.'

'All right, but you've got a funny accent!'

'I'm Belgian, lieutenant. My Tiffie was shot down yesterday evening. Can I smoke?'

'O.K. We knew that a Typhoon was shot down near here — in fact we're looking for the pilot — but we'll check your story at our command post. Please walk in front.' Then, almost apologetically, 'You do understand, don't you?'

Polo laughs — Polo laughs about everything — it's his way of reacting to spending his life helping the Canadians engaged in battle, and then finding them rather mistrusting him. 'Yes Lieutenant, I understand, but if you knew how funny it is!'

After ten minutes' steady marching the group reaches our lines and the field telephone soon clears our friend. Shortly after 10 o'clock a dispatch rider brings Polo back on the pillion of his motorbike, none the worse for his adventure. Slapped on the back and welcomed with a steaming mug of tea, he is pestered with all kinds of questions, jokes and congratulations. On the fringe, the Intelligence Officer waits to ask questions for his report.

Suddenly Polo fishes in his pocket for the magic compass-comb, sticks it under the nose of the 'spy', and asks 'Would you be so kind as to show me how the hell one finds the north with this stupid gadget, at night and in a forest?'

'Simple, my friend. You just pull a hair from your head and hang the comb on it: the fine side turns to indicate north!'

A look of incredulity spreads on the tired face of Flt Lt Cooreman, then his smile returns. But we — all the pilots — *we* saw a Gremlin that skipped away, jumping and clapping his hands. The Gremlin laughed and kept repeating, over and over again, 'A hair, Polo, a hair . . .'

Chapter 23
The Battle of Falaise

At the beginning of August the battle reaches its climax. We fly every day, going flat out, and successes mount: two tanks — flamers — near Flers, an SS battalion mauled near Aunay, two more tanks destroyed at Sourdeval, and five more the next morning at Couteville. The whole thing was crowned on 8 August by the start of the Falaise battle in which our Typhoons were to write a page of glory as the bells sounded the knell of the German armies in France.

That day Flt Lt Napier, B Flight commander in 164 Squadron, was killed during an attack on an enemy convoy. An hour later, Wg Cdr Walter Drink promoted me Flight Lieutenant and gave me command of B Flight. I was a bit surprised for there were other more senior pilots in the wing, but I was proud of this mark of confidence; now I would have my own flight to lead into battle as the war entered its decisive phase.

The very next day, 9 August, I can lead my eight aircraft in an attack on the outskirts of Falaise. The German 7th Army is being attacked on all sides. The plan is to trap more than 100,000 Germans in a pincer movement whose jaws would close on one of Hitler's best armies. The front line is reeling under the Allied attack and our job is to finish off the panzers trying to escape. The flak remains deadly, but irregular, as if the Germans had abandoned some units to concentrate their guns at selected points.

We arrive west of Falaise at 3000 feet, in radio contact with the attack control, called 'Cab Rank'. I'm surprised to recognise the voice of the controller — it's my old friend Mony Van Lierde (He returned to us in 123 Wing a few weeks later and took over command of 164 Squadron). There could be no better guide than Mony, whose calm voice gives me the form precisely and in a tone of close friendship as he mixes French and English.

'Allo, Charles. Tanks and staff cars in F4, behind the farm. Flak in the wood — *Bonne chance!*'

'Thanks, Mony. O.K. boys, orbit left.'

As we turn left, I plot the coordinates on my map, scan the ground, then pick out the poorly camouflaged targets round the Normandy farm.

No flak yet. As usual they don't want to show themselves before we go down, so as to take us unawares. Just wait, friends! In a moment, it will be your chance!

Three-quarters of the way round my turn, I am perfectly positioned up-sun to spoil the aim of the flak as we go down in our shallow dive on the Panzers. Now I can see the tanks clearly and I start diving with the first section. I send the other four Typhoons to look after the flak boys in the wood.

'Red section — we go for the armour. Blue section enjoy yourselves with the guns in the wood. Go!'

As soon as they realise that we have seen them, the Germans let go at us with everything they've got and tracers zip past on all sides. But nothing except a lucky shot can stop a Typhoon diving at 500 mph. Blue section neutralises the wood with rockets and cannon and we soon have a free hand. The first tank grows in my gunsight and I let go two pairs of rockets that get him on his left side. I pull up an inch, and fire at a staff car which goes up in smoke as the shells strike home.

A steep turn to port, and from the corner of my eye, I see my No. 2 climbing behind me while Nos 3 and 4 are busy shooting up a line of lorries that go up in flames. Down again and this time I choose a juicy half-track under a camouflage net and get a direct hit with my last pair of rockets. A little further away, a small, black Citroen jumps and explodes, as my guns go silent with the long hiss of compressed air that marks the end of my ammunition.

I climb back to 2000 feet to watch the slaughter. In a dozen places there are still sporadic explosions under the thick black smoke that billows towards the sky, and flames are coming out of the farm roof. I hope the French farmers are safe in the cellar, for all around it's hell let loose. Time to reform my Typhoons. I am very pleased to see my No. 2 keeping nicely positioned 50 yards to starboard. It's his first op. He's a Belgian Sergeant Pilot called Pol Mouzon, who will be my best No. 2 ever for many weeks, and become one of the best pilots I ever knew. With calm courage and clever as a monkey, little 'Mouze' is as imperturbable in the air as he is on the ground. It must be in the family, for his uncle is one of the pilots flying PRU Spitfires over Germany; equipped with a special camera they go all alone and completely unarmed, bringing back the most superb photographs.

This August sets a record in offensive sorties. My logbook shows I flew 37 ops in 23 days. 13 were flown between 15 and 19 August, the five days of the Falaise inferno. The Typhoon contribution was vital in the gigantic battle.

Those five days sealed the fate of the 7th Army, encircled, smashed, cut to pieces: 30,000 died and over 100,000 were taken prisoner. For us, ended three weeks of total effort from start to finish. It imbued all pilots with a kind of frenzy they had never known before.

In fact, it all started a few days before 15 August. We were operating around Falaise, the hinge of the German defence in the west. We had to take the city, which was the key of the road to Paris. On the 10th, we had attacked Bernay and chalked up a dozen vehicles and a few armoured cars. On the 11th, we hit Dozule and liquidated some motorised reinforcements. On the 12th, we paid a visit to a wooded area near Aily and gave it the usual treatment of a plastering with rockets and 20 mm

shells. A few days later, more than 200 German bodies were found there
— an SS company disposed of.

On the 13th and 14th, we were in close support of our own tanks
between Trun and Falaise, attacking strong points just ahead of our
armour. As always, this was the kind of mission I enjoyed most — first
because, technically speaking, one had to combine efficiency with
precision — to knock out a German Tiger just a hundred yards in front
of our boys was a delicate piece of work, and to smash an anti-aircraft
gun under rolling shell fire, at point-blank range, was a very exciting
exercise indeed. Secondly, it was a source of real satisfaction to know
that we were opening a way for our friends down there — those
marvellous front-line boys, advancing their tanks as the spearhead of
our forces. We were really proud to belong to the same army as those
soldiers who, without the glory attached to flying, were fighting and
suffering in far worse conditions than we were.

The balloon really goes up on the morning of 15 August 1944. The
whole wing is on standby and HQ has asked us to deliver a mighty blow
to the retreating enemy. Each of the four squadrons will put into the air
every serviceable aircraft, and as often as possible — a kind of shuttle
service at maximum effort. The Germans are sacrificing some of their
best units to hold the Falaise gap open. The Americans under General
Patton push ahead as the right jaw of the pincers, the British press on
straight ahead and the Canadians go all out on the left. On both sides,
no quarter is asked or given. The outcome will be of vital importance in
the war and, without being a great strategist, I have the impression that
should we win this battle the doors of France will be wide open to us.
News of an Allied landing in the South of France this same morning
adds to the euphoria and my morale goes up one more notch.

As 164 Squadron is still without a Squadron leader I have, as senior
Flight commander, responsibility for one-quarter of the wing. 609
Squadron is headed by Manu Geerts, 198 by a Free French pilot called
Pol Ezzano, while 183 still has Rex Mulliner, a charming, quiet
Englishman. The Wing Leader, our friend Walter Drink, is going to
earn his DSO in a few hours. All the squadrons are to operate singly,
with complete freedom of action within the prescribed area.

The first op of the day takes us to the Trun-Livarot-Bernay triangle
where the Germans are trying to escape from the bottleneck. With my
faithful Mouzon as No. 2 (a man I'm coming to appreciate more and
more for he seems always to be there when needed) I lead the squadron
into an attack on a convoy surprised in open country.

The sods are still well organised, with plenty of light flak to defend
them. But it takes more than that to deter a bunch of buccaneers who
are really enjoying themselves. Three, four, five strikes, and the convoy
is burning fiercely — decimated, smashed — while not a single Typhoon
is even damaged.

Early afternoon, we are back again, and it's the Trun road that is the object of our attention. Tigers! They are running to escape being surrounded. We have found them in the worst possible situation for tanks: in open country, with no line of escape. So the show starts like a well-planned ballet: the Typhoons go into echelon while turning, then dive on their prey at full throttle. Rockets whistle, guns bark, engines roar and pilots sweat without noticing it as our missiles smash the Tigers. Petrol tanks explode amid torrents of black smoke. A typhoon skids away to avoid machine-gun fire. Some horses frightened by the noise gallop wildly in a nearby field.

One tank tries to hide behind a bunch of trees. Stupid clot! Your hour has come. I don't know why, but of all in those heaps of iron it's you I have decided will perish in flames in that corner of France.

I'm surprised to find I am talking to myself. You Germans are going to pay, a hundred times, for all that we Belgians, the French, our English friends, all my pals, have suffered and endured for four years. You will die as proxy for that monster Hitler. You will die, ripped wide open by my rockets, and the blood of your crew will splash the red-hot sides of your tank. A kind of rage has come over me; I see only that grey object trying to escape by hiding behind the thin curtain of a thicket. But I have already regained my self-control. Coldly, with infinite care, I trim my Typhoon into a shallow dive, at reduced speed to lengthen my aiming time, to ensure that the red dot of my gunsight is centred on his belly. Caressing the firing button, I let go at those bastards who are about to meet their Maker.

A wisp of smoke, an explosion — then missing a collision by only a few feet, I shoot towards the sky while the ripped open Tiger emits a torrent of black smoke and bright yellow flames. For a few seconds I had forgotten everything; nothing else mattered but that tank, which for some unknown reason had suddenly appeared as the reason for my years of fighting, of privation, of blood and tears. All at once, my most primitive instincts had been let loose, had taken control of me and my avenging arm.

Then, mysteriously, as quickly as it has overwhelmed me, the excitement dies. Reason returns and I return to taking care of my boys, who seem to be enjoying the mayhem. It really is a slaughter, a deadly merry-go-round, with everyone playing a part. The outskirts of Trun have been turned into a cemetery for panzers, with raging fires and explosions throwing up clouds of black smoke. Even the flak has given up, silenced, leaving the Typhoons to roam at will.

Destroying, killing, sacking, setting on fire! I discover, with amazement, that I enjoy it, that it satisfies me; in fact, I really get a thrill from it! Like a wild animal whose mouth waters at the thought of getting his teeth into a long-tracked creature that is at last at his mercy. A dangerous reaction! Quite useful in the heat of battle, but it clouds one's judgement and liberating man's worst instincts can lead to mistakes. I realise that a leader has no right to fall prey to passion, that he must keep his self-control, be capable at all times of maintaining a correct balance between the goal and the means to reach it.

'O.K. boys, regroup at angels four.'

It's all over for today. There is plenty left for everyone, tomorrow, the day after — at least for those who will still be there!

The eight Tiffies climb into the Trun sky, leaving behind the burning wreckage of a Nazi division, and they follow me to our lines and to our airstrip.

On our return flight we pass other squadrons going out to battle, towards the kill, like vultures attracted by the smell of blood. We talk little. From the way everyone keeps in tight formation, I sense that these boys are full of guts, fed by their own success, and that we are a tightly knit family, grouped around their leader.

When we land, amid the general excitement everyone tells his story, talking loudly and quickly. It's the usual winding down, the relief valve after the fighting, the liberation of nervous strain built up during the action. All of a sudden, I feel old, very old — as if there were a generation between us, although I am one of the youngest. The weight of responsibility? The wear of 200 ops? I don't know. But suddenly it hits me that I have taken pleasure in a killing.

Chapter 24
Beyond Human Strength

August 1944. Things are reaching a crescendo. The hunt is on for the fleeing German army, trying to avoid our encirclement.

We take off at dawn, squadron strength; targets are 'anything that moves' within a five-mile radius of Falaise. Three sorties that day — a bridge destroyed, two dozen tanks and fifty-odd trucks. Flak is lively, but nobody is hit. We are lucky today for several Typhoons in nearby squadrons have been shot down.

On the last sortie we destroy a pontoon bridge across the Seine, near Vernon. The German engineers are wiped out like those little clay pipes in a shooting gallery. Memory strikes. As a child, I used to go with my uncle Fernand Demoulin each July to the big annual fair in Brussels-Midi. It was great fun to go round the stands, especially the one where, with an air-rifle, we shot at clay pipes and it triggered a camera if one scored a bull. My uncle was a veteran of the 1914-18 war with many distinctions and medals. If by chance I scored he was almost as proud of his protégé as I was of him. Now, I am all square with my hero of the Yser trenches.

On 17 August, we go back to the pontoon bridge on the Seine that the Krauts have repaired during the night. Although flak is heavy, we destroy again the fragile structure re-laid by the engineers. Pontoons that do not sink are swept away by the current together with the shattered corpses.

It takes us back to Vimoutiers, the second sortie of the day with 198 Squadron, led by Wg Cdr Drink. It is barely 10 in the morning and we find a mile-long convoy of ambulances, clearly visible on the narrow road. But, looking more closely, we see, spaced between the Red Cross vehicles, Tiger tanks and half-track 88 mm guns trying to sneak out. Found out, the Germans open up with a deadly ack-ack barrage even though we were only having a look.

Walter Drink's voice breaks in, loud and clear: 'That settles it boys. Give the bastards all you've got — and never mind those phoney Red Crosses!'

This gives us no qualms of conscience. As we dive on the convoy, the Red Cross 'ambulances' stop and armed SS men leap out to take cover in the roadside ditches. We heard last night that the SS had shot some Canadian prisoners of war in a farm courtyard, not far from Caen, so we can hardly be expected to spare those black-clad murderers.

By common consent, our squadrons separate:—198 goes for the head of the convoy, and with 164 I take on the tail end. Very soon the road is blocked at both ends and those between are ready for destination. High above, Walter Drink is co-ordinating the mayhem, guiding aircraft by radio to the places where they will do best, and calling forward two more squadrons to join in. Fires are burning everywhere, lorries and cars go up in smoke, tanks explode. When we have fired all our rockets, we switch to 20 mm cannon, aiming at the SS hiding in the ditches.

The flak has died down when, guns empty, we climb to 5000 feet to reform and go home. The whole thing lasted about 20 minutes. Now it's up to 609 and 183, who have come flat out to finish the job. I got a tank, two half-tracks, a score of lorries and an ambulance as well, which went up after a burst of cannon fire. I am sure too that many SS did not survive.

Immediately, our aircraft are refuelled and rearmed. We are ordered off again to the Lisieux area, where convoys are said to be escaping under cover of a swarm of Me109s. Well, well! The Luftwaffe is back! I hope that we meet them *after* firing our rockets — a dogfight with full load is no piece of cake.

Before take-off I warn my pilots that, should the Messerschmitts bounce us, they must turn towards the German fighters and keep right down on the deck. Low down, we don't have to worry but it would be suicidal to climb towards them:—the rails of our rockets would be a handicap in that manoeuvre. I remember that only one of my pilots has had any dogfighting experience — the rest have never met enemy fighters in battle as yet.

Nearing Lisieux, we can see a dogfight in progress, to our right just a few miles away. About 50 Messerschmitts are mixing it with a bunch of Spitfires — it looks like a big do. Calls coming from everywhere, jamming the radio with warnings and orders blocking each other. Unfortunately I can't go and join this fight, for we have to destroy another bridge on the Seine, to cut off a convoy of panzers in full retreat. It is lucky, for there would be no profit in meeting those fighters with a handful of green pilots. I decide to go down to the deck and head for the river. We arrive just in time to catch a convoy on the bridge. No messing about — we cut the pontoons to bits, gun the convoy and many vehicles fall in the water.

The whole thing is over in no time.

I carefully keep plenty of shells in reserve in case we are intercepted. We need something to fight with in case we have a nasty surprise. We set course back to Caen, still on the deck, when suddenly, on my right, I see a section of Spitfires diving on Blue section. 'Look out, Blue One, break right! Now!'

The four Typhoons swing starboard steeply, followed by the Spits with all guns blazing! Idiots, those myopic Spitfire boys, firing at friendly aircraft! As they climb away, I turn after them with my section, swearing like a fishwife, but they keep well away, probably having realised their mistake. Luckily, no one was hit, but some of us had a nasty turn. All this happened so quickly that I couldn't get close enough to read their squadron letters on the fuselage. A pity. I would have liked to frighten them to death. Even when I land at base I am still quite steamed up.

We learn that 183 lost four pilots this afternoon. All of them shot down near Vimoutiers by a bunch of over forty 109s: that was the big dogfight we saw going on. They are Fg Off Campbell-Brown, Warrant Officers Carragher and Humphrey, and Sergeant Gibson. All four were friends with whom I had flown a few weeks back when I was their temporary Flight Commander in 183 Squadron.

Four other Typhoons of 183 managed to stagger back to base full of holes and with pilots shaken but unhurt. The Germans bounced them while they were attacking a convoy. It was because the leader had not left a section above for cover and so the Huns were not seen coming. It was a miracle four escaped — probably thanks to the Spitfires' arrival. If it had happened just a few weeks earlier, I would have been with them . . .

August 18th and 19th: two days that are the peak of the battle: we fly three strikes a day, with three attacks per sortie. At that pace, it's impossible to keep up one's strength. A plane that has been damaged can be fairly easily patched up — but the human body rebels.

Getting up shortly after sunrise, after a night full of battle noise, I gather the pilots of the duty flight, go over the daily orders, and the Intelligence reports, then chalk on the board the names of the pilots to fly the first sortie. Before taking off, I hand over command of the squadron to the remaining flight commander, Flt Lt Thompson. He only arrived two days ago, and I trust he has been able to pick up enough gen in so short a time.

The battle is reaching its climax; we are still trying to close the gap between the British and the Americans and close the trap set for the German 7th Army — we must smash their escaping panzers and deny them the road to safety.

Vimoutiers, Trun, Bernay, Orbecq, Lisieux, Evreux: these names come up on every strike, like tombstones, marking the graves of two SS divisions. It makes a real charnel house of panzers. I fly like an automaton, I am tired beyond belief but success acts as a stimulant and I keep going. I feed on explosions, gunfire, burning lorries and broken caterpillar tracks. I am done in, out on my feet, and on 20 August at daybreak, my legs refuse to support me. I find myself in the sickbay, where the doc gives me a sedative that puts me out like a light for 24 hours on the trot.

On 21 August I am fit again and, after flying another rocket sortie, I meet the new CO of 164, Sqn Ldr Waddy. This pleasant man is returning to the front after a rest and doesn't know our sector. So, after being introduced to the pilots and checking over our area map, he says he wants me to lead on the next sortie and he will fly as No. 2 to get a grip of things. Which is the best way to get back in business.

Alas, two days later, old Waddy is shot down together with Flying Officer Trafford and Sergeant White — so there I am, back in command with three pilots short and only nine aircraft serviceable.

On the 22 and 23 of August, we fly another five sorties, mainly along the Seine, towards Quilleboeuf and almost to the outskirts of Paris, which is close to its liberation. We attack the remnants of the Germans still trying to cross the river and we decimate several enemy columns on their escape route to Rouen.

At the end of August, I look at my logbook and can barely believe my eyes: in 28 days I have flown 44 offensive sorties, of which 14 were between 15 and 19 August. The squadron has been credited with the destruction of 112 panzers, another 215 damaged, and more than 500 trucks destroyed. Add to that three trains blown up, 29 barges sunk and five bridges destroyed. My personal score since D-day is now 18 tanks, 26 armoured vehicles and over 60 trucks destroyed. As for the enemy put out of action, a conservative estimate for the squadron runs to several thousand German soldiers. It is interesting to note that, in 40 days, 164 Squadron has flown 82 separate missions totalling 656 individual sorties; 419,800 20 mm shells were fired and 5248 rockets were launched. We lost 11 pilots and 18 aircraft.

Since we arrived on French soil we have had two hectic months and everyone has dug deep into his nervous reserves so as to help our armies destroy the German armoured SS divisions.

I do not think any other military campaign has been so dependent upon a fighter-bomber to win the battle. The Tiger and Panther tanks could outgun and outfight our own tanks, British and American alike; it was the rocket-firing Typhoons that were decisive in beating the panzers.

It is the first time in military history that a ground-attack aircraft, the Typhoon, and above all the rocket-firing Typhoon, has been used on such a scale and with such effectiveness. The Ju87 Stuka dive-bombers of 1940 have been wiped from the western sky and are now used only on the Russian front. The Russian Stormovik is also operating as a dive-bomber, but neither the Stuka nor the Stormovik can compare with the Typhoon; its fire-power is much greater, its speed practically double, and its battle-damage resistance unequalled.

I am completely convinced that victory in Normandy is being achieved by the massive use of the Typhoon and thanks to the sacrifices made by the Tiffie pilots. As for the psychological effect, the Germans have said that their troops are terrorised by our diving attacks.

Over and above my conviction, I have to admit with regret that I have become an excellent killing machine, an artist in destruction. Will I ever regain my balance? The war is still far from its end . . .

Chapter 25
A Forced Landing

The last days of August 1944, and the front line is cracking in several places, the vice is closing and the retreating Germans are running for their lives to the River Rhine.

In Germany, the July attempt against Hitler's life misfired and has ended in cruel butchery. Rommel, wounded on the Normandy front by a South African Spitfire pilot, is recovering in Germany before being compelled by his Führer to commit suicide. Von Kluge has done away with himself before he could be ousted. In Normandy, the Falaise battle is over and the Anglo-Canadian armies are racing towards Belgium and the Dutch border. Paris has fallen on August 24th. General Patton, in his own personal cowboy style, drives his army towards Alsace and the Rhine. In the south, Toulon, Marseilles and Avignon have been liberated and General de Lattre de Tassigny has reached Lyon.

On the Russian front, the Red Army has reached the Danube and Bulgaria. Alas, in Warsaw, the heroes of the Polish resistance are dying, fighting from house to house, while the Soviets, with total indifference, stop their offensive only a few miles away and, monstrously, refuse to help the gallant Poles. The Lublin slaughter of many thousand Polish officers is genocide of one of the most courageous nations on earth. Only a few RAF aircraft based in Italy will fly all the way to Warsaw, at the cost of heavy casualties, to drop arms and bring hope to those men and women fighting to the death. Among those volunteers is a Belgian pilot, Baron Gérard Grendl. He will go back three times, each time returning with a plane heavily damaged by flak and once with an engine on fire. Operations without hope and which cannot change the final outcome of a battle lost from the start — because of the sadism of Stalin — but a hand offered to a dying nation by friends who can do little more than salute their tremendous courage.

We are now operating at the limit of our range. We should be operating from airfields just abandoned by the enemy, to support our forward units, but what we actually do on leaving B7 at Vaussieux-Martragny is stop near Lisieux. And, as soon as we arrive, the front line has moved forward so fast towards the north-east that again we are at the limit of our range. The armour is penetrating so far and so fast into enemy territory that — paradoxically — the air force has the greatest difficulty in keeping up and providing its normal support to our ground forces. In fact, it's a simple problem: a modern army, highly motorised, is dependent upon its supplies. When the distance between the forward elements and the supply base is lengthened, the efficiency of the forces in contact with the enemy goes down — because of the shortage of supplies, both ammunition and fuel. A tactical air force can therefore spend only a short time in the front line.

The only fuel supply available — blood without which a modern army dies — is from a pipeline starting in southern England and ending on the invasion beaches. From there, in jerricans, bowsers, or 40 gallon barrels, the vital petrol has to be taken to the front by long motorised convoys. The longer the distance the less chance of it arriving safely. The greed of some black marketeers, born of the German occupation, means that more than half the fuel disappears into thin air between Normandy and the front line. Bluntly, some of our top-notch units, our best fighting troops, are finding it difficult to get their supplies; many have halted pursuit of a fleeing enemy because the newly liberated people have pinched the much needed fuel — and used it for personal profit. This dirty little game was to cost many human lives, particularly during the battle of Arnhem. The days lost at the beginning of September lengthened the war by several months. And — who knows — in changing the face of Europe.

We are tired and our nerves are stretched to breaking point, but we cannot afford to let go. After four years of exile, of fighting, of loneliness, we are so near our homeland. If all goes well, I shall be in Brussels in a few days. I will see my family and my friends and will have achieved my aim: to win my war, to flush the Huns out, to be alive, to be free in a free world, and to live my own life — and I am not really making plans for the future; winning the war and earning the peace is still far away, very far away. There are honours to be won — and there are many more wooden crosses to be planted in the fields.

A batman comes to my tent with a message from Gp Capt Scott, in charge of the wing. I am to report to his caravan — that's odd, for usually he just telephones me without ceremony, to discuss the daily work. When I get to his office, I sense that the boss has already made his decision.

'Good morning, Sir, you wanted to see me?'

'Yes, Charlie. I want you to take a few days' rest. Fly back to Aston Down, and bring back a brand-new Typhoon that will be your own. Your friend Mony van Lierde is posted to 164 as squadron commander and should be here soon. A few days' rest will do you a world of good. And Brussels will be ours in a few days too. You must be in top form then — so off you go and enjoy yourself.'

It's an order, given gently but no argument. And yet I hesitate for, so near Belgium, I am afraid of missing the boat, of not being there on the day of liberation. But the boss is right. I don't like to admit it but I am nervous, jumpy, empty. Scotty is right; I need to recharge my batteries, to breathe the pure air of that marvellous Cotswold countryside, to be among the orchards full of summer promise and the centuries-old mansions, to visit the ancient pubs with their smell of hops, and love the pretty girls who welcome victorious warriors.

One standing order for returning to England is to fly along the safe corridor from Arromanches. A second says that aircraft have to go in pairs, so as not to be over the sea alone. But custom is that we empty our ammunition bays in the wings and load them up with bartered goods; champagne, bottles of Calvados, silk stockings, scent — and Camembert which can be got anywhere in the bridgehead, because its distribution is impossible since the landing. The slight risk of flying without ammunition is well compensated for by our grateful welcome at the other end; French goodies have been non-existent for four years, and are worth untold gold!

So, at around 4 p.m., I take off, heading for Aston Down. The weather is perfect and not a cloud in the sky. As I circle Arromanches at about 4000 feet, I watch the turnaround of ships unloading their supplies and rushing home for more. The D-day landing barges are like busy bees, providing a shuttle service between the cargo ships and the artificial Mulberry harbours where long lines of lorries wait for their loads. Here and there, wrecks of ships sunk on D-day are still visible at low tide, and, flanking the traffic, barrage balloons float lazily either side of the lane in which the busy bees work endlessly.

I am supposed to wait for another Typhoon to join me before I may cross the Channel. I wait a few minutes and call Control who seem totally uninterested. Then, becoming impatient, I decide to fly to England on my own. In the corridor, flying between identifiable pinpoints and in good visibility, it should be no problem to cross the coast near Portsmouth. I am on leave so, with a light heart, I set course for Gloucester to land at Aston Down nearby.

Soon I see Wroughton airfield right in front of me, dead on track, and flatter myself on my navigation. Suddenly, my eyes flicker, and even though I'm wearing an oxygen mask my vision starts to fade. A last reflex action — open the cockpit hood and I lapse into unconsciousness.

When I come to, I am gliding in a strange silence, one wing slightly low. I am still at about 800 feet and at once realise that I am not going to make the airfield about a mile dead ahead; I must jump at once or make a belly landing in a field. No time to decide, but I take a second or two — and I am at 500 feet, barely gliding. That settles it: a forced landing, and hope for the best.

Straps tightened, cockpit wide open, switches off. Muscles tensed, I prepare myself for the shock when I hit the ground at about 100 mph. I wonder about the engine failure; then I remember an ugly smell of glycol that filled the cockpit. A glycol leak sends the temperature up in no time, and the engine packs up without warning. Lucky it didn't go up in flames.

Although busy with a dicey landing, I feel confident. Not at all nervous, full of an Olympian calm, but a trifle worried that my champagne and Calvados might get spilt on the grass.

God! Ditches right across my landing path. Stick forward quickly to gain a little speed, then try to bounce just before a ditch, hoping to jump it, and stop skidding before the next trap. I hit at about 150 mph. The aircraft bounces like a ball, my head hits the base of the gunsight, a slide — and my Typhoon stops suddenly, but without catching fire or turning over.

It's 4.40 p.m. Not a single sound disturbs the peace of the countryside. I recover my cool, finding it strange to be sitting at daisy level, near peaceful cows who, quite undisturbed, go on grazing.

I climb out of the cockpit, remove my helmet and oxygen mask, disconnect the radio plug, and feel a large lump on my forehead — mentally exaggerated. An RAF staff car drives towards me across the field. It stops alongside my wrecked Typhoon and a cheerful Squadron Leader gets out.

'We saw you come down. Quite a nice landing, if a bit short . . .'

'Thank you, Sir. I'm fine. I am Flt Lt Demoulin of 164 Squadron, in Normandy. Engine failure — glycol leak I guess. Sorry for the trouble I am causing!'

'My name is Morris and I'm the CO of this airfield. You're no trouble at all, my friend!'

All this is spoken in the friendly tone of a neighbour who, with great urbanity and quite naturally, casually invites you for a cup of tea. It's time I worried about my load of booze! Borrowing a coin to use as a screwdriver, I start unscrewing the covers of the ammunition bays — I expect to see a mess when the panels slide open. Miracle! All six bottles of champagne and five bottles of Calvados unbroken — still neatly packed and looking great in their wrappings.

We transfer the precious loot into the rear seat of the little Hillman and go to the local HQ where I am made very welcome while the CO arranges for a twin-engined Oxford to drop me at Aston Down, still thirty minutes' flying time away.

While waiting, I offer my new friends a bottle of champagne and a bottle of Calvados, a drink of which my host says he has never met! So I decide to fetch another bottle of the 100-proof pick-me-up and open it for a tasting. Three glasses are produced and (knowing the stuff) I pour large slugs for the CO and the Adjutant, rationing myself to a thimbleful.

'To your very good health,' says the CO, taking a large swig of the fire water. A strangled cry, a paroxysm of coughing and eyes full of tears.

'Bloody hell! It's liquid explosive, this French stuff!'

We all laugh our heads off. My hosts finish their drinks, and most appreciative, have some more tots. By the time I leave the premises to board the Oxford, two RAF officers wave me goodbye rocking gently and with their eyes just a little too bright.

Smithy and Watts, my two old 609 pals still having a rest, meet me at Aston Down with the car that I left behind at 84 GSU when I went over to France. We drive off happily to recapture our local girl-friends.

Part Four
Crush Germany!

Chapter 26
A Wanderer Goes Home

After a lovely weekend, I report to 84 GSU where the factory will deliver my new Typhoon. I am thrilled to bits — like a little boy awaiting a new toy. It should be the latest model equipped with a special gunsight, and a new canopy of 'teardrop' shape, which greatly increases all-round visibility.

But it is not going to be ready for some time. So I give a hand to Smithy and Watts by testing a P51 Mustang just out of its cocoon. The reserve aircraft are stacked under plastic covers, like furniture under dust-sheets, and they must be fully tested before being dispatched to front-line units. It is absolutely fascinating to fly different types of aircraft, though sometimes with some surprises. It often happens that one is still looking for a particular flying instrument after one is airborne, and sometimes we have to use Pilot's Notes to locate the undercart selector or to find the right boost pressure to cruise with. It is not good practice, but we have reached the point where we treat an aircraft as basically a throttle and a stick, two items sufficient to make it fly. In short, we are getting over-confident, which is always a mistake. It comes from flying in the peaceful sky over England, devoid of danger compared to our usual flying operations.

September is just three days old when the radio brings news that the Brigade of Guards has reached the gates of Brussels. Hour by hour on that lovely Sunday morning, the news describes Montgomery's advance and the German retreat in Belgium. Everything has happened so fast that I have been caught napping, in England, and still without a plane. I should be over there, helping to liberate my country. I ring up the factory, beg the manager to get me a Typhoon, and even lose my temper with the staff. It doesn't help. The plane won't be ready for another few days. What can I do? I try to borrow a Spitfire or a Mustang from the reserve pool, but the much-needed planes can't be lent for my personal use. In any case, the officer commanding 84 GSU can't authorise diversion of an aircraft but, being sympathetic to my cause, he can arrange for a liaison aircraft to drop me somewhere in the south of England to try to get a hitch-flight to the Continent.

It is now Monday 4 September and Brussels was liberated yesterday. BBC war reporters tell the world about celebrations in the streets of the capital and describe the joy of a liberated people. I am beside myself with rage to miss those unique hours for which I have fought for four years. By lunchtime, I still don't know where to go in order to get to Brussels. I am on the verge of forgetting British discipline and letting my Latin temperament go, meaning that King's Regulations can go hang if they won't get me to Brussels.

Finally, old Smithy agrees to fly me to Manston in an Auster, hoping from there to get a seat in one of the Dakotas that fly to Amiens. With a slow aircraft like an Auster we will have to take off early on Tuesday morning and, once in Manston, it is up to me to do the rest . . . I manage to persuade the Mess Secretary to open the larder and fill a kitbag with white bread, spam, margarine, jam, coffee, bully beef and a bottle of whisky — and on Tuesday the 5th at dawn we are off to Manston.

We land at 10 a.m. and I manage to jump a Dakota that lands in Amiens around 2 p.m. The French airfield is newly liberated — and shows it. Semi-chaos everywhere. Tents are set up alongside the taxi-way and a crowd of would-be passengers are queuing up with a heap of luggage in front of the dispatch office. As I enter, I recognise the man in charge. He is sitting behind a table, looking really annoyed with a Dutch General. It's Butch Taylor, a Typhoon Squadron Leader who is spending his rest period as CO of a Com. Flight. A bit of a comedown on slow twin-engined jobs when one is used to a Typhoon but, every task is important in wartime. Butch certainly has a lot of work today with impatient VIPs stranded in Amiens. I find out that there is a steady shuttle service of American DC3s between the Wash and Brussels but no passengers are allowed on the fully loaded aircraft — top priority is fuel and ammunition. The other system, from Amiens, is by the Communications Flight, headed by my friend Butch.

As he sees me, Butch offers me a wry smile: 'Hello, Charlie, what are you doing here?'

'Butch my friend, I am trying to get home to Brussels, and I am so glad to find you are here and going to help me!'

'You're joking! I arrived here this morning with 12 old Ansons. Eleven crews have gone to Brussels with a full load of VIPs, but not one has returned. The bastards are having a ball, celebrating the liberation of your country and God knows when I'll see them again. Look at that bunch: three Dutch Generals, one with brand-new fishing rods, 15 war correspondents of all the leading London newspapers, a Russian diplomatic courier, and a whole lot of Belgian ministry officials: all of them have top priority red passes. They are all threatening to get me fired if they don't get to Brussels! What a cock-up this is!'

I seize my chance. 'Butch my friend, you said 11 Ansons went to Brussels? So you've got one left here?'

'Yes, Charlie, but no pilot — just an observer who flew in with me this morning.'

'Right, Butch. Give me that Anson — I'll fly some of your VIPs to Brussels, and so you can kill two birds with one stone. I get to Brussels and you get a few of these off your back!'

'Charlie, you are a fighter pilot, not a twin-engine bus driver!'

'Come on, Butch, I haven't got my logbook with me, but I've been fully qualified on twins for ages! No problem!'

I can see from Butch's eyes that — quite rightly — he does not believe one word of what I've said, but there is also a twinkle of understanding, the gleam of a solution to the problem of losing some of his worst guests. I can *feel* it would suit him perfectly to see them gone and I try to exploit his indecision.

'Butch old man, I can fly that kite like any other — you forget that I've spent two months as a test pilot at Aston Down?'

The truth is that I have never flown a twin-engined aircraft as a captain — but, as a co-pilot, I know a little about them. And on this occasion, a little white lie is of no importance to me compared with more than four years of exile.

'O.K., Charlie — you want it, you have it,' Butch says after a long pause. 'After all, I have to stay on the deck anyway! You take Fg Off Meadow as navigator. Your Anson is over there. Pick a load of these buggers and leave the plane at Evère where I will recover it when I can. Good luck, liar!'

It is my lucky day — I have a plane, now I have to get to Brussels.

At 4.30 p.m. the door closes upon a full load of distinguished passengers. The Anson is an old 1937 Training Command aircraft, rather tired and decrepit with a 130 mph top speed. But what of it? As long as it flies, why worry? The only problem I had was picking 12 VIPs from 40, all pretending that they had higher priority. Everyone has good reason for going to Brussels today and Butch has left me the dirty job of deciding who can come and who will stay.

My choice cannot be fair, obviously, but on board, next to God, I am master so let's decide: I'll take two of the three Dutch Generals (I refuse the one with the fishing rods; it's not every day that a Flight Lieutenant can 'forget' a General!), and I'll take 10 of the 15 war correspondents, especially the *Daily Mail*, the *Express* and the *Telegraph* men, hoping secretly that they will mention their odyssey in their papers. The man from the *Daily Mirror* is not among the lucky ones, it not being my favourite piece of reading. None of the Belgian bureaucrats is allowed on board; their front line never went beyond their ministry desks or the bar of the Antelope, near Eaton Square, Anyway, the plane is grossly overloaded with suitcases, bags, and cameras — not forgetting my own heavy kitbag full of food.

I make my way with some difficulty to the cockpit and get myself seated behind the wheel. Meadow, the observer is in the right-hand seat so, closing the communicating door, I tell him to start the engines.

From the way he looks at me I know he has his doubts about my ability to fly the aircraft so, before he objects, I produce a big smile and try to comfort him. 'Come on, Meadow, I just want to take things easy. Give me a hand and we'll have a joy ride!'

The fact is that I am not at all sure how to start the engines, I assume that Meadow, even though he is not a pilot, is quite used to the Anson and knows where the switches are. Once started, I'll take over.

'O.K., skip. Left engine.'

He pushes a button, sets the throttle, and the engine roars. Then the right-hand one splutters into life, and I take over. Throttles set, mixture on rich, warming up, brakes off. I briefly hope my passengers are happy — and unaware of my inexperience — and as soon as the chocks are removed, we taxi onto the rough grass field towards the end of the runway in use. A magneto check, and then full throttle. The heavily loaded plane feels as though it will never get airborne, only lifting at the very end of the runway when it was too late to do anything else.

Airborne! I concentrate on flying while Meadow pumps the wheels up — a very tiring exercise. Loaded and slow as we are, there is no question of climbing very high so I decide to keep down, flying at about 1000 feet all the way to Brussels. I follow a road that goes more or less in the right direction, noting the flags on church steeples and in the village streets, where hundreds of hands wave at our slow-moving rattle-trap.

Suddenly, an empty village, with no flags showing: that's strange. Then, a stream of tracer comes towards us from a little wood on my left. I realise the country is not yet completely liberated; there are still pockets of resistance. The only solution is to dive towards the ground and hedge-hop. I make sure that none of my passengers were hurt; I am pretty sure we were not hit for their aim was wild. I don't dare climb again and hope that further on we won't meet another retreating German unit that still wants to fight.

Around 18.00 hrs, we have had no more problems and we are not far from Brussels. I want to take a look at my home town of Wavre, and at the same time salute my parents from the air. So in a few minutes we find the River Dyle and I follow it home. There is the red roof that I know so well, and at full throttle I skim the tiles. My heart skips a beat: there are three gaping holes in the back wall of my house and no-one comes out to wave at us. A little further down the street, more houses have been hit; it looks like shell fire, probably 88 mm for there are no signs of bombing.

I fly over the house again as low as I dare but there is no sign of life. Anxiety is making my hands shake on the wheel.

'Something wrong, skipper?'

Meadow has seen the damaged house and has guessed that I am near breaking point.

'Yes, Meadow — the bastards have shelled my house and I am anxious about my parents. I don't know what's happened.

Neither does Meadow. He tries to be sympathetic by telling me that my parents must be staying with friends.

Nothing else to do, but fly to Evère. It is only five minutes to reach the circuit, where dozens of Dakotas are queuing up and landing in formations of three to save time. My radio is obviously not on their frequency, and I can't hear the control tower. As my speed is about 60 mph slower than the Dakotas', I find it difficult to join the circus. But I am not in the mood for good manners, so I make my final approach right in front of a flight of three DC3s which has no option but to go round again to avoid a collision. I can imagine the pilots swearing but I continue my approach and land, taxying quickly out of the way and stopping in front of the control tower. I don't feel like waiting to apologise to my American colleagues; my only objective is to find some means of transport to get to Wavre.

My passengers disembark, quite happy to be safe after our trip. Some of the reporters want to interview me: 'Sorry, gentlemen, but I have things to do' — I disappear, leaving the Anson with my friend Meadow.

In the control tower, a surprise. Two NCOs are coping very professionally with the traffic but through an open door I see Group Captain Jamie Rankin, officer commanding the base. Without hesitating I salute and say: 'Flt Lt Demoulin arriving from Amiens with the last Anson, sir.' 'Well, Windmill, I had the impression you were flying Typhoons!'

I tell my story, and the reason for my rather unorthodox landing. I also beg him to lend me some transport to get home.

'A car? My dear fellow, I don't even possess a car myself any more — everybody's gone mad. They're are all over town celebrating, and I've got to do the bloody work. Listen, I believe that we have some German buses that they are painting in RAF colours. Go there and, if you are lucky, you can requisition anything on wheels, including a driver. Good luck!'

At 7.30 p.m., with my heavy kitbag on my shoulder, I finally find the garage where a few airfield commandos are painting new RAF roundels over black crosses and swastikas on three öld buses. I see a corporal who looks a bright fellow and, without explaining I say: 'Corporal, I need one of these beauties — can you drive it? I would like you to come with me.'

With a strong cockney accent he says 'Sure thing, Sir. I used to be a cab driver in London!' The young man seems to be delighted to come along. He gets his battle dress jacket and his Sten gun, and then jumps in the bus, heaving my kitbag in too. As he does not know the road, I take the driver's seat and off we go.

I manage to keep the wagon on the road and head towards town. It takes almost an hour to get through Brussels because the crowds keep stopping us to offer drinks and flowers. All over town, the same thing happens, until at a cross-roads a jeep with two SPs, a bit suspicious, check up on us and our rather unusual transport. Apparently satisifed that an RAF pilot with a French accent is fully entitled to drive a German bus, they co-operate by clearing the road ahead and so, about 9 p.m., we arrive in Wavre. The small town has only just been liberated and I do not dare to go straight home.

I stop at the house of a friend, Doctor J. Scheen, a dental surgeon. We fall in each other's arms and, with great relief, I learn that my parents are safe. Our house was hit by the anti-aircraft guns of Beauvechain airfield, 88 mm as I thought, who fired on the defenceless town before retreating. My parents had left to go into hiding a few days before. They were on the Nazis' blacklist because of me — it seems the Germans knew that I was flying with the RAF.

In the street, a crowd gathers around my bus and my driver is besieged by enthusiastic people offering drinks, food and kisses. News of my return spreads like wildfire, old friends and new ones want to shake hands, to give me a pat on the back, and all the women want to kiss me. I hear that my parents have returned home but everybody wants to know if I did this, or if I was on that op! In minutes I am associated with every RAF deed that occurred over Belgium. Then, escorted by more than 200 people, laughing and clapping, my bus travels slowly the few hundred yards to my home. There too a crowd has gathered waiting for the return of the prodigal son.

My parents are on the steps. I can see them through the mob. My eyes are watering — then I fall in their arms. The neighbours laugh, cry, clap their hands, sing, shout, all at the same time. My father is speechless. So am I. He just looks closely to make sure that it is really me. I can feel he is happy — proud too — I can feel that he thinks I left as a boy and now he sees a man for the first time. Meanwhile, my mother tells everyone my life story, stopping to kiss me and then going back to her eager listeners.

Managing at last to get inside the house, with the door shut I open the kitbag and take out the white bread, tinned meat, coffee, cigarettes, soap and so on. I have not eaten since morning but my mother has already laid the table while my father brings out a long-saved bottle of Burgundy. From the larder comes succulent roast beef, country bread and a cheese soufflé: Ali Baba's cave — and I thought they were starving! So only the coffee, whisky, soap and cigarettes make a real impression on my family and friends — they have been short of those for years.

Just one evening with my parents is enough to wipe away five years of exile, hardship, and push the war into the background — till next day!

We eat. We drink. We are hungry, because happiness sharpens the appetite. We have so many things to talk about that dawn is breaking before we notice it, and the first light of freedom comes through shell holes into my liberated home.

Chapter 27
The Clairvoyant

After a long lie in bed, I find old habits coming back, and I also make my first acquaintance with Tiny, the little dog that my parents adopted in 1940 after my departure. She's a little fox-terrier bitch, clever as a monkey and loving as a mistress. My father is undoubtedly her God and, probably feeling some affinity, she shows her affection by much licking with a rough tongue.

I am told about daily life under the Nazi occupation, the rules imposed and the threats that the local collaborators were to my parents.

My mother is very proud and keen to show me some RAF leaflets dropped over Belgium. The first has my photo, quite recognisable, in uniform. The Allied propaganda machine dropped others showing four Belgian pilots grouped around my Typhoon. I appear in the company of Flt Lt P. Cooreman, Fg Off C. Detal and Fg Off P. Soesman. A lapse of security had allowed them to add 'Belgian volunteer pilots in the RAF, fighting with their British allies', followed by our ranks and initials. Several thousands of these leaflets were dropped over Belgium, and over my home town, on three or four occasions. Each time anonymous friends filled the letter box of my house with them to show their feelings. When I hear that our town Mayor, Mr. A. Bosch, and three of his secret army friends were shot dead by the Gestapo the day before the British troops arrived, I thank God that my parents, duly warned a few days earlier, had time to vanish and hide with friends. They had gone to the Cardinal Mercier College where a cousin of ours, Mr. J. Hanon, was headmaster. He hid them till the Germans had gone. I also hear of many friends killed and of those sent to concentration camps. For some, liberation is celebrated with joy, for others the war goes but fear continues.

For four very long years, my family and I have been separated. Pushed towards France by the German blitzkrieg, my parents fled in May 1940 as far as Toulouse, where the Germans caught up with them. In July 1940 they were allowed to drive back to Belgium, and their first worry was to find out what had happened to me. There had been no news since our goodbye of 10th May, when I went to war on my motorcycle. The last they heard of me officially was at St. Peter's Hospital on 16th May, after which I disappeared into thin air.

What had happened? Did I die as a result of my wounds? No trace was found. My father was absolutely — obstinately — determined to find out. As a last resort, he went to see one of my university professors, at the College of Notre Dame de la Paix in Namur. Father Lepers was not only a history lecturer but also a keen dowser.

So with his friend Doctor Alexis, my father had an interview. A big map was open on his desk and over it in his hand Professor Lepers held a swinging pendulum — which stopped swinging over Berck-sur-plage, a Channel seaside resort. The verdict: I had been buried in the military cemetery of that little town in June 1940!

Desperate, my father addressed his written request to the Germans to travel in the restricted zone of France to look for my supposed grave. Application refused; and a letter to the town Mayor did not help either, the reply being that my name was not on any grave, but six unknown soldiers were buried in that cemetery!

To try and help, good old Doctor Alexis decided to go with my father to see a well-known doctor in Brussels, Professor Mertens. He, apart from being a learned physician, was also adept with the pendulum. Professor Mertens did not know of Professor Lepers' finding. Same scenario: the pendulum moves, swings, then stops — over Berck-sur-plage!

This coincidence practically convinced my father of my death.

However, Doctor Alexis insisted that there was no certainty and proposed a visit to Madame Lagrange, a French clairvoyant who had had some fame in universities before the war. It was said that even the police had had recourse to this lady to solve some difficult cases.

Why not try her? Carrying a pair of gloves that I had used for motorcycling (for in this case the clairvoyant had to hold something the missing person had touched) my father, still accompanied by Doctor Alexis, got his interview.

'Sir,' said Madame Lagrange, 'I feel a pain in the right arm, on the elbow. It's *very* painful. I see a lot of water, probably the sea, and your son is beyond it, on its other side. He was injured, severely wounded, but he is now convalescent. Do not grieve, for he is alive!'

The clairvoyant looking very much like the French authoress Colette, with her hair undone, her pinched face and with an eternal cigarette hanging from her lip added: 'Your son travels a lot, I can see him in the air. He is very resourceful. He is the type of boy you could throw naked into a river and he would bubble up with a new suit and his pockets full of fish! Furthermore, you will get some news soon — before Christmas — probably a letter written with his left hand for he still has difficulty with his right. Don't be alarmed, Sir, I am sure he will come back, but it will take a long time!'

Hope — like faith — belongs to those who want to believe, so my father took his leave of Madame Lagrange feeling much happier, even if he did still have some degree of doubt!

About the same time, at Woodlands Cripples Hospital, near Birmingham, a nurse carrying the ward mail stopped by my bed and, for some unknown reason, deposited the lot on the blanket at the foot of the bed. Some letters lay flat and some others stood up. One facing me showed on the back of the envelope the sender's address: Madame

Yvonne Dumoulin, 5, Avenida d'Ottubro, Lisboa, Portugal. This intrigued me and I memorised the address. I got the idea of writing to the unknown lady in Portugal whose name was so much like mine and ask her to get in touch with my parents. Portugal was neutral, but I still had to go through British censorship and, after Portugal, the German censors. The only other way of communicating with Belgium was by 25-word messages transmitted by the International Red Cross, but they took ages to arrive.

I wrote a letter to my pretend 'Auntie Yvonne' telling her about her 'nephew' being convalescent in England and asking her to give news to her 'brother' in Belgium. I then gave my parents' address, pretending that they had moved and that this was their new location. Auntie Yvonne cleverly understood perfectly what it was all about and, with her help, my parents were overjoyed to get my first letter two days before Christmas 1940. Madame Lagrange was invited to celebrate with my parents and the first Christmas under the German boot was, strangely, a really festive one.

Throughout the war, Madame Y. Dumoulin was postwoman between my people and me — both ways. After the war I met her in Portugal and found a beautiful young woman, born in Costa Rica, married to a Belgian engineer, manager of the Solvay Company in Lisbon. He had become Belgian Consul there and both of them spent time helping Belgians during the war.

The story of the clairvoyant might have ended there and then, but the sequel was even stranger. Later, in 1946, I learned the whole story which has been checked by several sources and it is even more amazing.

Madame Lagrange belonged to the Resistance and was taken by the Gestapo in 1943. She was sent to a concentration camp at Ravensbruck. She shared a tiny dark cell with two other women. Later, they were all moved to a larger cell and one day Madame Lagrange said to one of the others, 'You said you lived in Wavre before being captured. I know that you were a friend of Charles Demoulin before the war. Do you want to know what he is doing nowadays?' The lady was my tailor's wife — I knew her well, but neither she nor I had thought about the other since 1940. Nevertheless, 'Francine' was thrilled to talk with Madame Lagrange about a mutual friend. She described my life in the RAF to her room-mate, including details of my flights from the autumn of 1943 to the end of 1944, She even told her that I had seen my father in front of the house in 1943! Francine noted it all down in an exercise-book diary.

Both survived the Nazi camp and came back in June 1945 to Belgium in poor health, but alive. One day in 1946 I happened to meet 'Francine' who invited me to her house — and there she gave me the account she had kept in the camp of Madame Lagrange's stories. It was so astonishing that I went back later to her place with my logbook and we compared the dates and the diary. There was not one error; the two documents matched *exactly*!

It was not till 1948 that I met Madame Lagrange. She was giving 'consultations' in the small parlour of a bistro on the corner of Avenue Legrand. I thought it only natural to stop by and thank her for what she had done for my parents. I did not propose to discuss my future. When I got there, she skipped the 20 ladies waiting their turn in the bistro and I was rushed in by the waiters: 'You at last! I was expecting you!' Amazing woman! Clairvoyant? Certainly — hadn't she proved it to many people?

While I was thanking her for everything, she was looking at me with her large, green, shining eyes, giving me a strange feeling. Could she read my mind? She seemed to be digging into me; her eyes penetrating and her hands fidgeting. I felt she was about to say something — but what would it be?

'You know, Charles, all human beings are like radio transmitters: they send out waves. But not many people are like receiving stations, and even fewer can read the messages. For instance, I see you in the middle of a pile of building materials!'

As during our conversation I had told her about my life, about leaving the Air Force after the war to join the family firm as a contractor, building highways and airports, I took that as superficial, not needing special intuition.

'No, my friend, I know you are thinking it's general knowledge I've told you. But you are wrong. What I meant is that today you started to build your own house!'

Incredibly, not an hour before, the first lorry-load of bricks had been brought to the plot I had bought for my future home!

I take off my hat to Madame Lagrange, and I must admit that this little lady knew many things — enough to make me shiver.

'Don't worry, my son, I'm like a sun-dial — *horas non numero nisi serenas*!'

Quite, Madame Lagrange! You only give the good news!

Chapter 28
The Tragedy of Arnhem

The war goes on. After two happy days in the bosom of my family I have to leave my parents, forget about my enthusiastic friends and go back to fighting. Some of those 'friends' before the war looked down on me with a measure of superiority, their condescension plain to see. In their eyes, I was king of the non-conformists, individualist, strong-headed and one of the long-haired boys. Today the same so-called friends are the first to applaud and to court me. I suppose it's normal: the flock always follows the leader . . .

So, a quick goodbye to my parents and I step into a local police car. The lieutenant in charge drives me to Brussels/Evère airfield. From there an Auster takes me to Northern France, where 123 Wing should be stationed. After enquiring in Lille, I learn that they are a few miles away in Merville, coded B53, and I soon find 164 Squadron and my friends.

The Germans had no time to destroy the airfield or the buildings, so there are two complete wings based on Merville: 123 Wing with Typhoons, and another wing with Spitfires including the two Belgian squadrons, 349 and 350.

With more than 150 planes on the station traffic is very heavy, making formation take-offs and landings very dodgy. There is plenty of work for everyone, because although the Germans are retreating and Antwerp harbour has fallen into our hands undamaged, the River Schelde giving access from the North Sea is still in enemy hands which prevents any ship getting there. Moreover, Dunkirk, Calais and the island of Walcheren are still solidly held by the Germans. So our main task is to free Antwerp, to crush Dunkirk, Calais and Walcheren, and participate in the coming battle of Arnhem.

123 Wing, after a few days of celebrating the liberation of Belgium, gets back to its usual daily operations. Group Captain Scott and Wing Commander Drink get their squadron commanders together and give a general briefing on the present situation: priority is on the left flank in support of the Canadians. We must strike at any armoured forces, flak positions or artillery that hinders their advance. But our wing has lost many men in the last three months: Squadron Leaders Waddy, Scarlett, Harbutt and Beaky, more than 25 other pilots, are missing or dead. This, added to those who have been wounded or who have been sent back for a rest, leaves us with very few old hands. The great majority of the pilots are green, straight from training and with few hours on Typhoons. There's no time to train them further, they will just have to

learn by trial and error, on the spot — and we know that most casualties occur on the very first op — through lack of experience.

I am sorry for these sprogs, who will probably not get past their first ten missions before 'going for a burton'. The average survival rate for a rocket-Typhoon pilot since mass missions at low level were introduced is around 17 ops. After that, he lives on borrowed time. Veterans stand a better chance of living than the younger ones, whose average number of ops before 'buying it' is no more than five.

Old hands do not always get away with it. A few days after the liberation of Belgium, Sqn Ldr Lallemant, who took over 609 only a few weeks earlier, belly-lands at Merville and is badly burned. He will have a painful recovery — over six months — getting back to the front line only a few days before the end of the war. A South African, Sqn Ldr Wallace, takes over command of 609, and once more, as a flight commander, I take command of 164 Squadron while Mony Van Lierde goes on leave.

On 11 September I had just landed from an attack on Dunkirk when a car flying the flag of the AOC 84 Group stopped not far from my kite. Getting out of it were Air Vice-Marshal L. M. O. Brown, AOC of 84 Group, with Group Captain Scott and Wing Commander Walter Drink. While I unstrapped my parachute, the 'brass' came up, smiling. I stood to attention and saluted as the AVM walked up to me.

'Good morning, Flight Lieutenant. I'm pleased to meet you.'

'Thank you, sir, me too!'

'How was the op?'

'Lots of flak, sir, but Dunkirk is softening — we hit a few 88 mm batteries and destroyed three pill-boxes.'

'Well done! Now let's get on with rather better things!'

He turned to his ADC, took from his hands a case and opened it, then extracted a blue and white striped ribbon, on the end of which hung a silver cross: 'I particularly wanted to present to you personally the Distinguished Flying Cross, awarded to you by King George VI. You can be proud of it; your citation is very flattering and you have earned every word of it. I do congratulate you!'

I managed to stutter a thank you, in front of smiling Scotty and Drink, who were obviously pleased by my distinction, awarded in front of the British pilots gathered around us. Then there were drinks at the Officers' Mess, and lunch where I had the honour of sitting next to AVM Brown.

Next day with my mail was a very charming letter from a wonderful person, Baron Cartier de Marchienne, our ambassador in London, and another from our Defence Minister, Mr. Camille Gutt, who was always very kind to me. There were telegrams, one from the C-in-C, Air Chief-Marshal Leigh-Mallory, and another from Air Marshal Coningham. It was a field day for me; I was joining a most exclusive club, the holders of the DFC — a silver cross that no Belgian could ever remove from my chest!

Scotty calls me, half smiling, half serious, 'So you haven't sewn on your ribbon next to your Croix de Guerre yet? I suppose you would like your mother to do it properly? So, take the Auster and fly home. Come back tomorrow morning — there will be plenty to do!'

'Whoopee! I am already on my way. Thank you, sir.'

I change into best blue and, DFC in my pocket, jump into the Auster and fly to Wavre. With a little airmanship and a good headwind I would be able to land in a field near my home. That done with barely a hundred-yard run, the local police are entrusted with guarding the aircraft till next morning. At home, my mother is as proud as can be, sewing the white and blue striped ribbon on my uniform while I tell my father about what we are doing. I am thinking — and don't really want to talk about — that with luck she may soon be sewing on the third ring of a Squadron Leader, with me as CO of 609 Squadron.

When I land the next morning at Merville everybody is very busy. The ground crews are rushing around, the pilots are in the briefing tent, and the Intelligence officers are displaying large maps in front of the squadron commanders. My CO, Mony Van Lierde, gestures to me frantically.

'Come on, Charlie, get cracking! We are taking off in twenty minutes.'

Target: Arnhem! Montgomery's daring plan: airborne divisions to be dropped behind the lines. We get the map sorted out: gliders to land in Zone A, paratroops dropped in Zone B. A few gliders will land right by the famous bridge and our job is to neutralise the bridge defences with a low-level attack on the guns and machine-gun posts. We absolutely *must* silence those guns, whatever the cost, to allow the gliders to reach the bridge area. Several dives will be necessary, first with rockets, then with canon fire to finish the job. As we will be operating near our own troops, it will be a precision job — as usual, reserved for Typhoons only. The targets will be marked by red flares, while our own forces will display orange smoke to mark their perimeter.

'Give 'em hell, boys! Our paras expect you to do the job,' are last words from the Groupie before we take off.

Everyone knows the score and what is expected from each pilot. This is the crunch of the campaign. Another Falaise, but this time it will open the way deep into Germany. If we can shoot the bolt we can cross the Rhine and the Ruhr will be wide open to us. And then the war can't last much longer.

We take off second, just after 198 Squadron led by my friend Sqn Ldr Pol Ezzano. Twelve aircraft to each squadron, which is all we can scrape together. Mony leads 164 Squadron with Blue section, I am leading Red section. Mentally, I size up our strength: three veterans, five semi-experienced pilots and, unfortunately, four green ones on their first op. As the reception committee will be on the alert, it's bound to be dodgy!

After Antwerp, climb to 6000 feet and follow the road that leads to

Arnhem. We know that General Dempsey's 2nd Army is trying to join up with the forces dropped in the Nijmegen area. Not far from there, two airfields, Gilzen Ryen and Eindhoven, are still in enemy hands. We keep an eye on them, although they are the Spitfires' job. We press on along our route. Allied tanks can be seen on the road below, advancing into Holland.

Soon, on our left, big black puffs fill the sky. It's a fascinating sight! Without deviating an inch from their course, the Stirlings towing the gliders roar on through the killing flak and release their tows over the scheduled spot, as if they were on an exercise. Many are hit, some are shot down but the stream never falters. The crews show the utmost gallantry and extraordinary discipline. Among them, as usual, the Poles set a fine example.

We leave our four-engined friends to their unenviable task, and position ourselves behind 198 who are starting a shallow dive under the leadership of Pol Ezzano. Group Captain Scott is flying No. 2 to the sparkling Corsican. Wingco Drink is following with 183, and 609 is led by Wallace. It's tradition in the wing that the Groupie, and sometimes the Wingco, always fly as wingman to a squadron commander, letting him make the decisions. If necessary they can take charge at any time and have things done the way they think best. This is not a disappearing act by our senior officers, but more a tactical move to let squadron commanders use their initiative. At the same time they can assess their competence — and, probably, prepare them for leading and commanding larger units in the future. On the other hand, in the Spitfire wings, which are fighters rather than fighter-bombers, the Groupie or the Wingco lead the bigger formations themselves.

198 has gone down, strafing the machine-gun nests defending the approaches of the Arnhem bridge, about a mile short of the river. The rockets squirt towards the individual posts and strong points while the flak lets go at us. Then Mony makes a steep turn left positioning us up-sun which hinders the gunners' aim. Our speed goes up for our dive as a 198 aircraft leaves the fight with a long smoke trail behind him. Another Typhoon will not last long, but perhaps he will make it to our lines or bale out if he can.

'O.K. Digit aircraft, diving now!'

Everyone is ready to turn down to the inferno. Spaced about 100-150 yards, we dive using all our 2400 hp. A little rudder to stabilise the red dot on target, a touch of trim to ease into the dive. The ASI needle sweeps up — 450, 460, 470 mph. First, rockets, then spray the guns with cannon fire. Finish by coming out of the dive as close to the ground as possible.

Eight hundred feet — target 700 yards — first pair fired. Six hundred feet — target 500 yards — second pair gone. Then the third — 300 feet with the target at 200 yards. The last pair goes at point-blank range! I pull hard on my stick and shoot off towards the sky, blacking out as centrifugal force thrusts me down into my seat.

Many shouts in my headphones: parts of sentences and orders blot each other out.

'Down we go again Digit aircraft — now!'

I obey, swinging my Typhoon into the dive as I check that my section is following. I barely miss a crossing plane and down we go again, emptying our ammo on strong points full of smoke although it's impossible to see the German gunners clearly. The ground is a pattern of craters and the flak has gone quiet.

We swing slightly left to reform around Mony, making room for the other two squadrons following us. Arnhem bridge stands intact, spanning the dull and deserted waters of the river. Thousands of men are going to die and many thousands more will be wounded for the object of the whole battle — possession of this plain iron framework.

A few miles away, the Dutch fields are covered by the multi-coloured silk mushrooms lying on the ground. The men who dropped from the sky are going to fight for the next ten days, encircled, short of ammunition, dead tired, for conquest of a bridge. When they get there, and take it in one piece, they will hold it for days and nights on end, outnumbered thirty to one, then a hundred to one, hoping against hope for reinforcements that never come. A bridge too far. That's the price. Ten thousand dead and missing — for nothing.

We fly back to Merville, like a practice formation. Two Typhoons are missing but my squadron has returned complete — a good baptism for our sprogs, and I am sure they will remember it. If they come back next time . . .

During the next few days, we listen anxiously to news on the radio. The speaker's tone prepares us for bad news.

'Our glider forces are meeting renewed resistance from enemy armoured reinforcements around the town . . .'

'Our paratroops are still holding the far end of the Arnhem bridge against tremendous opposition . . .'

That 'still holding' is a bad omen for the coming hours. It means in military terms that we won't hold it much longer. I don't understand why we are not flying day and night to help them, but it seems that the task has fallen to other groups of Typhoons. For us, our daily work is round the Breskens pocket, along the Schelde river, where German flak is creating havoc among the heavies trying to drop supplies to our Arnhem forces. Our top priority is to neutralise those flak batteries although we feel somewhat left out of the main battle.

Nobody can save our Army friends in the trap — only an early breakthrough from Antwerp could have saved them, but we got there too late. Partly because of the German resistance, but more than anything else because our tanks were delayed due to lack of petrol; a consequence of the black market. A bridge too far.

September is ending; we attack Calais, Dunkirk and Breskens day after day, beating down the German last stand a little more each day. However, the war of rapid movement is over for the time being. We are facing rivers and the Allies must take another breather before crushing the enemy on the Schelde. Walcheren, Flushing, and Breskens are going to suffer in the coming weeks.

With the autumn come clouds, rain and wind. My logbook shows 800 hours of flying, of which 500 are on operational missions at the enemy. I am still there, but familiar faces are becoming much rarer. I feel lonely and tired; fatique weighs heavily. It sticks in my bones like cold showers of October rain.

Chapter 29
The Breskens Pocket

With my squadron, I was a frustrated witness of the Arnhem defeat.
Soul-stricken, we didn't even join the last days of battle because we were
diverted to other tasks. Now there is another major objective for us: to
clear both sides of the River Schelde, opening the way for ships to bring
supplies in to Antwerp. The front line runs from the Breskens pocket on
the North Sea to Antwerp, with the island of Walcheren solidly
defended, and the Germans can deny the river to the Allies. In addition,
the enemy garrisons at Dunkirk and Calais are still holding out inside a
strong defensive perimeter and they are not to be overcome until long
after our September breakthrough.

Our wing is ordered to clear the North Sea coast. Our base is still
Merville, near Lille. 609 Squadron is still commanded by our South
African friend Sqn Ldr Wallace, 198 by the flying Corsican Pol Ezzano,
and 164 by Mony Van Lierde with me as his deputy. With little Mouzon,
we are the only three Belgians in the squadron but we are an experienced
team and for a long time we have felt more British than anything else.
We share the daily tasks, Mony Van Lierde leading one show and I the
next. Exceptionally we both fly on the same operation; perhaps if the
whole squadron is required, or when only the experienced old hands are
chosen for a special mission.

To fly with Mony is to be sure of a busy day. For the whole two years I
have flown with him, I have found from experience that he believes the
best defence is attack — whatever the odds. Except for a few months
when he was on Tempests in the middle of 1944, I have had every
opportunity to appreciate the qualities of this fighter-pilot: high
courage at all times, extraordinary dash, sharp eyesight, coupled with
an expertise that ensures he seldom misses his target. He is one of the
few RAF pilots to have been awarded a DFC and two bars.

In 609, Mony earned a complete set of German aircraft. He started
with an Fw190 over the Channel in January 1943 and followed it with a
juicy Junkers 52 shot down near his home in Lessines — where Mony
was sort of 'visiting' his family. Then, a few days later, in a dogfight
along the Dutch coast, he forced a Messerschmitt 109 into a fatal dive
ending in the sea. Flying a night Rhubarb, he saw a returning Heinkel
111 in the moonlight. A short burst of 20 mm cannon fire turned it into a
last flight by some young Teutons. Then the 'free-for-all' when there
was a sweepstake open on the 200th victory in 609: he missed winning it
by a few minutes. Mony, had gone hunting on his own and shot down a
Junkers 88 — but, unluckily, after Pinky Stark had also disposed of a

lonely Ju88. And to conclude his list of air victories Mony made sure of a Messerschmitt 110 coming back from night patrol.

At the beginning of 1944, our friend van Lierde left 609 to take over a Flight in a new Tempest squadron under command of our former boss Roland Beamont. Roland was now a Wing Commander, DSO, DFC and bar, and had well earned command of the first Tempest Wing to be formed. In June 1944 he led his new wing against the V1s that were launched against London. During that singular battle, Mony Van Lierde achieved the fantastic score of 37 V1s destroyed. Some he got by tipping up their wing tips with his own — at great risk of being blown up by the bomb.

Mony, ordered to take a rest from flying in July and August 1944, chose to become a controller at 'Cab Rank' in Normandy, where he was positioned in an armoured vehicle right in the front line, directing by radio the close support given by Typhoons to our armoured forces. This was the man, posted back before the end of his rest, who came to head up 164 Squadron. It was a joy for me and a slice of luck to be able to fight alongside him again. The two of us intended to forge this squadron into one of the best on the northern front.

Most of our present activities are directed towards cleaning up the German coastal strongholds, with priority on the River Schelde. It will culminate on 1 November with an assault launched on Walcheren. The ports of Boulogne and Calais become of secondary importance because from a military point of view, they cannot influence the outcome of the war — but they do have a nuisance value. On the other hand, Antwerp, liberated early in September with its harbour undamaged thanks to gallant action by the Resistance, must become our forward base for much needed supplies. Clearing the approaches is therefore our number one objective.

However the German flak together with some last-ditch troops are making a fine stand, causing us to pay dearly for our attempts to seize the river banks. As they represent a difficult target for the heavy bombers, because of the nearness of our forward armoured units, the honour of subduing these defences falls to the Tiffies. The most important ones are on Walcheren, the island lying below the level of the North Sea and with many dykes and an elaborate system of lock gates. Any seaborne landing would have to be made in the face of strong defences that will have to be softened up by us first.

Near Flushing, a radar station has to be put out of action before anything else. The concrete buildings resist any kind of bombing but, with rockets, the armoured doors can be blown in. Also, the radar aerials can be put out of action by a low-level attack driven right home. This is the target given to 164 Squadron.

Mony leads six Typhoons and I take the other six. We will attack from sea level in order to be a more difficult target for the enemy defences. And we shall have a better chance of approaching undetected.

In doing so, we will have to fly through the flak barrage — and hope!

We cross the coast near Ostend and fly straight on to the island that takes shape in the morning haze. Next to me, Mouzon flies with his wing tucked close beside me, like a watch dog. I know that anywhere I go he will be there, calm, determined, and formidable to our enemies. Never in the war did I have a No. 2 who combined better great piloting skill with such determination to drive his attacks home. In RAF slang one would say that he was a 'buster' — nothing would stop him. So feeling him next to me, ready to cope with anything, left me free to deal with other problems.

We have arranged for Mony to take the command post while I deal with the flak. I therefore go in first, and I position my Typhoon some way east of the radar, then do a steep turn left so as to present a front of six aircraft covering the whole width of the target.

500 yards away, the tracer comes up at us. 88 mm shells explode on the water, throwing up geysers of green water and glittering splashes in front of our noses. But already our rockets are on their way towards the enemy guns. Then our 20 mm shells pepper the gunners, who collapse like broken toys. I keep on firing until within a few yards of the flak muzzles, flying through the explosions of our rockets which shake my aircraft for a second or two — then I am clear and turning away sharply over the sea.

From the corner of my eye, I can see the other group attacking the aerials and the buildings. From all around the target the fireworks criss-cross, climbing in multicoloured arabesques and falling back in gentle curves to the sea.

Another steep turn and we are facing what is left of the radar installations: it is our turn with the last of our ammunition. I see two revolving aerials grotesquely sheared off at their base, and a door blasted open in the nearby casement.

The main building in the middle of the shambles seems to be untouched — let's go for it! A long burst creeps towards the windows, the sparks reach its front, and finally the roof. I clear the house at the last second, skimming over the chimneys and get down again to ground level. Behind me, my friends also use up their shells and then quickly reform around me.

The radio is silent until Mony joins us and we regroup the squadron in close formation. All Typhoons are accounted for. Ostend beach is under our wings, with the windows of houses facing the beach boarded up. The blots of abandoned concrete pill-boxes spoil their view of the sand dunes. People in the streets wave at us, and frightened seagulls disappear in all directions as we set course for Merville.

In the near future we will deal with the Breskens pocket.

A Polish tank regiment is operating at Bar le Duc, its advance halted by some very strong opposition. Some 88 mm guns cover all lines of approach at point-blank range over flat open land, preventing tanks advancing and compelling them to use narrow, winding country lanes. The fields in the neighbourhood are under water, so that alternative is also denied. Well entrenched behind the dykes, some well camouflaged Tiger tanks are defending their positions — this is where we come in.

Before take-off, we look carefully at some aerial photos taken the day before, and plot the enemy gun positions on our large-scale maps. Five 88 mm batteries — meaning 20 guns — and half a dozen dug-in tanks, barely visible under their camouflage nets, are selected and circled on the maps. Our radio is on the same frequency as the one used by the Cab Rank forward observer.

Our aircraft take off from Ursel, an airfield near Eckloo in Belgium, which is within a few minutes' flying of the front line. In the morning sky fringes are still hanging from low clouds and patches of haze stick to the flat ground. I plan to take the Huns from behind, at low level, hoping to catch them unawares.

At 10 o'clock precisely, our Polish friends mark the targets with mortar smoke shells. Yellowish mushrooms blossom near the batteries as we dive on them, and the slaughter begins. Calmly, as if on exercise, everyone takes his target, firing rockets in pairs, then spraying the batteries with cannon fire.

I concentrate on the central one, which disappears under my explosions. In a split second I see a tank leaving its hide-out: a steep turn, level off, just time to get the red dot of my gunsight on the caterpillars, and whoosh! — a pair of rockets flash down . . . At this range, less than 200 yards, the panzer doesn't stand a chance. A gout of flame; the tank stops and throws up dark, dirty smoke that marks the death of a Tiger.

I fly through the dark cloud and find myself in a carousel of twisting Typhoons, enjoying themselves in the middle of fierce but inaccurate flak. As usual, Mouzon is glued close to me, and I can imagine the smile on his face.

A lone battery seems to have escaped our loving care. I have two rockets left and a lot of 20 mm, so let's take it. My number two has understood and flies a bit further out as he joins in the attack. Coming in, I spray the battery with cannon fire while I stabilise my Typhoon and not waste my last two rockets. At about 100 yards I release my weapons and climb at once towards our lines to observe the results.

On the road, sheltered by a dyke, a long line of Churchill tanks show their appreciation by making sweeping gestures of friendship while in my earphones the Slav-accented voice of the Polish controller is shouting with joy. I reform my Typhoons and make a wide turn above our Polish friends who are going into their attack, and making the most of the shambles we have created. In a matter of minutes, our armour is in the middle of the enemy positions and advancing without apparent opposition.

We fly low over the battlefield, but it seems that we are not needed any more for the Poles continue their advance. I call the controller to ask him if he wants more help and an excited voice comes back: 'Zank you, no Typhoon. Jerry kaput. Very gut show — 'Zank you!' A last turn and back to Ursel.

Soon after landing, a message from the Polish brigade tells us that the position has been taken and sends us their thanks. They found nine guns and three Tigers destroyed when they moved in, with several more damaged. Bar le Duc has fallen.

During the afternoon we go back to the same area. This time it's Saint Kruis that has our attention — and we are going to support the Canadians.

This corner has become well known to us in the last few days and the climate is not healthy; it is stuffed with multiple barrel 37 mm guns and manned by men who are going to sell their skins dearly. For them there won't be any retreat and surrendering to the Canadians is not a long-term insurance policy. Since the tied-up bodies of 18 Canadian prisoners were discovered in a farm in Normandy, executed by the SS, the Canadians don't take many prisoners.

By contrast, whenever I meet Canadian tank officers I am warmly welcomed. They really appreciate our Typhoons' support and never miss an opportunity to show their gratitude. They invite us to visit the front line in their sector to show us the results of our attacks and often give us war trophies. A Colonel of a Quebec regiment offered me a Luger pistol complete with holster and spare magazine, taken from a dead German officer in a tank destroyed by our Typhoons. In return we invite them to bistros in Zoute.

The ops on Saint Kruis are not exactly a walk in the park. As I buckle on my chute, I think about the last attack in that corner, when I came back with a holed petrol tank and an aileron half severed by a lucky 37 mm shot. The Tiger and Panther tanks defending the Breskens pocket along the Belgian border have kept their mobile flak units with them; we have difficulty in locating them by photographic recce as they are never in the same place twice.

I climb to 5000 feet to get a general view and be able to dive out of the sun. We are a formation of six Typhoons, spread out to allow each pilot to dive with sufficient time to find his target with certainty. This way the flak shows itself as soon as the leader of the formation dives, allowing the others to aim accurately at the gun positions revealed.

A small town asleep among canals and deserted roads, Sluis lies on my right. My No. 2 today is Flt Sgt Teather, newly arrived in the squadron, and I want to give him some experience with an op near our own lines. It was with a tinge of regret that I left Mouzon on the ground, but each pilot has to take his share of the work. Before take-off, I explained clearly to Teather that I wanted him to stick with me like a shadow. Even so, I feel sure that when the flak opens up, he will be surprised at his baptism of fire.

The Controller has given me the supposed location of the German tanks. A glance at the map on my left knee, followed by a long look at the ground below my wing, and I find the cross roads that serves as the pinpoint. I look at it carefully, but find no trace of the enemy. Not far away there is a little wood, still with leaves at this time of the year, and something tells me that it's not a healthy spot. Behind, the village of Saint Laureins looks deserted, with a little road leading to Saint Margriète, near the Belgian border. You would think we were in the waiting room of Paradise, there are so many saints around. But, here comes the yellow smoke to mark the front line; once past that little coloured cloud, we may shoot at anything that moves. But nothing moves.

'Hello Control, Red One here. I have had a good look at A3 F7 but I can't see any jokers. Please confirm your instructions.'

'Hello Red One, Control calling. I confirm A3 F7 — probably behind the farm courtyard. Out.'

If I can't see anything then it's because they are well camouflaged, so the only thing to do is to go down and see what happens — but keeping ready to fire instantly.

'Digit Red and Blue sections, I am going down alone. Wait till they open fire, then give them hell.'

Now, down we go at full throttle and take a good look while my five Typhoons orbit up top.

The wing goes down, the engine roars and the ground comes up at full speed, while the red dot sits over the suspicious orchard: 400, 425, 440 mph and at 500 feet the merry-go-round begins. A curtain of fire is thrown at me from the orchard, and from the little wood.

At the same moment, I fire my cannon and let my rockets go, aiming at the dark patches I can now see under the fruit trees. I spray them all the way down, then steep turn away near the ground, keeping well clear of the little wood.

Great! Everything going to plan! Those sods were playing dead until the last moment — but now some of them will be dead for quite a while. As I climb up for another attack, my friends dive, one after the other, on the orchard. All but Teather. He hesitates a moment then goes for the wood.

There's no time to warn him by radio; his plane is already a ball of fire, and he hits the ground near the road. An explosion, then the horrid black smoke billows up. That's all that's left of a young sprog meeting battle for the first time. Bad luck maybe. But why go straight for the lion's mouth? I had warned him about the wood. But, inexperienced, he probably thought only of avoiding the flak coming from the orchard — and so he fell into the trap.

With rage in my heart I dive at the inferno. My guns bark. I would like to kill all those Huns, open their guts, but deep down I know it would be irresponsible to use up my last shell.

All Digit aircraft reform at angels 3.

I spat out the order. Enough damage for one day. Temper is a bad counsellor and one must keep a cool head. A good shepherd brings his flock back safely.

During the return flight not a word is spoken. We land quickly and at debriefing I make my report to the spy. Then I call the adjutant whose duty it is to collect the dead pilot's earthly belongings. I haven't the heart to pen the details to his family, but I dictate a letter for the adjutant to send to his next of kin.

All Saints' Day is approaching and organ music in a village church somewhere in England will accompany the terrible sorrow of a father, a mother — then another name will be added to the local war memorial.

Next day, I get my car and decide to take a 48 hour leave with my family. I won't tell them what I feel, nor about our losses; useless to worry them too. On the contrary, I will speak lightly and brush aside the dangers. But I realise that my life has become tougher than it was when I fought from England or from Normandy. It is more difficult psychologically because of leaving the warmth of one's refound family to go back to face death — then return to the affection of a home, only to return for the battle — it's against nature. As long as the fighting was to liberate one's country, to free one's family and friends, the incentive was there. Now this has been achieved, it's different. This 'softening' is prejudicial to our main goal — the complete defeat of Nazi Germany. But, each day, those that fall leave us sharing a loneliness more and more difficult to bear.

As soon as I get home, I hold my parents in my arms, then find an excuse to leave as I cannot bear to enjoy the family warmth. I am afraid of being unable to leave them, yet I also fear being cowardly. I am afraid of fear.

Late that night, I am back at Ursel airfield — to my tent, my sleeping bag, my lack of comfort. This is where I belong and, though the lonely autumn night does not offer much, I am happy not to have gone soft. Perhaps there is little difference between doing one's duty and becoming a coward: just a tiny moment of doubt, a slight hesitation in a decision . . .

Chapter 30
In Command

With autumn comes the rain. The war has stagnated into boredom and the front has bogged down along the old German river. In the last days of October, the left bank of the Schelde has finally fallen into our hands and the other bank has collapsed before our drive. The Huns defended it yard by yard, selling their lives dearly for every piece of this front, but everyone knows that the last offensive will not come before the spring. It takes months to bring in supplies, to stock up the necessary human and materiel reserves. And there is still Walcheren to crush, then Dunkirk on the Canadian front which is supported by a Czech brigade and a Polish division. In Italy, the Allied thrust towards the Alps progresses slowly, with Kesselring achieving wonders in maintaining a coherent defence. At the centre, in France, the Americans and new French armies are re-forming before the final assault on Germany.

Nobody suspects that Von Rundstedt will take his big gamble, a last desperate attack in December at the point where the British and American forces meet in the Ardennes. Moreover, precisely where a green American division is holding too large a front. And, at a time when meteorological conditions prevent the Allies from using their tremendous air superiority. Nobody foresaw that 15 divisions, some of them armoured, will break through and get almost to the Maas River, and very nearly to Antwerp. The Americans will write a glorious chapter at Bastogne and Montgomery will close the gap while Patton turns round to nip off the dangerous breakthrough.

As for us, in late October we are doing odd errands such as attacking V1 and V2 launching sites in Holland while we prepare for the invasion of Walcheren.

From 27 October it has become a shuttle service, two or three times a day, softening the defences to the south-west of the island, mostly in the area of Flushing. The heavies have struck at the inner dykes with 10-ton bombs, to breach them and let the water flood the roads to stop all movement. It was a partial success, but gun positions on the coast are still operating because they were built above dyke level. Our task is to silence the large numbers of 88 mm, 155 mm and 37 mm guns on the perimeter which would endanger any landing. Those batteries are surrounded by light flak, mostly 20 and 37 mm with quadruple barrels — particularly deadly because, at this time of year, the cloud base is down to 2000 feet; allowing perfect aim on us for the enemy gunners.

There are only two ways to get at them: either just below the cloud base, where our silhouettes are clearly visible against that cotton wool background; or at wave level, where our camouflage makes it more difficult to detect us. The first solution allows one to pinpoint the targets accurately while manoeuvring, at 350 mph, a group of aircraft and positioning them for a synchronised attack. Naturally, it's the more costly one as it gives time for the defences to aim accurately.

On a low-level attack, it requires a perfect knowledge of the target layout, plus very precise navigation and an attack from point-blank range. Should an aircraft be hit low down, the pilot has practically no chance to bale out.

So, one can get a pretty good idea of the thoughts we share when about to go on that kind of op — either way, the chances are not good.

The old hands know the score well, but the new boys are easy meat for the flak gunners who are real experts at their trade. They have had live training on real targets for years. Experience is the one thing that cannot be passed on. It's the price that is paid by all who hope to survive this never-ending war. Even experienced pilots do not always avoid mistakes. Becoming over-confident is as dangerous as lack of experience — and some chance their arm once to often. It's probably the law of averages that counts finally.

In what could be called a routine attack Squadron Leader Wallace, who arrived to take over 609 only six weeks ago, leads his squadron on besieged Dunkirk. The German-held perimeter narrows daily, and by now is back to the suburbs of the port — so the flak is more dense than ever, as it is grouped in a smaller area. With their backs to the sea, and no escape route, the only end for those gunners is kill or be killed.

Wallace has to silence some field guns harassing the Czech brigade on the eastern side of the town. He has chosen to make his dive from the land towards the sea so as not to endanger our troops. But, this tactic will force him through the main flak-barrage when pulling out after his attack. Warned in advance, the Germans had all the time in the world to adjust their aim and get him right at the end of his dive. The Typhoon, mortally damaged, plunged into the waves near the beach at high tide and disappeared. Our friend Wallace will never be seen again.

A year and a half later, in 1946, Wallace's mother came all the way from South Africa to Brussels and visited me. She was trying to find out exactly how her son was killed and trying to find his body, not yet recovered. She had visited the Air Ministry without result and had then gone to all the Allied cemeteries in France without finding any trace of her son's grave. On that day I was second-in-command of 164 Squadron, and Wallace was CO of 609, so I had not seen the crash but I had heard what happened. I therefore gave her what details I remembered, particularly that the aircraft crashed not far from the beach at high tide. A mother has the determination to win where man has failed for years: patiently, she persuaded the special unit of the RAF that was still searching the battlefields for missing RAF crews to send a party to Dunkirk and she went with them, searching for long days on end. One day, on that beach, she saw a piece of metal sticking out of the wet sand. A team from the RAF recovery party started work at once and finally recovered the Typhoon with the PR-B markings. In the cockpit were the remains of the pilot, and his mother went back to her far-away land with the body of her son, to bury him in the shade of a South African tree.

When Wallace did not return I was landing after an op over Holland when Group Captain Scott told me to report to his command van. Walter Drink, the Wingco Flying was with him and there was a twinkle in his eye even before the boss had said anything:

'Sit down, Windmill. Did you hear that Wally had bought it? Well, you will replace him. Congratulations, you are now CO of 609 Squadron!'

I had mixed feelings and, for a moment, I remained silent, then I realised what Scotty had said: I am a Squadron Leader, CO of one of the most famous squadrons in the RAF. The West Riding of Yorkshire Squadron. The six-o-nine! I must be dreaming, but Walter Drink smiled and gave me my new sleeve ring.

'Better have it sewn on at once, Charlie, because you take over this afternoon and go to Dunkirk to finish the job. Good luck! By the way, don't get yourself killed . . . we are short of experienced pilots!'

The black humour of the Wingco is his way of scorning death — with whom he had a date a few weeks later. His Typhoons were called to help the Americans besieged in Bastogne during the Battle of the Bulge. He landed at Chièvres airfield on an icy runway, skidded and overturned. By the time the crash crew arrived, Walker Drink, my friend, was dead.

I must get my squadron together. There are only three veterans left — Georges Jaspis, Polo Cooreman and Pinky Start — and they are due for a rest because their tour of operations is over. My first job as CO is to write the usual letter of sympathy to Wally's next of kin, then to sign Georges Jaspis' recommendation for a well-earned DFC. With the adjutant I must get Wally's belongings together for sending to the RAF depot.

Then I call my two flight commanders and lay down the form for the routine work: Starky will be my deputy, and 12 aircraft have to be ready for the afternoon. Nothing better than action to shake up a depressed bunch and boost morale again after a shaky do.

In the mess at lunchtime, Mony Van Lierde of 164, Pol Ezzano of 198 and Rex Mulliner of 183 pull my leg gently by way of congratulation. It's also one of the last times that we shall be together, for Pol and Rex are soon to be posted to other duties, and Mony Van Lierde will be sent to the new Belgian Air Force HQ in Brussels. In a matter of weeks, I shall find myself the most ancient squadron commander of 123 Wing, even though I have only just been appointed to command 609: war consumes men very fast!

I am lucky still to be there for, the afternoon I take command I have another narrow escape. The flak at Dunkirk is still very fierce; a 40 mm shell hits my left wing and my fuselage is holed by two 20 mm shells that blow my radio set to bits. The good old Tiffie gets me home safely and the other Typhoons are spared.

During the days following we mount a non-stop attack on Walcheren in foul weather. Remembrance Day is the time of the year when the weather seems to match with human sadness: fog, sleet, or steady cold rain with low cloud. Add that to the falling leaves and it produces a cold feeling deep in one's bones. And yet, for some unknown reason, although flying conditions are worsening and the last resistance at Walcheren is very bitter we haven't lost anyone for over a week. Just a few hits here and there, enough to give our fitters and riggers some work but nothing really serious.

With my usual luck, I have barely painted my CO's insignia on a new Typhoon when a few machine-gun bullets manage to find an oil pipe and cause minor damage to my engine. Chiefy takes a dim view of my bad fortune but repairs are quickly made.

Why did I decide on that November morning to test fly the repaired aircraft before doing an operational mission over Holland? It's difficult to explain, but maybe it was a premonition . . . So, at 11 o'clock, I take off alone and climb rapidly over Ghent, then go to Wavre and salute my parents from the air. It takes only a few minutes to get there, and I cannot resist beating up my home — showing off what a Typhoon can do; or rather what I can do with a Typhoon, so that my compatriots will admire the RAF birdman . . .

A dive at full throttle, a beat up, a slow roll, a stall turn, and . . . silence. My engine stops without warning.

At 3000 feet above the small town, a decision has to be made in a hurry. Belly land if I can find a nearby suitable field, or bale out over open country. From the corner of my eye, I can see under my left wing a field by the side of the Chaumont Gistoux road. I know the area well, for I played there often as a child. My decision takes a split second: I will save my aircraft and belly land as neatly as possible in that field. I lose height, gliding gently while I open the cockpit, fasten my straps and steer the seven tons of steel and alloys towards Mother Earth. Contact off, seat lowered. No time to be afraid, for I am busy preparing to hit the ground at 150 mph.

I start levelling off at about 50 feet, aiming at the small field bordered by pine trees. Hell, I am going to overshoot, and finish in those trees! Got to push her on to the ground as soon as I can — and there is a stupid haystack in my path . . . better hit the hay than finish in the trees. I gently push the stick forward and neatly cut the haystack in two with my right wing. The Typhoon does not even notice it, and touches the ground perfectly straight and level, sliding to a stop in a few yards. Just the propeller blades bent, no other damage — once lifted on a trailer, the plane will be repaired in no time, as soon as the engine trouble is sorted out.

I get out of the cockpit, undo my parachute straps and smoke a cigarette until my friend the police lieutenant arrives with his car. Many people run across the field to see what has happened — or to rip souvenirs off the plane. So much so that an armed guard has to be sent to prevent the plane being stripped. I am driven to my home where my parents are surprised to see me. My father, as usual, opens a bottle of wine to celebrate and my mother fusses about, telling me to be careful about catching cold in this rotten weather. She worries because the pullover she was knitting for me is not finished. It's wonderful to see how parents can busy themselves with trivial things when what it's all about really is to live just one more day — but maybe it's their way of hiding their fears.

Kisses and goodbyes; I manage to ring up base to tell them that I am O.K., and will be back as soon as I can. This means getting to Beauvechain airfield, an American base, where our allies kindly airlift me back to Ursel. I suppose that my escapade has washed out any hope of promotion on the next list, but I start wondering how long my luck will hold. So far, I have belly landed four times and baled out twice — and I am still as fit as a fiddle, and in one piece. For some unknown reason, I have always believed I had nine lives, like a cat — but having used up six of them, at least, I am living on borrowed time. After 800 hours of wartime flying, when shall I meet up with fate?

When the American Fairchild dropped me at Ursel, in the early afternoon, I arranged for my Typhoon to be loaded on a trailer and brought back to base. Next day, when it arrived, the experts found an oil pipe had been severed by gun fire and had been missed during the repairs . . . again I regret the passing of our mechanics of the old 609 days — this would not have been missed by them! And I bow to my personal Gremlin who got me to test fly my plane when I did. If not, the engine failure would have happened above the German lines and I would by now be a prisoner — or dead.

The bad weather is back, stopping most of our flying. There is also a possibility of a move from Ursel to Gilze Rijen in Holland. I take advantage of the enforced lull to fly to England and pick up a brand-new Typhoon equipped with the latest type of hood.

The GSU at Aston Down has changed so much that I don't even know a single pilot there. So I fly straight back to Ursel and get my plane lettered PRA with my insignia painted on its side. It's a privilege of rank to have one's personal aircraft and I feel a sense of childish satisfaction to know that nobody else is going to spoil that expensive toy. This one is my eighth aircraft since I began operational flying, and I soon have a very strong affection for it. After all we fly together, for better or for worse . . .

On 20 November 1944, we leave Belgium and Ursel to cross over the Gilze Rijen in Holland. As soon as we arrive on the German-built airfield, we are welcomed by snow storms and it seems that all the sadness in the world is reflected in the surroundings. The hangars are half destroyed, the billets are cold and wet, and there is mud everywhere. This kind of war wears me out; the cold penetrates to my bones and the boredom is demoralising. I'll have to overcome this insidious torpor, but the place does not help one to stay enthusiastic. If only the front would become more lively — perhaps an offensive to keep us busy — but nothing worth talking about is happening. In front of us, the cold grey water of the Waal speaks of a winter that promises to be long and dreary.

Even our operations are not especially exciting. The advance from Normandy to Belgium was lively, and war seemed full of adventure — risky but exciting. Here our task is limited to the destruction of some distant target, often badly suited for Typhoons and always heavily defended by flak. As soon as we cross the lines, we fly through flak alley, and we can do nothing about it — not even prang them. It's a wonder that, so far, we have lost no one since we came here — but I have a feeling — something like a premonition — that things will change for the worse soon. Everything is too static, too idle and, in a word, unimaginative.

I make use of this time to build up my squadron and try to reach the same professional level as that in the old 609 days. Not easy with the green pilots. They are very willing and doing their best, but the fact remains that we do not have the same brilliant individuals as those of a year or two ago. Maybe I am prejudiced but I feel that the atmosphere has changed and the keenness is not what it used to be. I try to analyse the situation and I think it is because we are operating under quite different conditions. First, there is the change of scene; this part of Holland in winter is downright depressing. The people have suffered so much and the war has lasted so long that they don't communicate any warmth. Our living conditions are appalling: we are billeted in an old girls' school, with no heating, no hot water, and nowhere to go off duty — no pub, no dance hall, not even a cinema. Our mechanics have to work in the snow, in the mud, and more often than not enveloped in fog. What can one do to lift morale?

November ends with an attack on the Reichswald forest. All we know is that supplies and petrol reserves have been stored there; what we don't know is that this is all being built up by the Germans for their Ardennes offensive, so we plaster that snow-covered forest with rockets without being able to see any targets and even less to observe the results. A very boring kind of operation, executed by very bored pilots fighting a very dull war and living a very dull life. Once in a while we are lucky and start a fire in the forest, leaving a long trail of black smoke billowing up towards the low clouds. But most of the time we see nothing worth mentioning apart from heavy flak, which discourages even our most disciplined pilots.

December does not help either, with the same dull life and the same boring ops. To make things worse the frost has come, making the mud hard and icing up the runway while the fog becomes even deeper, all adding to the difficulties of flying. Before starting the engines, our unfortunate mechanics have to keep warming them up by lighting fires in cut-down barrels filled with waste oil. In the Officers' Mess the beer is rationed and the food is poor quality. We eat to live, but our stomachs are tired of the same tinned bully beef day after day, with an occasional variation of tasteless spam or powdered eggs. Still no heating anywhere and our windows are white with frost. All the old hands have gone; the new ones are barely able to keep a Typhoon in the air — and my morale is far from brilliant. If only I could get something worthwhile to do, I might have a chance to stir them up, but everybody seems to sink into lethargy.

I don't know it yet, but my days are numbered. After 2041 days of war, we are told to destroy an oil refinery near the German border, at Schoonebeek. I have the whole afternoon and evening to plan the attack. Wg Cdr Drink being on leave, I will lead the whole wing, four squadrons, all equipped for the first time with phosphorus rockets.

Chapter 31
Mission Without Return

We climb in the cold December morning. The Dutch soil disappears in a light wintry fog and ahead the Rhine unrolls its long ribbon of dirty grey water.

Twenty-four Typhoons, spaced widely, are climbing hard before crossing the enemy lines. Our Spitfire XIV escort is above us on our left, to deal with the German fighters. Foot by foot, we gain height with a maddening slowness, heading for a curtain of cloud before entering the concentrated flak waiting for us around Arnhem and Ede.

I glance around to make sure that everybody is in position and that no aircraft is lagging. Higher, the billowing clouds are in a hostile sky. Now 4000 feet. Soon the Rhine. At 5000 feet we cross the front line.

It's too low — or too high, for at this altitude we are going to collect every calibre of flak, from the 20 mm to the infamous 88 mm, and the 37 mm with quadruple barrels. I have no choice since, in spite of our extra tanks, we shall be short of fuel for this op which is at our extreme range. If things go well, we shall have two, maybe three minutes to identify the target in the snow and destroy it with phosphorus rockets, a new weapon used for the first time — 1500 degrees C guaranteed. A thousand yards' flat trajectory and the necessary precision to blow up the reserves of petrol that Von Rundstedt has stored for the coming Ardennes breakthrough. But first, we have to find the well-camouflaged target, assuming we get through the best-trained and densest flak concentration the Germans have yet set up.

Now 6000 feet — Arnhem lies slightly to my right. Here it comes! In front and to my left, at the right height, 12 black smoke mushrooms mark the first salvo from the Ede batteries.

I pass through the area of the explosions and my plane rocks in the shock waves. It's much too close for comfort. The gunners down below are not just enthusiastic amateurs — they must be using a rangefinder coupled to the radar firing director. Speed, altitude and range are automatically computed to provide the necessary corrections.

We are still climbing too slowly, but there is nothing to be done about it. My orders are to get through, whatever the cost, right through flak alley. To go round the defences would mean using too much petrol and aborting the mission. It's freezing cold in the cockpit and yet I can feel the perspiration dripping as I turn my head to see what is happening to my chickens.

'Blue leader to Blue One, get your section in battle formation. Out.'
'Roger, Blue leader. Out.'

The 24 Typhoons are lined up on a wide front of more than half a mile and the 12 escorting Spitfires are stacked up, higher to the left, and slightly behind. If the Huns have the right height, the next salvoes will be deadly. But, one advantage of command is that there is no time to be afraid; there is too much to worry about — maintain the right course, watch for the pinpoints on the map, check the wind direction, verify oil pressure and temperature and, above all, keep one eye on the sky in case the new jet Messerschmitts try to jump us.

Strange — a few seconds ago the first salvo sought us out, and now the black puffs are but marks in the sky, trailing far behind us. Why are they waiting to start the usual barrage? We are flying at 6500 feet, climbing slowly, which should be ideal for them . . .

A sharp shock, an icy slap in the face, and all hell breaks loose.

I never saw the second salvo. Under my feet there is a gaping hole. The stick, cut off at the base, hangs uselessly in my right hand. The engine is running wildly, far beyond its 3800 rpm limit. My kite, mortally hit, rears up to the sky; then howling like a wounded beast, the engine explodes. The sky swings wildly, the earth starts revolving, the fuselage holds me prisoner in a flat spin.

Jump! Yes, I've got to jump; fast, very fast, for I must have lost a lot of altitude. I strain to heave open the plexiglass canopy with both hands. In vain. It must be stuck fast by the explosion which has twisted the airframe. At last I find the explosive cartridge that blows the canopy off in an emergency. It too is stuck. I push the red button again and again but nothing happens. And I still go round in my flat spin, body glued to the back of the seat.

Up to now, I have had no time to be afraid, being too busy to sort things out, but I can feel panic creeping up and it would be fatal. I must stay calm, but act fast.

I can't go through the gaping hole in the floor, with its metal edges like sharp knives. As a last resort I push the rocket release button located inside the now useless throttle, thinking stupidly that I had better get rid of them before hitting the ground. As if it would make any difference in the inferno of fire and petrol that will blow-up on impact! Unconsciously I make a last choice on the manner of my death, hating the idea of being burned by the phosphorus . . .

A huge flame, a big bang as my rockets leap out crazily into an empty sky — and I feel myself falling freely, still in my bucket-seat, freed by the explosion.

The Typhoon has split into several pieces, now pirouetting around me. A wing spirals to my left, the fuselage a little further away, and lower down the engine drops like a stone while the tail unit somersaults nearby.

My chute! Thank God it's still there! But first let's get rid of the belt still holding me in my seat. Then, a pull on the ripcord and the white canopy blossoms above my head as the straps cut into my shoulders. Under my feet there is about 3000 feet of fresh air, the long ribbon of the

Rhine and the town of Arnhem sunk in a misty December morning.

The sky has emptied suddenly. I am alone, hanging from a chute falling towards beautiful Mother Earth. Alive! Yes alive, but crushed by the utter loneliness.

I soon realise I am going to land not far from the lines, where the Rhine itself is 'no man's land'. With a bit of luck, if the wind carries me to the west, I can land in the Canadian lines, or at worst fall into the Rhine and swim towards our side. Quickly I pull on the parachute cords so that it slides me towards our lines and freedom.

The Huns don't agree with this; they don't want their prey to escape, and a long line of tracer climbs towards me. I can do nothing to avoid it. Seen from the ground, the show must be interesting. As the target it gives me a most disagreeable feeling that all those will-o'-the wisps are converging towards a point exactly between one's eyes. Not very funny when one is travelling at 500 mph and protected in front by a huge engine, but it is really disconcerting when one is hanging like a puppet on a string and feeling very, very exposed . . .

I let go the cords, shrink as much as I can, bend my legs and hope the tracers will miss me. What a bunch of bastards! But let's admit it — it's a cruel war and it's all part of the dirty game. It's difficult to be objective when one is hanging in the air, unarmed, at the end of a parachute. Didn't I myself firing from point-blank range kill dozens and dozens of Nazi soldiers jumping from burning transports? If I get the wind to help and if I escape I will fly again, and maybe soon shoot down another Hun or smash another Tiger tank. But war leaves no choice for the gunners firing at me. My only hope is to pretend I am dead, to hang loosely without a move, but thereby giving up any hope of falling into our lines . . .

Only about 100 feet now before I hit the ground. The firing has stopped because the gunners are sure they have won. I don't make the river and the murky water, for I am coming down in a town. A bare 150 yards from freedom, but on the wrong side!

A deserted street, roofs with red tiles. A shock. The parachute silk falls on me, I roll down the roof but miss the gutter. Emptiness, cobblestones, a last try to hit the pavement feet first. Another dull shock — then the long silence of unconsciousness.

When I come to, eight hours later, I am lying in the back of an Opel car driven by a German soldier. My bleary eyes stop on the SS insignia of the officer seated next to me, who is looking at me coldly, impersonally.

Part Five
Guest of the Third
Reich

Chapter 32
The Cage

Wetzlar in the Black Forest. Wetzlar, a small country town famous for the Leica, the marvellous camera that is produced there and whose fame is worldwide. In the RAF Wetzlar is well known too but for other reasons. Since 1942 Frank Ziegly, our Intelligence Officer in 609, has been alerting pilots to tricks used at the Dulagluft — the Luftwaffe interrogation centre for aircrew prisoners. First its position. It's next door to the optical factory that works for the Kriegsmarine, producing periscopes, and for the Luftwaffe making all their photographic equipment — both of the finest quality. It is not stupid to have such a plant next to a prison camp. It is the best way of protecting the Leica works — for proximity of Allied prisoners precludes any mass bombing.

We had also been warned by Ziegly of the techniques used. They are tidy, methodical, reliable. The aircrew prisoner is first conditioned by a 'softening' process — a progressive melting of his will. It is achieved by alternating 'cold' and 'warm' — a hard labour regime followed by recreation — with the purpose of getting the prisoner 'to spill the beans'. No physical brutality, at least not to my knowledge, as we are not in the hands of the SS. Our interrogators are 'gentlemen' of the Luftwaffe or even from the Kriegsmarine — sometimes it's a civilian, a Herr Doktor who asks the questions, university professor and psychologist. But the prison regime is very tough, especially at the end of January 1945 when the thermometer shows minus 20 degrees Centigrade.

Little by little, I come to. The straw, the attic, the wire grille and the old sentry sitting with his back turned to me. A hurricane lamp throws a dim light on this set for a horror film. I remember falling over Arnhem. The night, the coma, the open car. The SS officer. God how my head is aching and my leg hurts every time I move it. I check my pockets: empty. It suddenly hits me that I have become a prisoner! A terrible weariness comes over me; better to let things go, to give up. No! That would be stupid.

First reaction: how to escape? I know that now is my best chance, while they believe that I am groggy. Later it will become more and more difficult. Where am I? Somewhere in Holland, surely; or perhaps already in Germany? No watch, nothing in my pockets, and my gun, well hidden in my flying boot, has gone too. I think hard. Only solution: try out my keeper — flannel my guard — and grab a chance if it comes.

'Posten, bitte, haben sie ein Zigarette?'

The Jerry is an old reservist, well into his sixties. He looks quite human.

'Ach ja, Herr Major, Zigarette!'

He comes over, gives me an ersatz cigarette through the wire grille and lights it with an old lighter.

'Trinken, bitte.'

'Nein, Herr Major, nicht zu trinken. Morgen, ja, nach Lazareth!' Then, as if he had discovered a great truth:

'Das Krieg ist Scheisse!'

You can say that again, friend; the war *is* shitty, especially for you, well on the way to losing it!

I get up, but my leg gives way under me. I can barely walk. An excruciating pain marks each step. I don't know it but I have broken a bone in my leg and cracked my skull — no use thinking of escape tonight. I can barely walk — as soon as I make the effort, everything goes round and round. A pity, for my Jerry could have been overcome easily.

I lie down and, incapable of sleep, wait impatiently for dawn to show its first dirty grey light. God, how long can a night be!

I think hard, dreaming up the most impossible schemes. Only one solution: make it look as bad as possible, pretend that I am in a bad way, and get to hospital. It's the best place to escape from.

So, when the platoon comes to fetch me the next morning, I put on an act, refusing to march and speaking with the voice of a goner: *Kranke*, *Kopfsmerze*. My knowledge of Goethe's language is elementary, but good enough for my play-acting.

I can hear them discussing my case, and finally an NCO decides to take me to hospital. Stretcher; lorry. When I am unloaded without ceremony I read on a board: 'Saint Joseph Ziekenhuis. Enschede'. That registers with me. I am still on the Dutch side of the border, at Enschede. Better than being in Germany.

Now, I have got to play it smoothly. The Medical Officer is no fool. An X-ray — my uniform is taken away. Then I find myself in a large ward on a bed with clean linen. The scene is horrible. British paratroops, Polish and German soldiers each in a bed are all mixed up: amputees, the burned. Some are completely inert, others cry, their faces distorted by pain; everywhere is that sour smell made up of old blood and new disinfectant.

A German matron, helped by a sick bay orderly with only one arm, rules everybody with a rod of iron. She pushes me unceremoniously into a bed. I've won; I am now a patient. One thing at a time — the first act is over.

The doctor comes back and talks to me slowly while examining the X-rays. I understand that I have a cracked skull and a slight fracture of the bone next to the tibia. My leg is bandaged and I am given some milk and two aspirins.

I think myself into the part of a wounded man and make sure that I look twice as bad as I really feel.

The days go by. I am well treated, though the horrible smell in the ward makes me feel really sick. Some men die. Others sometimes scream — his bed is screened and a drug administered. Then it happens again in another corner and another wounded man dies without a friend to hold his hand.

At the door of the ward, an armed sentry keeps guard on the wounded and on the hall entrance. They are old soldiers — some look as if they fought in the 1870 war! Their rifles would be better as crutches.

The pretty young Dutch nurse who looks after me at times tells me she is 19, and was evacuated from Arnhem during the Arnhem battle. Most of the wounded have been here since September, Germans, Allies, paratroops and SS. When the German matron is not around I try to speak Dutch to my nurse. I ask her about the Resistance and decide to trust her by telling her that I want to escape. Two days later she tells me that she has been in touch with some Dutch patriots and that they are willing to help. Marvellous! I dream — I have nothing else to do — about an heroic escape in which I meet the Dutch resistance during the night and find shelter in a barge on a frozen canal. My fertile imagination sees me disguised as a German pilot, penetrating a German-held airfield and stealing an Fw190 which the mechanics are warming up. Under the noses of the Germans I take off at full throttle without looking behind and down-wind if necessary. They shoot at me — missing of course — but I am already in the air, flying low towards our lines, towards freedom. No parachute of course — just an important detail. As for piloting an Fw190, I remember that the throttle works in the opposite direction to ours. As for the undercarriage and petrol gauge, I will cross those bridges when I come to them. I am day-dreaming but, after all, a plane is made to fly so it should not be too difficult. Next, I guess my friends, supposing I get that far, will shoot at me when I arrive! So I'll have to fly low, hope for the best and land straight ahead when I see a friendly airfield — before being shot down by my own people . . . My dreams are so vivid that when I come back to earth I am almost shocked still to be lying in the hospital bed I've occupied for the last three weeks. Soon I will be sent to Germany — I must act now. From my little nurse I learn that my uniform is kept in a locker next to the bathroom. I'll have to get it and dress when I go to the bathroom. Then, open the window and disappear into the night. As far as I know, there are no sentries outside. Walking west, I should be out of the town quickly and should find a farm to hide me before morning. The only promise I have is that the Resistance will be waiting for me as soon as I hit open country.

Right! No more hesitation. It's on for tonight. Let's hope the alarm won't be raised too quickly and that my unknown friends will be there to help!

It's already the third time that I have been to the bathroom, with a pretended lame leg and holding a painful tummy.

I pull myself slowly along in front of the guard, hoping that my pitiful face is expressive enough. Ah, that Spanish tummy! Those rolling eyes, and then the pretended haste to get there in time . . . It's a great act, one that should one day get me the lead in a play. It is so true to life that the sentry is convinced.

Seated on a three-legged stool, his Mauser rifle against the wall, my guardian does not move and goes back to his Teutonic dream while I am in the bathroom with my uniform. It's all there, except for my boots! Good God, where are my goddammed leather boots? I have to accept it: only my big white woollen socks are there. Too late to do anything about it: let's run.

The window slides open noiselessly. A low wall. Then the night — and the trampled snow, which squeaks a little and penetrates a lot. Frozen. My shoeless feet are frozen in less time than it takes to say it. Not a soul about. Nothing but the night, with a swirling fog which clothes everything in a misty dress. My heart pounds. I'm shivering with cold, maybe also from nerves. Where do I go? Left? Straight ahead? The only thing that's certain is I've got to hurry, before the alarm is raised. Later? We'll see!

All the loneliness in the world falls on me, in a silence broken only by my footsteps in the snow.

'*Wer da?*'

Hell! A patrol, right in front of my nose, at a cross-roads. I say nothing. They come out from behind a house where they were sheltering, without hurry, not even lifting their rifles. My poor frozen feet refuse to move: no possible escape. And in any case, where would I go? There are three of them, an NCO and two men. They surround me and lead me away, without brutality, like some workmen doing their job conscientiously. The NCO must be thinking of the special leave he might get for this capture. Personally, I know it is not my day!

But I also know I'll try again, as soon as possible, this time with shoes on.

In the cooler I have plenty of time to meditate on a badly prepared attempt to escape. I despise myself for an amateurish piece of work, but was there any other solution? The problem is how to profit quickly from any little chance one gets. With a bit of luck, it could have succeeded — but I really need a certain minimum of equipment and some outside help to make it. Otherwise, it's a dead duck.

My prison is damp and I am frozen. I try to massage my feet to restore the circulation. A pale blue lamp illuminates the naked walls, a bit of straw and a dirty blanket.

But the Germans are not going to leave me there for long: a key turns in the lock, the hinges creak and a matter-of-fact voice says '*Raus, raus!*' — out! Just time to put my socks on and I am ready. An officer in leather gloves and a long overcoat watches me as I am pushed into a gas-fuelled lorry.

'Rather shabby, the Jerries.' I spoke the words as a kind of challenge. The officer understands. He says, quite slowly in perfect English: 'You might be sorry for being so witty, Herr Major, for your case is not a good one. Our Führer has given orders to punish by death all escapes in the front line.'

Very polite, my Hun, but menacing. He adds that I am being transferred to a prison camp, where there will be no chance of escaping. So be it. I will keep a low profile for the present.

The lorry moves slowly, brakes and stops in front of a small railway station. In the waiting room there is a stove full of glowing coke. It's good to feel the warmth flowing through my freezing limbs. I feel dirty and lonely, ground down by a large impersonal machine.

In my condition I recognise that I was getting off rather lightly. Even admit that I am feeling grateful to my captors who were treating me correctly, with a rough humanity that was quite unexpected. I also sense that they are treating me with deference, even with respect. Is it due to my rank, or is it because they respect a man who won't give up and who keeps on fighting in line with his beliefs? So far I have been treated according to the rules of war, without brutality.

A slow train draws in, brakes squealing and belching plumes of white smoke. A third-class compartment is isolated from the rest of the train and smells of stale tobacco and rancid sweat. As a bonus, I get four guards with packs on their backs and old rifles on their shoulders. The officer hands over some papers to the NCO who snaps out a smart '*Zum Befehl, Herr Leutnant*' and we are off.

Once seated, my guards pull out sausage, black bread and margarine. One of them hands me a lump of bread. That evil-tasting bread goes down with as much pleasure as a delicious cake. My feast ends with a kindly offered cigarette.

The four old reservists are anything but warmongers. One can feel that they have had enough of this war — that they probably hate it — but they carry on like fallen leaves blown by the wind. I feel really sorry for these old wrecks. At best, they are like hostages — prisoners of their fate. They will never escape. Where are the proud Teutons now who paraded in the Champs Elysées in 1940?

The train puffs its way across wooded countryside. Then night falls, with stops several times in open country, then moving on a few miles, and stopping again. Sirens can be heard, planes fly over at great height and, far away, is the continuous noise of loud gunfire. One can make out the bark of flak, followed by the dull thuds of heavy bombs. It goes on all night.

When day breaks, a railwayman tells us to leave the compartment because the line is cut. So we march. We march for hours along the rails, in Indian file. Two guards in front, then me, and two behind; a sorry human convoy on its way like sheep to Frankfurt-am-Main — the town the RAF has bombed all night.

Dog-tired and dirty, we circle bomb craters and climb over twisted rails to reach what is left of a platform in a station. There some civilians wait patiently for an imaginary train.

I am uneasy for the looks given me are not exactly friendly. I çan imagine that they hold me responsible for last night's raid. Suddenly, a man in uniform, a civil policeman with a black leather belt, runs to me shouting loudly that I am a 'terrorist flieger'. He not only shouts but, happy to get at an English murderer, starts hitting and kicking me. No use fighting back — I would be slaughtered by the mob. I duck the blows as best I can, hoping that my guards will come between us before I go out for the count. Maybe because he's behaving like a madman, maybe because they will eventually have to answer for my safety, my guards finally intervene and free me from the mob.

God! A little more of that and it would have been too late. My head must look like a cauliflower, my trousers are torn, and I don't feel very proud of myself. We move away from the crowd. Then a train comes slowly into the station and my guards hustle me into a reserved compartment.

At Wetzlar, the cage opens, then closes on a prisoner in a very poor state.

Chapter 33
The Interrogation

Brick-built barracks. Narrow paths bordered by snow-covered lawns. The whole place is built with everything in sharp right angles, something like a model factory. There are watch towers with sentries wearing coal-scuttle type helmets.

A passage. A hall. A door opens and I am shown into my cell. The key turns in the lock. Six feet by four, bare walls, no window, a wooden board and a blanket, an electric heater against the wall. Apart from that, an electric bulb lit day and night and a closed grille in the door. Nothing else but freezing cold and silence. And hunger. But I am so dog-tired that I drop on to the board — and shiver under the blanket.

Everything I had on me was removed when I was caught at Arnhem, but I saw my guards deposit a big envelope in the prison office and the clerk made a list: watch, signet ring, fountain pen, money, cigarettes — and the wallet I stupidly carried on operations when I should have left it at dispersal; everything listed and confiscated. And, before I entered my cell, my shoes, belt and tie were also removed. Now, I have to occupy my mind — dream, invent, imagine, so as not to go mad. Days pass, one, two, four, and then I lose all sense of time. Except for one visit a day. The guard opens the small hatch and pushes through a bowl of soup. It's a horrible stew that at first I can't swallow — but after a day or two, I manage to gulp it down somehow with my nose firmly ignoring the smell. Every day, too, the door opens and two Russian prisoners put down a lavatory bucket half full of strong disinfectant and remove the other one, all under the watchful eye of a guard.

Unwashed, unshaven — I am sure I stink. Fortunately I have been warned about the scenario by Ziegly. When they decide that I am properly 'softened up' they will take me out for interrogation, with many apologies, and then the whole process will start again.

Until they give up, for I am not going to give in.

At least, I hope I won't talk.

Was it on the fifth day? The sixth? I don't know, for time becomes as immobile as the ice that clings to my walls. Once every 24 hours, the electric heater on the wall is switched on, becomes red all over, and heat permeates my cell. The ice melts and water droplets flow down the walls. They hesitate and stop about one hour later, I guess, when the heater is turned off. Then they freeze and stay there till next day.

Sounds of heavy boots in the passage. A key turns in the lock. A Luftwaffe officer comes into my cage. An admin type, for he is not wearing wings. Stick under his arm, shining leather boots and cap at just the right angle. He speaks to me in clipped English that doesn't hide his German accent.

'Major, what's happened to you?'

He's a good actor with the right touch of incredulity, his face showing great surprise. Let's play the game, according to the rules.

'Herr Leutnant, judge for yourself! May I remind you that I an a senior officer and I expect to be treated according to the Geneva convention?'

A smile is quickly controlled but my Hun plays it out in full.

'But of course, Squadron Leader, please follow me! The bathroom is at your disposal. Please have a shower and shave. Then we will go to the Officers' Mess.'

A corridor, a door, and indeed, there is a bathroom — with soap, towel, comb, Gillette razor and shower. I even find my boots and my belt, but no tie. I take my time to clean up, to feel human again and to be back on form.

When I come out I walk beside my host, with an armed sentry close on my heels. Comes the first try by my Hun.

'If you agree to give your word as an officer not to escape I will send the guard away, and we can even go for a little walk!'

'Sorry Leutnant, I regret to tell you that, given the opportunity, I will of course escape — or try to! So I cannot give my word.'

How's that! Boasting even! But I know that as long as I keep my cool I will stay on top.

'I am rather pig-headed, Leutnant. I don't like the kind of hospitality you provide. At the very first chance, I'll have to say goodbye.'

Obviously he does not like the joke but says nothing. We arrive in front of a barrack block and go in. The sentry stays close behind.

On the door a name and rank: 'Oberst H. Mueller' Then I am in front of a walnut desk, all very neat and tidy. Standing behind the desk is a Luftwaffe officer, a slightly greying pilot, who salutes me very correctly. He ranks higher than me, so I return his salute — a touch of military etiquette; got to show I'm a gentleman, though still keeping my distance.

'Please sit down. A cigarette?'

'Thank you.'

I take the cigarette and smoke it with real pleasure. The Lieutenant has gone, but the sentry can't be far away.

'I have your file, Squadron Leader. A brilliant pilot — squadron commander at your age is not bad at all!' He hands me a sheet of printed paper and a pencil. Then with a smile, 'The Geneva Convention permits you to send this Red Cross message to your next of kin. Twenty-five words are allowed. Please fill it in, Squadron Leader.'

I see at once that the printed form has nothing to do with the Red Cross, and disregarding the questions, I write down my name, number and rank — nothing else. The questions will remain unanswered. I hand back the blank form.

'Have you lost your memory?'

'One could easily lose it after the treatment you have quite wrongly subjected me to, Sir.'

'Wrongly? According to international military law, you deserve 28 days' solitary confinement as punishment for attempting to escape. I am told you refuse to be put on parole — you are a stupid man. If you don't fill in the form, I'll send you back to your cell. Your stubbornness is ridiculous when we know all about you!'

He looks very angry. He opens a big file marked with my name and shows me two newspaper cuttings with my photo, one from an English newspaper and the other from a leaflet dropped over Belgium. Then he goes on to say that I was a flight commander in 164 to such a date, and made CO of 609 on another. He's just trying to bluff me — and almost succeeds for everything he says is true. Only is he wrong when he boasts that I took off from Eindhoven the day I was shot down. It was from Gylze Rijen — just 15 miles out!

'Since you know everything, Colonel, why ask me any questions?'

'Just routine! Good will! Nothing secret, but if you refuse to be courteous you will be treated as you deserve!'

Threatening now! After the carrot, the stick; what childish psychology!

'I fully appreciate your courtesy, Colonel, but if we exchanged seats, I would also understand your refusal to answer.'

'Guard!'

The door opens and the guard comes in. I am pushed out roughly, marched back to the solitary confinement block and back to the limited charm of my freezing cell.

Shoes and belt removed. Two days, four days, maybe more. Dirty, hungry, getting thinner, and with morale rather low I wait for the next interrogation. Then, one day, the door opens: my little lieutenant is back again, still pretending it's all been a mistake and exuding charm. Same routine with bathroom, etc. I even get a clean shirt and find my uniform has been pressed when I have finished my shower. What will be the price for that service?

Quite soon, we enter the Officers' Mess. It's dark outside and heavy curtains hide the brilliant lighting. Classical decor, a bar like a night club, a white-vested barman and, glasses in hand, a group of officers drinking. We approach the group, who welcome us cheerfully.

'Ach so, Herr Major, come and have a drink with your German colleagues!'

They are all very civilised, introduce themselves and offer a whisky that seems to have been poured ready for me. With a little imagination I could be in an RAF Officers' Mess, at night after returning from ops.

'Prosit.'

My glass slips to the ground and the whisky spills. Just in case it contains a drug, prepared beforehand, to get me drunk and garrulous. More difficult to do it in front of me while I'm watching the barman.

O.K., another whisky. We drink.

'Typhoon, nein?'

Yes, a Typhoon. You have the scattered bits of it. So, yes; Typhoon!

In English, at times in German, they talk shop, discuss their planes, ours, comparing their respective merits and slowly, gently, they drift towards technical points.

'Launching your rockets from 5000 feet?'

There we are! From this, we shall come to frequencies, to names of pilots, to artful questions that seem innocuous — all normal procedure. I can already feel that we are soon going to talk about the Tempest, the new British aircraft.

A curtain is drawn back slowly — a well rehearsed move. It reveals a beautifully laid table, a lavish display of food — and other delights. Two girls, lightly dressed with dancing eyes and a deep cleavage hinting at perfect breasts, seem to expect us to join them. There is no doubt about the looks they give. One would have to be blind not to understand that a silent promise is being conveyed by our pretty hostesses.

'*Späte*! Later, Squadron Leader, you get all that after we eat and drink! Have another drink now!'

I feel my mouth watering. I want nothing else but to eat, to devour eggs, sausages — any kind of food. My head is spinning but I know that the play is nearing its end. The final act is coming. One more drink, and I have had it!

'No thank you, Hauptmann. I don't want any more!'

An incredulous look, then a direct question, with a touch of menace in the tone: 'You refuse to drink with us?'

A perfect portrayal of a country gentleman, hurt, shocked, as though my refusal is an insult!

'Sorry, I can't drink any more. I am hungry!'

'Guard!'

The guard is never far away. I am removed without ceremony, back to the hell of my cell. I could have cried, I am so hungry and cold, cold to my soul. But somewhere, deep down, I am proud that I did not give in.

No, I *won't* talk.

The days go by but I have lost all count of time. I exist like a robot. I hear noises in the cell next door but can't make out what they are. Then, one day, there are repeated knocks and I realise it's a kind of morse. Is it another poor unfortunate trying to get in touch, or a German trick? I can read the message: it says, over and over, 'Who are you?' I can answer that, and do. Then the response. My neighbour is a USAF Colonel. Soon, the morse is interrupted. I hear nothing more from my unfortunate companion.

I smell awful and, from my beard, I must have been locked in for about 10 days since the last time I was let out. If the punishment is 28 days in the cooler then it should soon be over. I find myself hoping again — the worst must be past. My uniform just hangs on me, I have lost so much weight. I sink into a permanent cold night, although the bulb continues to provide its miserable pale light.

Footsteps in the corridor. They stop in front of my cell. Same routine, complete with the bathroom act. Then a small room with a wooden table and two nasty-looking black-clad civilians in leather overcoats and felt hats. I never saw such sinister-looking individuals. Brutes with hard faces and broken noses, and looks as cold as razor blades.

'You are Belgian!'

It's a statement, not a question. The tone is threatening, the French halting and heavily accented. The one who spoke seems to be in charge.

'British, and a Squadron Leader!'

I hang on. My only chance is to stick to my story — stay behind my shield.

'Your parents live in Wavre! Our soldiers are already in Namur. Soon we shall take all Belgium and get your parents. You are a terrorist!'

He spoke the word with barely concealed hate. Cut off from everything, without news, I know only that weeks ago the Germans launched an offensive in the Ardennes and met with some success. But I have had no idea of what is really going on since my time in the hospital in Enschede. The bastards are lying, I am sure, but it may be partly true. I am tortured by the thought. What are they after?

'You are a liar! You are Belgian. You will be judged as a terrorist. We are Gestapo, you understand?'

This dirty little game goes on for two whole days; part of the time in my cell, then more conditioning at the hands of the hoodlums.

I am confused. I don't know what to do; more so since the Luftwaffe officers haven't shown up, and the SS don't seem to ask proper questions. They just threaten, pretend that Belgium is out of the war and that, technically, I am just a terrorist.

Like a machine, I give only my name, rank and number — and I claim to be British. I won't answer any other questions.

This cruel game must be part of a process of intimidation — but to what end? The absence of Luftwaffe officers is proof that the Gestapo is in charge and yet, no physical torture — not even the slightest brutality — has been tried on me. I will never learn the reason for their attitude because, after a final session, I never see those brutes again.

The next interview takes place in a kind of salon, with a senior officer and a middle-aged civilian who introduces himself as the former Consul General of Germany in Brussels before the war. The atmosphere is completely relaxed. Earlier I had been taken to the usual bathroom where I shaved, had a shower and found my pressed uniform, a clean shirt and socks. There is definitely something special in the air — and I find the two Germans in front of me much more agreeable than the two Gestapo agents.

'Squadron Leader, I have come specially from Berlin, where the opinion is held that you could be quite useful to the cause of Europe. In short, we want to send you to join King Leopold III of Belgium and his family, presently living in a castle near the Austrian border. You would be free, as an ADC to the King, provided you give us your parole. What do you say?'

If a bomb had exploded behind me I could not have been more surprised. So the Gestapo business was all over? And I am now being asked to collaborate, even to give my opinion . . . ?

'Sir, I am your prisoner, therefore I have no choice. It's out of the question for me to be "on parole". It's a matter of honour, and I won't discuss it. As far as joining the King, I have no objection, provided I do so as a prisoner and as a British officer.'

Though I was taken aback by the proposal and I answered without hesitation I had at the back of my mind that it ought to be easier to escape from a castle than from a prison camp. So, I am all for it. But my attitude towards the King of Belgium has changed considerably since 1940.

When I volunteered, on the first day, to fight the Germans, I was an ardent royalist. Later on I had difficulty in understanding the King's behaviour — his order to lay down our arms after 18 days? Sad but logical. Impossible to act differently. Our forces were totally disorganised and total slaughter had to be avoided. Even then, the King could have left the country to continue the fight from England. But he chose, at that cross-roads of our history, to share the fate of his beaten army and declare himself a prisoner. I had to agree that his attitude was humanly understandable even if, politically, I thought it was a great mistake. But my pledge of fidelity to the King was still intact when I reached England in 1940.

Only in 1941, when I heard about his marriage to a certain Miss Baels, made Princess de Réthy for the occasion, did I find myself with a conscience problem. Was this true to his promise to share the fate of his soldiers, now prisoners? Could they too get married behind barbed wire? And that fat Cardinal Van Rooy, who blessed their union? But I could take no more when I learned that our sovereign was shooting game with certain people and that the new princess had chosen an Austrian dentist! No, a thousand times no. We were not facing death every day for that kind of thing!

Since the liberation of Belgium my opinion has not changed even though the Regent, Prince Charles, now fills the void left by King Leopold's departure to Germany: I don't believe that this kind of royalty is what Belgium needs. It is a half-baked solution, probably not the best for a badly shaken country where part of the population resisted bravely and another part collaborated willingly with the Germans. As far as I am concerned, I took an oath on the Bible of allegiance to the King of England. Wounded, I was invalided out of the Belgian forces in 1940 and now I belong to the Royal Air Force. O.K., I was born Belgian and the Belgian Government in London considers that I am of Belgian nationality although a British officer. I would not want to deny my roots or my country but my sense of duty and the final sacrifice of so many of us must be recognised.

The proposal just made does not fill me with enthusiasm — only the possibility of an easier way of escaping attracts me. And, perhaps, curiosity at meeting one of the key figures in my country's history.

'We believe, Herr Major,' continues the speaker, 'that the Allied powers must see where their interests lie, which is also where the interests of Europe lie. The English and the Americans must clearly realise that the Russians are the real danger to our civilisation. We must unite our efforts to crush Communism which is only the tip of an iceberg called Russian Imperialism. We also believe that King Leopold, with his British connections, can play an important part as mediator. We want you to be our go-between and obtain from King Leopold his agreement to this plan! As you are the only senior officer of Belgian birth who has fought in the RAF and who is now prisoner, the King will be informed best by you.'

So, that's the idea! They are doing me the honour of believing that I can change the course of history by agreeing to such a scheme!

As I think over the whole thing I realise it's a trap. First, because my enemy is Germany with her allies such as Japan. But the Russians, communist or not, have fought well. They are our allies — why should I do anything against them? Indeed, I have great sympathy for the Russian people even though I don't agree with their political system. Therefore I could not be party to a German plan dictated only by their realisation that they are beaten. I choose my words carefully before answering.

'Mr. Consul General, I am and remain a British Officer and a prisoner. If you sent me as ADC to the King of Belgium, I would refuse to convey ideas that are contrary to my own. Germany must pay for her crimes, as we paid for our mistakes. I am an officer not a politician. Please treat me as a soldier. That said, if you insist, I will tell the King about your scheme, but also warn him of the complete determination of the Allies to go on to the end.'

'Please think it over, Major. Your personal fate is also at stake. My Government would be grateful for your intervention — with all the advantages that obviously would go with it. We shall meet again tomorrow — and I hope that a good night's sleep will change your mind.'

My interviewers rise to indicate that the meeting is over. The senior officer takes me to a different room, simply furnished but, even so, the relative luxury seems like heaven.

'Tonight, you sleep here. You are now to be given a hot meal. Good night!'

Definitely, life is an eternal adventure! Here I am, almost courted after having been to some extent roughed up for weeks. A bed with white linen and a soft eiderdown. Soon a tray comes with steaming sauerkraut, cakes, and a beer! Ten cigarettes too, and some matches.

I luxuriate on the bed. I eat slowly, savouring each mouthful, and I ponder. What exactly do my captors want? Probably to create the right climate to get me to agree to be their messenger to the King. Well, enough for tonight, let's sleep.

The next day, the usual routine with bathroom and pressed uniform — the guest regime — then the interview with the Consul.

'Well Major, I hope you enjoyed our hospitality?

'It all depends on the price I have to pay for it, sir.'

'Frankly, Herr Major, I believe that Germany offers the last chance to save Europe. I am not a Nazi. Neither are many people around me. Europe must be saved. The Nazis will rightly be punished, but Europe will be saved from Communism if at long last the Allies can be made to understand. But time is short. You could help to change the world's future. Will you accept our offer?'

'Don't count on me to defend your thesis, Mr. Consul. First of all, I will let the King know what I think should be his choice. Then, I would have to get instructions from London through the Swedish Consul, whom I would need to talk to personally. Thirdly, if I get the opportunity to escape, I will do so. Please understand that I am grateful for my favourable treatment and quite honoured by your proposal. That said, I have nothing to add.'

A faint smile; the man knows I won't play his game. Maybe he things I am stupid. Hesitantly he offers me his hand with, it seems, a tinge of regret in his eyes as he wishes me luck.

'Auf wiedersehen, Herr Major. Maybe one day you will remember our talk.'

The corridor, another building. Then a door marked 'Oberst Kunecke'.

It's the office of the camp commandent of Dulagluft. On his desk is my file together with my personal belongings. Still inside is my half-smoked packet of Churchman's No. 1.

'Herr Major, you are to be transferred to Barth, to a Stalagluft. That's in Pomerania. You are going at once. Those are my orders. Here are your personal belongings — please sign here. The money is confiscated I am afraid, but I have given you a receipt for it!'

'Thank you, Colonel.'

I sign — and I wait, stiffly to attention

The German gets up. Looks at me for a while almost in a friendly manner and then, with a heavy German accent that makes the words more detached and more meaningful, 'Herr Major, you did not talk. Even when we made things a little tough. You are an officer. May I shake hands with you?'

'Yes, thank you, Sir.'

I shake hands, salute, and before I leave add, 'There are not enough Germans like you.'

Then I turn about and go, escorted by my keepers. 11 February 1945 is the date on the office calendar.

I walk down the frozen lane with my escort towards a railway station covered with snow and surrounded by trees. The war has so far spared that little town. The rare passer-by doesn't even look at me, and neither do my guards. Each of us marches towards his fate, lost in a private dream, and for a moment the war seems so far away.

Chapter 34
Stalagluft

I have the honour of being transferred from Oberursel to Barth under the viligant eyes of an escort armed to the teeth. This kind attention is the result of my liking for unauthorised walks while a guest of the Luftwaffe. So far, I haven't succeeded, but they are taking no chances. The NCO has warned me that they would shoot at the slightest sign of an attempt to escape.

In this 1945 winter everything is the colour of desolation in the bloodless Germany that we are about to cross — at the whim of uncertain steam trains and over a partly destroyed railway network. The train moves lamentably slowly and at each stop everything seems to be collapsing around us. Hungry civilians show no spirit, no reaction, like ghosts. The once-proud soldiers of the German army go about with week-old beards and torn uniforms.

It takes four days to cover 500 kilometres. Before they hand me over to the camp administration, the NCO in charge of my 'bodyguard' hands me a packet of cigarettes and adds that 'Kriege ist Scheiss'! I have heard that before but it's a bit late to find out now.

The barbed wire of an ugly Stalagluft closes round me. This POW camp houses 8000 RAF officers and 2000 USAF officers in several compounds separated by more barbed wire. The whole is guarded by watch-towers equipped with machine guns and searchlights. To get a complete picture, add the standing patrols going round the wire all the time with police dogs, and a few 'ferrets' (stooges) who wander all over the camp and even under the wooden barracks to test the ground for tunnels.

In this month of February, the temperature is somewhere around minus 20 degrees C and there is little or no heating in the barracks. Each prisoner is entitled to two shabby blankets, a mattress filled with straw. The bare walls are relatively clean. After having fulfilled my obligations, such as having my fingerprints taken and annoying the goons, I enter the world of a prisoner for the second time. Many of the guards are old reservists but they have been reinforced by an SS company which seem to be there to keep up their comrades' fast-diminishing enthusiasm.

I am taken to the first compound on the left, then led to a room where there are four bunks and three American officers. I am delighted to share this accommodation with Lieutenant Colonel Gabreski, the American Mustang fighter ace, and two Yank majors. Old Gabi is the Americans' top scorer with almost thirty victories to his credit and the most cheerful character I met in the camp. The three of them welcome me as a brother, immediately share their Red Cross parcels and make me feel like one of the family. I will never forget that human warmth, which made such a difference after the loneliness of the last ten weeks. There are a few questions to check whether I am genuine, which is standard procedure and to be expected when I am only a French-accented English speaker. Then, as always with Americans, a friendship is born. Colonel Gabreski enjoys telling me about his home, and takes me daydreaming to Santa Monica, California. In a very short time I find myself free, far from my prison and wandering about those heavenly places which he is talking about. A man can be deprived of physical freedom, but as long as his mind can escape and fortify his will to endure, nothing is lost. To this day, I am grateful to my friend Gabreski and his two pals for the tremendous kick I got from the few days in their company.

After about ten days, I was fished out of the American compound and shifted to a room in the British camp, where I shared accommodation with a British bomber type Squadron Leader, Squadron Leader Bogdan Artz, a Pole and CO of the famous Polish 303 Squadron, and another Squadron Leader, also of Bomber Command. I must confess that the atmosphere was not very cheerful, probably because the two moustachioed bomber pilots are not mixing types. If they ever had one, they have lost their sense of humour, maybe because they have been prisoners for over two years and are out of touch. Luckily, the Polish fighter pilot, who was a well-known journalist in civvy street, shows himself as a true friend and a great human being. So, the little food we get to eat and the cold we have to endure has not killed our fighting spirit or our strong determination to hinder the Huns in every possible way.

A favourite game, during the early morning or the evening parade, is to move from one rank to another during the counting, so that the goons are either up or down a prisoner or two. This means being counted all over again, sometimes three or four times. Quite brave on our part to stand in the cold, but we have a good laugh at the infuriated Jerries' expense. The usual punishment is eight days in the cooler if you're caught. I never was, but then, some people are lucky . . . But some people are victims of new rules made by the camp commandant. For instance, when there is an air raid nearby, which happens more and more often, the alert is sounded and everyone has to run inside the barracks and close the shutters. At the second blast of the siren, the sentries in the towers will shoot at anyone still outside. In a matter of a week several prisoners were killed that way — just normal Nazi cruelty.

Life in prison camp is dull — so one has to keep busy. Trying to keep in shape physically is the main problem, especially when hunger is the daily norm. From the time I was put behind the wire until my departure, I never saw a single Red Cross parcel or any food other than the ridiculous daily rations the Germans allowed. One slice of black bread with an unidentifiable grease, a little barley sometimes and one cup of watery soup — not much to keep alive on, but enough for me to lose over two stones in six weeks.

Having gathered that if we are to be liberated, it will be by the Russians as they are a lot nearer than the British or Americans, I decide to learn some Russian. My Polish friend Bogdan is teacher. It is all oral so, at the rate of ten words a day, I can soon say short sentences with my vocabulary of a few hundred words. This could be very useful later on, even if I am unable to understand Russian. For the time being, I have become the barracks' official trader with the German guards. Bribing them is not easy but the more the Russians advance, the more some of the guards become nervous and co-operative. So we use the reserve of cigarettes collected by the escape committee as barter, or Parker fountain pens, or chocolate bars sent in earlier Red Cross parcels. In return, we get onions, potatoes, a little sausage, and pepper. That spice is not only to make food tasty but stacked away to put off the guard-dogs when escaping.

The Senior British Officer in the camp is a Canadian bomber Group Captain named Craig. He must be in his late thirties, and has been a prisoner for many, many months. A very regular Air Force spit and polish type — most useful to keep the Germans at a distance and ensure strict discipline among the prisoners. Around him, we have an escape committee, five or six senior officers, each with his own duties. A Wing Commander is in charge of the secret radio that gives us the BBC news each day, and which the Germans never found. Even a news sheet is printed and circulated quietly to each room. My duties are not very demanding because since February escapes have not been permitted by the committee. The Russians are getting nearer and nearer and we have been officially warned by a German poster in English that anyone caught in certain zones will be shot on sight. The poster says in large letters, 'Escaping is not a sport any more!' followed by a list of death areas which, as expected, are all located around the prison camps. So, for the time being, planning is going on, but nothing more. A rumour, unconfirmed but quite probably true, circulates: Himmler has ordered all aircrew prisoners to be shot if they cannot be evacuated before the Russian advance. This means that a massacre is possible. It also means that we must be ready to fight, and if possible not with bare hands should it come to that.

As March goes by, we hear about the crossing of the Rhine by the Allies and, soon after, Marshal Rokossovski takes Stettin. A map is not necessary to realise that the Russians will reach us first. This news does not really please our Polish pilots for they know better than us what our Red allies can do. The first thing is to remove their Polish eagle and sew on RAF wings instead.

One day, I get the surprise of my life. Around mid-day just as we are about to sit down to our meagre meal the door opens and in walks my old 609 pal Robbie. He had succeeded me as CO of 609 when I was shot down and then had himself been shot down over a Dutch North Sea island. Sqn Ldr Roberts, DFC, managed to hide for a while but had the bad luck to be captured at the very moment when the RAF had despatched a special rescue party to bring him back.

He was able to fill me in with the true story of events over the last three months and shared our room for a few days until he was transferred to another block. A member of 609 since 1942, Robbie was to live through the war and later become a BEA Senior Captain.

Towards the end of April, I and a South African fairly fluent in German get authority to escape and join the Russian forces if possible. I have already prepared the way, first by getting a Walther 7.65 mm revolver from an Austrian guard who was a 1914-1918 veteran and who begged me to sign a 'good conduct certificate' to be produced to the Russians when they came, and secondly I also have about two pounds of pepper for the dogs. I also have some cigarettes, worth four German marks each on the black market, to smoothe things along if necessary. To complete our plan, we need a car. We have seen a car every day for weeks, driven by the now-dead SS captain who was so keen to start shooting the POWs who were slow to return to barracks during an air raid alert. It is a nice little yellow 6 hp Adler coupé.

We depart with the refuse, collected each afternoon by an old horse cart, and somehow manage to convince the widow of the SS Captain to 'lend' us the car. Travelling in the opposite direction to the retreating Germans, we end up at a farm where French soldiers, captured in 1940, had virtually become the owners. It was amazing what those farm workers in uniform had achieved. Not only had they taken the place of conscripted farmers in harvesting the fields of Pomerania, but they had obviously replaced them at home too. They enjoyed relative freedom, a very full larder, and in most cases, their own guns. With their help we reach the front line, which has become very thinly defended. The Wehrmacht has fled, leaving small groups of SS to defend the main roads. The Russian steam roller takes little notice, advancing at a speed limited only by their petrol and vodka supplies.

About 20 miles from Barth we meet up with the Ivans, manage to dodge a few bursts and soon celebrate at their local HQ. We have some difficulty explaining that we want their advance guard to hurry to our camp, to save some 10,000 Allied prisoners. Finally they get the point and with roars of laughter they send us with about a company of men to liberate the Stalagluft.

Most of the Russians are Asiatic troops, and women in uniform are common. As to their equipment, a gas-fuelled captured German lorry seems to be the most up-to-date transportation. My first impression of re-found freedom is puzzling: a mixture of relief and gratitude to our barely known allies together with a feeling of surprise at the way we are welcomed by the Red Army. We find that the front line troops are very primitive, ruthless and often 'high spirited' — if one takes that to mean courageous as well as boozed up. They show very little interest in newly-liberated Allied prisoners of war. Provided we stay put in the camp, they do not bother us — but neither do they offer to feed us. Their orders are simple, brutal and not exactly designed to promote reciprocal friendship or understanding: no one, apart from a dozen exceptions, is allowed outside the barbed wire. In return, no Russians will enter the camp.

I am one of the exceptions. Given a special pass written in Cyrillic characters, it says that the bearer is allowed to circulate within a radius of 10 kilometres of the camp. I use it to best advantage, and go unmolested in the following days during which we organise our life as 'liberated-hungry-prisoners-still-detained-if-not-locked-up'.

A ten-man delegation representing the 4000 French prisoners working in farms in the area comes to the Stalagluft, asking to come under our protection! It seems that their meeting with the Russians was not exactly a success. At best they were ignored and the delegates ask to be allowed to bring their men inside our camp. This is impossible for lack of accommodation — and probably would not be allowed by the Russians. Group Captain Craig instructs me to take 'command' of the Frenchmen and organise things as best I can. My first decision is to take over all the empty houses in a nearby village and tell the French to camp there if they want. This has a rather agreeable result. The French bring a herd of cows, plenty of poultry, wheat and farm produce, all by horse and cart — and plenty of firearms which we store in camp under the responsibility of the joint camp committee.

Soon our American friends organise a slaughterhouse (an American aircrew prisoner was formerly at an ultra-modern Chicago slaughterhouse), and a bakery. With all the farm produce, the food problem is largely solved. There still remains the problem of organising our transfer to the Allied lines, and this is not an easy matter.

Although the news of Hitler's death has now been confirmed, and the end of the war is an evident fact, there are still SS pockets fighting between us and Monty's spearhead, and there are alarming reports that Marshal Rokossourski's troops take a very dim view of the British army advance. Some rumours even leak through that both sides are adopting a threatening attitude occasionally when they meet . . .

Chapter 35
The Concentration Camp

In a grey Opel, freshly added to our list of war prizes, the British army medical colonel and his No. 2, both former prisoners who have been detached to Stalagluft, are trying to make face masks from bandages. They have agreed to come with me to a concentration camp, a few miles from Barth, led by a French sergeant. About 4000 prisoners there are slave workers. Some of them in an underground secret factory where deadly gases are produced and the rest are the necessary manpower for a Messerschmitt factory next to an airfield.

I drive slowly in open flat countryside along a dirt road. Soon we come to an open gate. The camp, circled with barbed wire, is a long rectangle, very neat in design with the usual wooden watchtowers. The guardroom is empty. Not a human being in sight. Nothing moves in this deserted place — and yet thousands of concentration camp prisoners were here a few days ago according to the reports we have. The Russians don't seem to be interested in this area, so we enter the camp without meeting anyone.

The door of the first barracks is open. We walk through a corridor: in the rooms alongside, the white wood furniture is in perfect order. Not a sound anywhere and everywhere this oppressive, almost threatening, silence.

In the second building, some decoration and the same absence of noise. The camp, is sinister, empty. On a table, the remains of a meal; on a chair, a scarf awaits its owner.

At the centre of the camp, a stone building. The only one with a second storey. These are the administration buildings and they also house the central kitchen. We walk in warily, guns in hand. Through a half-open door I can see the stiff bodies of three prisoners, veritable skeletons, clad in the now infamous striped pyjamas and lying on the floor — no trace of violence. But their stomachs are big round balls as if they were pregnant! The immediate diagnosis of the medical officers is that they died from over-eating — they ate too much after being starved. The huge balls that are their stomachs contrast grotesquely with the emaciated state of the rest of their bodies. It's horrible — those poor creatures died at the very moment when freedom was at hand. Worse still, they died *because* of their new freedom, by putting to poor use their first actions as free men.

Where are the others? Probably evacuated by the SS at the last moment. To clear our consciences, we go down the staircase to the basement. In a dark corridor we discover a man moaning, his face completely blank, his body covered by rags and with ankles and wrists chained. The rags are what is left of a uniform, a Spanish Lieutenant's uniform from the Azul division, which fought on the Russian front.

The man wearing it is no longer human; he's a repulsive blind animal, stained with blood. We hear later that he was a Spanish deserter, but the poor thing will die in a few hours, not even knowing that he is liberated. Perhaps death was his true liberation. Horror has no limit, and the 'human condition' is mocked when such atrocities are revealed.

We now go to a hut from which comes a terrible stench. Although we are wearing our improvised masks because we are afraid of typhus, we can hardly bear the bitter smell of death mixed with the excrement of the dying. There are about ten bodies, stiff, seated on benches next to a white wood table or lying on their bunks. Some of them are still breathing and the same striped pyjamas hang on skeletal bodies. The doctors get busy, providing whatever help they can to these human beings whose life is already leaving them. We have no drugs, and good will is not enough.

The French sergeant looks at me without a word. I can read on his face his incredulity, his disgust, and the murder in his eyes. We go out for fresh air, to breathe, but also to avoid the horror of the scene. We are ashamed of ourselves but there is a limit to what one can endure — though I feel a coward not to be able to stand the sight of it.

We haven't finished. Another building is drawn to our attention: it's the sick bay, which is next to the hut. As we walk in, more stiff bodies and more of the dying. There are about twenty barely alive and one dragging himself to quench the thirst of the others still breathing. In halting words, we hear the full story. There were about 4000 prisoners, and the SS got them together, in haste, a few days ago. They drove them out of the camp. A death march!

A few managed to hide, some on the roofs, some in the cellars. Others used the chimneys. In their haste to run, the guards did not have time to comb the camp. That's how these living skeletons escaped — and found themselves alone. Like a flock of frightened sheep they emerged, dazed by the light, intoxicated by the silence, numbed by the unexpected freedom. Then came the rush to the kitchen and the pilfering of abandoned food. Those starving people followed only their instinct: eat, eat, eat. A feast of raw potatoes, fat, musty bread, all swallowed barely chewing and without the slightest thought. They killed themselves eating, after almost being starved to death!

The doctors are with us in the infirmary and their fears are confirmed: typhus is all through the camp! We must get the corpses together and burn them or cover them with lime, disinfect the barracks, transport the dying to the sick bay, treat them — but first find drugs and help.

After washing our hands in antiseptic my French sergeant and I drive down to the nearby village.

Numb with horror, blood chilled by such bestiality, we close the concentration camp gates. It is completely unbelievable that human beings in the 20th century could act in such an inhuman manner, such a savage way. So, very angry, and with guns in hand, we enter the local Burgomeister's house. No Russians are in the village, though the area has been in their hands for at least three days.

Shaking all over, the fat flabby-faced Burgomeister agrees to everything we demand. Yes, he will gather all the inhabitants together: men, women, and children — all to assemble in the square, with shovels, lime and buckets. The chemist bows in front of us, accepts our requisitions without demur and we fill the car with drugs. Hate must be showing in our look and the Huns know perfectly that the slightest wrong move on their part would be followed by swift, summary justice.

The silent crowd starts their journey to the camp, not too sure about their fate, but willing to demonstrate their unquestioning good will: it would not be propitious to do otherwise. We lead a procession of about four or five hundred villagers along the country road. The unhappy column hesitates at the gates, draws back a little, then stops, awaiting my orders. My French friend moves to the head of the line and sorts out the cowed villagers until they themselves — slowly at first and then with typical German discipline — walk to the central building. These Huns must see this hell for themselves. They must realise that the people of the Great Reich are collectively responsible for this ignominy. They will feel the shame of a nation, of the *Herrenvolk* as Goebbels used to say. What we want at this precise moment is to get into the thick heads of the people beside this concentration camp, the conquerors of yesterday, what levels of bestiality the Nazis have sunk to.

With bowed heads, they try not to look and they say they were never aware of the existence of such a camp or, at least, of the living conditions here! They move around the compound of death, with sullen faces, resigned, pretending surprise. Strange, isn't it, to live so near and yet to be unaware of what went on behind the barbed wire?

I have allotted the tasks: some are to dig a common grave, others to transport the corpses. Yet others will throw in the lime while the shattered women at the grave side cry silently, holding their puzzled children. About sixty bodies are piled up, stiff in their striped pyjamas — without names, without means of identification, without a religious service, without even a wooden box. It is absolutely imperative that we avoid a typhus epidemic. What more, now, can we do?

Two of the women come forward. In broken German they explain they are Russians, that the Germans took them from their native Ukraine in 1942 and brought them to Germany for forced labour. Both of them are trained nurses and they volunteer to help our doctors. I have no way of checking their story, but the doctors are happy to get some competent help and soon the two volunteers are working hard to look after and save the thirty or so prisoners still alive and lying in the infirmary.

In front of the huge grave, now filled in and silent, the villagers await their orders with heads down. Not one dares move. What can we do with them, apart from sending them away to be hanged somewhere . . .

Bit by bit, we learn from the escapers that the camp was mainly filled by prisoners from Central Europe — German communists and Poles. We find no trace of Belgians or French. The more able-bodied were selected for the Messerschmitt assembly plant adjoining the small airfield; the rest were used in the underground factory where the French sergeant was an administrative employee.

Before fleeing, the SS blew up the factory. Then they gathered the prisoners together and marched them off towards the sea.

An unconfirmed rumour had it that they were piled aboard a cargo ship that was sunk a few miles out to sea. Another frightful piece of information was passed on to me. In the factory, the Germans tried the toxic gas on some of the slave workers who were considered unable to maintain normal output. A dozen at a time were chosen, segregated from their comrades and then invited to a meal served in a special dining hall — which had special pipes through which the gas was pumped at the end of the repast. The sadistic torturers watched from outside through small windows built in the walls, noting the effect of the poison and carefully measuring the time it took for the prisoners to die. Guided by the French sergeant, I visited the remains of the blown-up factory a few days later and saw for myself the walls of the torture chamber that the explosives had not demolished.

I have had enough of all these abominations and I decide to go back to the Stalagluft and report to the camp commander about the concentration camp. Also I want to hear the latest news about the war. Though my friends and I have been liberated, and though Hitler has been dead for two days, we still have no exact information about what goes on in the space between the Russians and the Allies because the news we receive on our radio is rather vague. At our end, the Russians are ignoring us, apart from insisting that we stay confined to camp.

As I mentioned, I am one of the few senior officers with a pass allowing me to move about within six miles of the Stalagluft. So far I have experienced no limitation on my movements. But the behaviour of the front-line Russian units, mostly composed of Mongols, is so unpredictable and their mood so uncertain that I am always on my guard.

Once I took an American Major with me to look around the area. We were stopped at a cross-roads by a woman soldier directing the traffic, who relieved the Major of his gold watch. A gun pointed at his head made her message clear. Another time, having been invited together with an American war reporter called Bennet to a banquet by the Russians, we sat for five hours at a table with a number of high-ranking officers, eating far too much and drinking vodka between each dish. Toasts were proposed to Stalin, to Roosevelt, to Churchill, and to so many other people that our Russian hosts were soon drunk. I quickly learned to spill my vodka before its contents reached my mouth, so I managed to stay fairly sober.

At night, the soldiers were normally drunk, letting guns off at random and terrorising the German women. Though I was far from approving their behaviour and lack of discipline, I was aware of what the SS had done in Russia. So? Like Pontius Pilate, I washed my hands of it. For another very good reason too, that I could do nothing about these Asiatic Russians and, secondly, because this could be a price the beaten Germans had to pay for their crimes.

At the Stalagluft, Group Captain Craig and the American Colonel Zemki are in charge. Today, as every day, they hold a meeting at which the situation is examined and decisions are made. But this time there is something special for two American officers have reached our camp. They bring us an up-to-date picture of the general situation. The Allies have stopped on a predetermined line. There are German pockets still fighting in many places against the Russians, but for many it is only to surrender to the Americans or the British. The Russians have vetoed any move from our camp towards the Allied lines, giving as pretexts the lack of transport and the general insecurity of the area. So our orders are to wait, to avoid all incidents, to stay together and to try to hide our arms. The tension between Monty's spearhead and the Russians is confirmed but so far there have been no clashes. The utmost care must be taken to avoid an unfortunate incident . . .

Towards 4 p.m. we arrive back at the sick bay where two Russian lorries are parked, full of infantrymen. At the door of the building a Russian officer is arguing loudly with the Medical Corps Colonel. Seeing his gestures, it is obvious that the discussion is becoming heated and trouble is in the air. As we get nearer we see the two nurses from the sick bay — dragged by some soldiers with beaming faces.

The Colonel moves towards them shouting: 'They are going to hang them! We must stop them, it's sheer murder!' He is stopped dead by the Russian officer who, finger on the trigger, points a gun at his chest. Several soldiers surround him threateningly, guns lifted.

We stand like stone — no one dares move. Under threat of guns we witness, horrified, the departure of the lorries carrying soldiers and nurses which soon disappear from our sight.

Deeply moved, the doctor tells us about the tragedy. The soldiers are security troops and the officer in charge is a German-speaking political commissar. He explained that the Ukrainian girls were traitors, that they had collaborated with the Germans, and that they were to be hanged on the spot. This is our first glimpse of the Russian Secret Service who seem to be well informed, and I will quickly decide to keep clear of them.

The incident leaves a nasty taste in my mouth and, after a rapid tour, Gp Capt Craig and I, still with the horror of the concentration camp in our minds, start the journey back to the Stalagluft to avoid being out after dark. Going through the gates we take a short cut that avoids the village and pass through a wooded area. A lorry is stopped there. Soldiers are eating their meal round a fire. On the low branches of a tree a little back from the road the bodies of two young women hang, immobile, at the end of two short ropes.

We pass by slowly without saying a word, without turning our heads, but I will long remember the shiver that went through me as if the cold of death had penetrated me deeply.

Chapter 36
Towards Freedom

We have entered the ultimate phase of Nazi Germany's agony. We are living through the last days of the war and somehow, in Barth, we organise our new life — men freed from the Germans but still dependent on the Russians' good will. We try to be ready to move to our own people and to rejoin our former units.

We are taking things as they come, not completely sure about the attitude of the Russians although they leave us alone under the authority of our own senior officers. The main problem is still that they won't allow us to go. Are we going to be hostages, a prize for bargaining? At the moment we feel safe enough and there are unconfirmed reports that Allied transport is being organised from Wismar, 150 miles away, where Monty has now arrived. But, pockets of SS are still fighting in some places. Then come rumours that incidents between Russians and British forward troops are becoming more widespread every hour. It is said that the Russians have issued an ultimatum to Montgomery to move his troops back out of Schleswig-Holstein so that the Russians could occupy that territory. And that Monty has of course refused, threatening to shoot the first Red Army unit moving an inch forward. Should things get serious we would indeed be hostages of the Russians!

On the other hand, the Russians who have been prisoners of the Germans since 1942 or 1943, and have now been liberated by the Red Army advance, show no enthusiasm for rejoining their compatriots. Most of them are hiding in the woods and trying to reach the British lines. Many of them make no secret of the fact that they are afraid of being shot by their own troops, accused of being deserters.

We have also noted that a day or two after the first-line troops had gone through — most of them primitive Mongols — the new occupying troops are more sophisticated. Probably they are members of OGPU, the Russian equivalent of the Gestapo, and these units have things well in hand.

As I can go outside camp to look after my bunch of French farm-worker prisoners, I enjoy full freedom within my six-mile radius. I take advantage of it to go out every day, with my car, to see that we are kept well supplied by my French connections. Every day, a cartload of potatoes and other vegetables comes into camp together with a few cows. 'My' Frenchmen are very proud to help, and I soon find myself with several thousand men under my (somewhat theoretical) protection.

One day, a French NCO comes to me, reporting that he worked at the gas factory as a chemist. He says that before the Germans blew it up, he buried some samples of the latest gas in a nearby wood, with the idea of handing it over to the Russians. But, after seeing their attitude, he would rather give us the benefit of his war trophies, or 'secret weapons' as they might be. The trouble now is that the Russians are in occupation of the factory and its surrounding area and it is strictly forbidden even to go anywhere near it.

I have also seen that the sugar refinery is occupied by Russians. They are rounding up every technician who worked in the Messerschmitt factory and, I suppose, other local plants. After screening them they have put them on a goods train bound for Russia. I guess that the chase for war criminals is on and the civilians are being treated like cattle.

Rape is a common occurrence, day or night, and in full view of any passer-by. Not the slightest restraint, quite unconcerned, coolly, as it if were a right. Needless to say, refusal means death.

Even though the Nazis have committed horrible crimes in Russia, including genocide, I am deeply shocked by such behaviour and my first reaction is to interfere. Soon I find that it would only mean being shot, without the slightest hesitation, by these beasts.

Altogether, I have had enough of this, and I make up my mind to take a chance, to hit the road towards our lines, for I cannot stand any more passive waiting. Furthermore, I have a good reason for going, after what I learned today.

Urged on by me, the French chemist agreed to go and dig up his gas samples. We went together, managed to avoid the Russian guards and the samples are now safely in the Stalagluft. Two hours later a Russian officer came to enquire who had been near the factory and, although he went away, he clearly was not happy that he did not find a culprit. It meant too that I was in trouble. Apart from this, we were having to hide the Polish fighter pilots from the Russians. So, all together, I had sufficient incentive to act swiftly.

After a short meeting with Group Captain Craig, it was decided that I should make a bold run for it at dawn the next morning, taking with me my disguised Polish friend Sqn Ldr Bogdan Artz, the gas samples, and enough petrol and arms to have a chance of finding our way to the British lines. We also were told to pass on to the Intelligence people, without fail, the true situation in the Stalagluft.

Bogdan, having removed his Polish eagle and medal ribbons and replaced them with RAF wings, was disguised as a British Squadron Leader. He sat in the little Adler with our armament, and I took the wheel. In our frame of mind it was better to assist fate than to wait patiently for something unpleasant to happen. To be honest, I felt much better doing something than sitting on my backside and accepting the inevitable. The eternal Don Quixote I suppose — but a much nicer way of spending one's life than being a careful, reasonable, calculating type! With two hand grenades, two revolvers, and a Schmeisser machine pistol, we hope we can blast our way through if we bump into the SS. I have my lucky Walter 7.65 mm at hand, and also the famous Russian pass allowing a six-mile ride. The plates on the car are painted with my number: RAF 134769.

At dawn on 5 May we hit the road towards Wismar with a rough sketch map, and the names of the small places we are supposed to go through written on a scrap of paper. We foresee three possibilities. Either we get through unmolested and get to our lines in Wismar — or we bump into the SS and have to fight for it — or, most likely, we are stopped at a Russian roadblock and have to negotiate our ride. In any case, there is bound to be some sort of a checkpoint before we can cross over to the other side. It's necessary that I do any negotiating, even with my very limited Russian vocabulary, for with his Slav accent my Polish friend would be found out at once. Anyway, we are both of a mind to get out at all costs, even shooting our way out if necessary. Only much later did I find out how foolish we were to be prepared for such a thing but, at the time, it was just straightforward friendship; two people in the same boat, for better or for worse. It was a time when friendship and a strong feeling of solidarity still bound human beings to a particular course whatever it might be. As a British officer, I personally was safe, at least in principle, but my Polish friend risked being added to the anonymous victims of Katyn. Neither of us gave a second thought to the outcome: we were quite happy to stick together to the bitter end.

Luckily, there was no bitter end. The only Germans we met were unarmed deserters, running for their lives, and the few roadblocks were only stopping people coming the other way. After hours of crawling along in the gallant little 7 hp at a steady 30 miles an hour, my navigation proved to be correct and we saw the road sign 'Wismar 2 km'.

We stop to make sure that our artillery is handy under our coats, then to refill the petrol tank and throw away the empty jerricans. With a full carton of Lucky Strike cigarettes and two bottles of German schnapps, off we go towards what we hope will be the last roadblock between us and freedom.

Round a bend in the road, the way is barred by some oil barrels and farm machinery. At the side of the road, in a house bearing the scars of local fighting, is a troop of armed soldiers. Two or three Russian guards are standing by the road, and look kindly at us as we stop the car a few yards away. With cigarettes and schnapps in hand, I get out of the little Adler and go towards them with a large smile, calling out the few words of Russian I know.

'Tovaritch, ruski? Tovaritch angliski! Polpotnik. Djin dobre. Papirosa. Schnapps!'

A glimmer of recognition, of understanding, and then of comradeship appears on the soldiers' faces as, one by one, they take me in their brotherly arms and kiss me full on the mouth! After the kisses comes a great deal of back slapping.

After these Russian niceties, they offer to swop an open packet of Russian filter cigarettes, twice as long as mine and made from sweet tobacco. These NCOs obviously have not the slightest hesitation in fraternising with a senior British officer at a time of communal victory. I certainly don't resent the demonstration of friendship. Even the kisses, rather unusual in the West, are quite welcome! But there are still those barrels and things to get through . . .

Not knowing how to say in Russian that I want to go through, I use friendly gestures to show what I expect from them. A deal of shouting — and four nondescript types run out of the house to start clearing a path for the car. I am almost delirious with happiness!

'Thanks a lot, comrades!'

Just as I am about to move the car the tallest of the sentries shouts at the top of his voice: 'Angliski!'

My heart misses a beat. My legs won't move. I stop and look back. A second of uncertainty, and then I see the Russian NCO coming towards me with the opened bottle of schnapps, offering me a swig.

'Nasdrovie! — Good health!'

I drink — and I laugh nervously. God! No papers shown, no firing. Please, no more roadblocks! Just let me on that little road that leads between the obstacles to freedom, leaving those two goons drinking Schnapps! I am terrified in case I stall the engine. I drive at walking pace, with Bogdan praying. Thanks a lot comrades!

Half a mile further on, a huge Irish Guardsman yells at the top of his voice: 'Halt! Advance and be recognised!'

'Friend — 134769, CO of 609 Squadron!' I shout my identity while walking to him. The sentry salutes punctiliously. I want to kiss him, too.

'Very well sir, kindly report to the guardroom with your friend!'

I drive slowly to the guardroom, where the red and white striped barrier is lifted by another guard, and I enter the office with Bogdan.

'Well, I suppose you are a prisoner of war. Welcome home! Care for a drink? Take a seat while I contact HQ. By the way how did you get through the barrier? You are the first the Russians have let through . . .'

It takes only minutes for the Guards officer to check our identities and we are cleared. We tell him our story and stress the plight of 10,000 Allied air crews and French soldiers collected in Barth. Our host makes it clear that tension is high along the line and says a conference at the top is going on at this very moment. Would I please go straight to Luneburg where I am to give information to Intelligence HQ — and there is an airfield with a direct link to England!

So after a drink and thanks for the welcome, we are on the road again to Luneburg, eating welcome cheese sandwiches as we drive. We have an armed jeep as escort and an Intelligence officer as shepherd. The 'brass' are waiting for us. But, safe now, my only thought is to drive home to Belgium, to reassure my family, who may believe me killed, then to see my pals and celebrate victory!

Strange: a few hours ago, my only goal was to be free. Now that the nightmare is ended, and I am free and alive, other priorities have taken over, almost equal in importance to matters of life or death.

In Luneburg, Bogdan and I will go our separate ways. I am offered a flight to England. As soon as I have reported to the brass about the Stalagluft situation, I choose to have Bogdan go to England and convey the gas samples to the War Office, while I drive home. I won't even stop here to sleep at the Officers' Mess, but set off immediately on my long road journey to Brussels. It may have been the wrong choice, for I heard later that my Polish friend was decorated for carrying such important information to the War Office laboratory. But who cares? I have had enough of playing Boy Scouts now that the war is over.

Along the autobahns, at night, I cover many miles and, on 6 May at dawn, reach the Ruhr. Everywhere I have seen desolation, ruins and the scars of war. Only some parts are less badly damaged, where the Allied advance was swifter. But the towns are totally wrecked by Allied bombing. In Düsseldorf, then Cologne, the sight is unbelievable in the first light of a May morning. Bulldozers are busy in the ruins, opening up roads between barely standing walls which sometimes fall into the rubble with clouds of dust. Everywhere a sweet rancid smell: the smell of corpses lying under the rubble which conscripted German workers are laboriously clearing. Traffic is down to walking pace, often completely stopped by the huge yellow machines. A world has been destroyed; another world is to be built.

My brave little car goes through holes, round obstacles and over tricky patches in the tormented road. The Belgian border at last. The air of my homeland stirs my tired senses. In spite of my tiredness, I feel fine — in an oversized uniform that hangs on a body that has been more than a little slimmed by the months in prison. What of it? I am alive, and spending the last hours of this war driving home.

Just 2191 days have passed since the first cannon shells fell on us, and now the nightmare is over and done with, to be replaced by the sweet music of the armistice that should occur any day now.

For 37 hours I have been at the wheel, from Barth to my home, during which time I have crossed Russian-occupied Pomerania, half of Germany, part of Holland and then half of Belgium. I had no way of warning my parents, and my arrival takes them by surprise. Great joy keeps us painfully silent. Mother sets the table. She says that I have lost a lot of weight: 'Please, eat. You must eat well!'

My father looks at me, reflecting. He offers me a drink, starts to say something, then lifts his glass, and says nothing.

All three of us are struck dumb by emotion.

Then, in come the neighbours whom the bush telegraph has somehow warned. It's celebration time. Everybody has something to say, and each one congratulates the other. The wine and beer flow and kisses are standard procedure. I am happy. I am tired. Feeling a bit apart from the crowd I can't help thinking of all the blood so liberally spilt, of the beer that so many friends won't drink, of fires, destruction, the misery of war.

A dark vision comes suddenly: I see clearly the German pilot I killed at 20 yards range, above the trees, over the French forest of Compiègne, and who threw me a last look . . . That was on a May evening long, long ago. An evening when I realised that my youth had gone, unnoticed, even before I had learned to value it . . .

Chapter 37
The End Becomes the Beginning

Not far from the airfield a tranquil trout stream flows bordered by willow trees with old birches in the background. By the river an old watermill slumbers, whose wheel has not turned in years. A decaying footbridge overhangs a terrace covered in moss, which eats away the crumbling flagstones and time alike, inexorably.

As far as the eye can see, a tranquil sky lazes above quiet fields, spreading its blue canopy like an umbrella over a Gainsborough painting.

Enter the artists! Lift the curtain over my actors, who make their entrances, speak, declaiming or stuttering their lines, disappear almost without trace, trapped in a void.

May 1943. In the cool evening, the scene is set.

A strange peace has come over me, nibbling away at the seemingly never-ending war. Introspection. Flashback over one's life. Summing up the past, wondering about the future. What future, when death is one's daily escort in the present?

For two whole days, I have been living in this rustic calm, in this forgotten corner of East Anglia. The gods of war have forgotten us, left us on the edge of the battle. During the two days we have been grounded, we have felt no fear and are no longer as tense as a tightly strung bow. Already I have reverted to the bad habits of a normal life: fixed meal times, long hot baths, mind wandering in a dreamy haze.

But it would be wrong to yield to this seductive idleness. I have to confine myself to certainties. Not ask myself questions. And even more not to seek answers. Everything would have to be reconsidered if doubt were to enter my life through a door left ajar. Once faith has been shaken and taboos turned upside down, I would become easy prey for my sleeping devils. What am I? Where am I going? How? Why? . . .

Twenty odd years. A man, born too late into a dying world, I already know that I shall always be an 'old child' whom neither time nor events will shake. A drifter I suppose, living intensely each moment and trying to protect an inner dream.

Here am I immersed in a double life: as a wartime fighter pilot I am an enthusiastic amateur — perhaps even a gifted craftsman — amongst professionals, regular warriors honouring contracts signed in days of peace. Their valour inspires me and their example leads me on. Like them I kill methodically — without hate and almost without regret. But, like so many people who entered this war and became brave overnight, I am only a temporary soldier and will never become a military man.

As a man I try to hide my doubts, my weaknesses and my pain. I cannot afford to let my true self be exposed. I must fight the enemy, but myself even more. Already I know that if I live through this war I will not stay in the Air Force, for everything will seem dull after the exaltation of the hours we are living through. I shall have to fight other battles to face other challenges and win other conquests.

But first of all, this war has to be won. I must bear my share of the common task. More than my share, to distinguish myself from the herd. A matter of pride, of elitism to a true Aries. My head in the clouds from preference, my feet firmly on the ground from necessity.

My Achilles heel is a strongly felt need for human warmth. I am vulnerable to loneliness. I was selfishly generous until the day I passed through into the inner circle of true friendship and discovered that one had to learn to receive, simply so that others may enjoy the pleasure of giving. A lesson in humility. Not easy to accept.

Neither is death. It's another lesson in humility. Not to be afraid but to court it with serenity, to challenge it, to push it back as long as possible. But to be aware that one always loses the last battle. Die with dignity as a matter of self-respect, and out of consideration towards those who go on living. The ethics of elegance; a problem to be solved with delicacy.

Love. A hunting ground reserved in theory for better days. Proscribed at the present time. A devouring passion would inevitably require a change of priorities. The impossibility of such a compromise. Admit only the desire, and satiate the animal with the help of the female species. But gently, with good humour and good manners.

This war, almost lost by short-sighted politicians before it began, will be won by our determination — and by our emotions. It's with our hearts that we cling to liberty. It's with our guns that we make history while others more prudently write it with a flowing pen. It's with our certainties that we push back both doubt and fear. For to doubt would be to renounce. Renunciation is entirely foreign to me. Live at 400 mph, taking all the necessary risks, but never the other kind. A matter of judgement. Balance.

Soliloquy on a May evening, with the war fading away for a few hours. The personal thoughts of a man pushed around by an inferno that is destroying a world. Yet the earth goes on revolving with or without me. Every day I set my soul upon the anvil of the flak that hammers the warning bolts of destiny. My soul must be tempered like steel, forged like iron, shaped by fire, but also it must be mine, entirely, and I should never be ashamed of it, be it before God or Man.

Nonsense? Just as I was talking nonsense yesterday beside my little river, am I talking nonsense as I write this page today? I realise now that I spoke nonsense about 'certainties'. So, when doubt invades my soul, doubt in God and doubt of mankind, I jump back in time to my river bank, asking nothing of anyone.

Of anyone but you, my friends, who shared the same hours and died the same deaths, and kept intact for me, through the years, your friendship.

In the steeple of my life, sixty bells have rung. With tranquillity. Happily. Along the quiet roads that I follow, I still treasure — carefully, delicately — a little flower named Hope.

Appendix 1
In Memoriam

One hundred and ten pilots, of whom 72 were British, 22 Belgian, four Americans, three Canadians, three from New Zealand, two Australian, one Norwegian, one Frenchman, one South African and one Rhodesian were killed, while serving in 609 West Riding of Yorkshire Squadron.

More than half of all the pilots who served in this legendary unit during the 1939-1945 war lost their lives in defence of freedom. This means that, with an average strength of 25 pilots, the squadron was practically wiped out four and a half times in a matter of four and a half years. The battle honours of this outstanding squadron included 232 air victories, together with many probables and others damaged, besides probably the highest score of ground targets such as tanks, armoured vehicles, gun positions, troop concentrations, bridges, barges, enemy cargo ships and flak ships. Railway engines were destroyed by the dozen, at least 11 troop trains were left burning, and a Gestapo HQ and six other headquarters were heavily damaged.

Adam R.	F/Sgt	
Agazarian K.	F/O	
Amor H.	P/O	
Ashworth R.	F/Sgt	
Ayre	F/O	
Baillon P.	P/O	
Baldwin	G/Capt	DFC
Barker T.	W/O	
Barran P.	F/Lt	
Bennet G.	Sgt	
Bliss L.	F/Sgt	
Boyd R.	Sgt	
Bramble K.	Sgt	
Buchanan	Sgt	Canadian
Buchanan J.	P/O	
Carrick M.	F/Lt	
Chestnut G.	Sgt	
Choron M.	F/O	French
Crook D.	P/O	DFM
Cropper D.	P/O	
Churckin J.	P/O	DFC
Daix D.	F/O	Belgian
Davies I.	Sq/Ldr	DFC
Dawson J.	F/O	

de Blommart		
de Soye	Sgt	Belgian
de Grunne R.		
(Comte)	P/O	Belgian
de Hemptinne B.	F/O	Belgian
de Selys-Longchamps		
J. (Baron)	F/Lt	DFC Belgium
de Spirlet F.	F/Lt	DFC Belgium
Detal C.	F/O	DFC Belgium
Drummond-Hay P.	F/O	
Dopère R.	F/O	Belgian
Dundas J.	F/Lt	DFC & Bar
Ellis R.	F/Sgt	
Feary A.	Sgt	
Fidgin I.	F/Sgt	
Garton J.	F/O	
Gaunt G.	P/O	
Gibson R.	F/Lt	Australian
Gilbert J.	F/O	
Goblet	F/O	Belgian
Goodwin H.	F/O	
Grant R.	P/O	
Haabjoern E.	F/Lt	DFC Norway
Haddon A.	F/Sgt	
Henrion L.	P/O	Belgian
Hickman G.	Sgt	
Hill J.	P/O	
Holmes R.	F/O	
Howen F	F/Lt	DFC
Hugues-Rees J.	P/O	DFM
Innes J.	Sgt	Rhodesian
Jackson W.	Sgt	
Keough V.	P/O	U.S.A.
King G.	F/Lt	DFC
Leslie J.	P/O	
McConnel J.	Sgt	New Zealander
McKenzie	P/O	
McSherry P.	Sgt	
McLaughlin J.	P/O	New Zealander
Mamedoff A.	P/O	U.S.A.
Matheson A.	F/Lt	Australian
Mercer R.	F/O	DFC Australia
Miller C.	P/O	Canadian
Miller R.	P/O	
Mitchell G.	P/O	
Nankivell	F/O	

Nash P.	F/O	
Niblett	Sq/Ldr	DFC
Offenberg J.	F/Lt	DFC Belgium
Ortmans C.	P/O	Belgian
Ortmans V.	F/O	DFC Belgium
Osborn B.	P/O	
Palmer A.	Sgt	
Parthoens R.	Sgt	Belgian
Payne R.	F/O	
Persse-Joynt D.	F/Lt	
Pollard E.	Sgt	
Price P.	F/Sgt	
Proudman	F/O	
Raw P.	F/O	DFC
Robinson M.	W/Cdr	DSO DFC
Roelandt R.	F/Lt Belgian	
Rouse S.	Sgt	
Rowland C.	F/O	
Russell I.	F/O	DFC U.S.A.
Seghers E.	P/O	Belgian
Shelton M.	F/O	
Soesman P.	F/O	Belgian
Spallin S.	P/Sgt	Canadian
Staples M.	P/O	
Stellin J.	F/Sgt	New Zealander
Taylor F.	W/O	
Thornton-Brown P.	Sq/Ldr	DFC
Thorogood	F/O	
Tobin E.	P/O	U.S.A.
Van Daele J.	F/Lt	Belgian
Van Neste M.	P/O	Belgian
Vamn Shaick J.	P/O	DFM
Van Zuylen van		
Nijvelt (Baron)	Sgt	Belgian
Wallace T.	S/Ldr	DFC S.Africa
Wilmet B.	F/O	Belgian
Wiseman J.	P/Sgt	
Wood R.	F/Lt	
Zegers J.	Sgt	Belgian

Appendix 2
The Typhoon

During the 1939-1945 war, Hawker-Siddeley produced 3317 Typhoons, a single seat fighter, powered by the Napier Sabre engine, developing from 2200 to 2400 hp. The original version was equipped with twelve .303 machine guns. The operational aircraft was equipped with four 20 mm cannon, firing at the rate of 640 shells/min. The total all-up weight was 13,250 lb. The prototype flew for the first time on 24 February 1940. But it was not until 1942 that the Typhoon made its operational debut, when 56, 266 and 609 Squadrons were re-equipped with them.

Although the Typhoon was the fastest aircraft at the time, with a 40 mph advantage over the Spitfire, it experienced many problems, both with its 24 cylinder engine and even more with its air-frame. The tail unit and ailerons created many headaches and were responsible for many crashes.

At the beginning of 1943, the Typhoon proved its superiority over the Focke-Wulf 190 at low level. Reaching over 500 mph in a dive, it could maintain 420 mph at sea level. Later equipped with two 250 lb bombs, and subsequently with two 500 pounders, or with two long range petrol tanks under the wings, it became for the Germans a most fearsome intruder. Later, with the invasion in prospect, it was equipped with eight 60 lb rockets and became an assault aircraft specialising in ground attack. As such, it was the most successful tank and armour buster ever produced.

In Normandy, the following squadrons of the RAF were equipped with Typhoons: 137, 164, 174, 175, 181, 182, 183, 184, 193, 197, 198, 245, 247, 257, 263, 266, 438, 439, 440 and 609.
These 20 squadrons formed five Wings in Nos. 83 and 84 Groups of 2nd ATAF.

Appendix 3
The RAF Typhoons in the Normandy Battle

When, at dawn on 6 June 1944, the Allied forces launched their attack on the Normandy beaches, Air Chief Marshal Sir Trafford Leigh-Mallory, Commander-in-Chief of the Allied Tactical Air Force, was able to call on 4766 aircraft and establish total air supremacy over the bridgehead. He also gave powerful direct support to the ground forces chosen to launch the Second Front.

The Americans were entrusted with establishing air superiority at altitude and hammering enemy communications in the south-east area, as well as dealing with what was left of the rail network around the invasion zone. To do this, they had 2645 aircraft, the majority P47 Thunderbolts and P51 Mustangs, plus a force of Boston twin engined bombers. On the British side, the 2nd Tactical Air Force numbered 2121 fighters, fighter-bombers and rocket-firing Typhoons, four squadrons of 'Bomphoons' and a force of Mosquitoes for night intruder work. Their task was twofold: to achieve air supremacy on the left wing of the invasion front, and to give close ground support to our invading forces. For the 20 rocket-firing squadrons of Typhoons, the main task was destruction of enemy armour and strong points. To their formidable fire power of four 20 mm cannon and eight armour-piercing rockets, the Typhoons added their diving speed of up to 500 mph to become the spearhead of the invading Tactical Air Force. The heavy night bombers of the RAF Lancasters, Halifaxes and Stirlings, and the USAF day-time heavies, B17 Flying Fortresses and B24 Liberators, had since 1942 been used by the Strategic Allied Air Forces to destroy the German war production by deep penetration into the heart of Germany and the occupied territories. The attacks made by the Tactical Air Force bore directly upon the fate of the battle in progress from the landing beaches to the Normandy plain.

A few weeks after the initial landings, 30 Allied divisions (15 British and Canadian, 15 American) were in action against 62 German divisions of which 12 were armoured. The 15th Army Group was based in the Pas de Calais and the 7th Army operated south of the River Seine. Expecting the main thrust in the Pas de Calais, and respecting Hitler's personal orders, the 15th Army Group was held back from joining the main battle. The 7th Army, deployed from Caen to Avranches with Falaise as pivot, bore the whole weight of the fierce battle. That decision by the German HQ proved to be a fatal error for the Third Reich and greatly facilitated consolidation of the beachhead and, later, allowed Patton to break through near Falaise.

Like any landing in enemy-held territory, the success of such an operation lies initially in the effect of surprise and depends on the air superiority established over the given area. Then, upon the capacity to reinforce rapidly and enlarge the bridgehead, so as to put ashore enough invading forces to counter any strong attack on a limited front. Subsequently, the break out comes from building up a sufficient superiority at a carefully chosen point of the perimeter, causing the defending positions to crumble.

These different factors were effectively exploited in Normandy, thanks just to the air supremacy gained by the Tactical Air Force. Next, by the exemplary logistic support provided by some 5000 naval craft, and, needless to say, by the legendary valour of the soldiers who bravely made the initial assaults planned by Field Marshal Montgomery's headquarters. It was the Allied plan to let Montgomery take and contain the brunt of the German counter-attack in order to allow Patton to break through at Falaise, swing eastwards and make the historic drive that ended in the liberation of France and Belgium within two weeks of our Falaise victory.

Against this force, the Germans had some 6000 fighter aircraft scattered over the different fronts: about 1500 were trying to contain the Russian drive, some 3500 were kept to defend Germany itself and the remaining 1000 were sacrificed against the invading Allies in Normandy.

The Allied air superiority in that theatre of war was therefore in the order of 5 to 1. The Germans could not accept open battle with the prospect of being wiped out in a matter of weeks. Their tactic was to operate in packs of more than 40 aircraft with the hope of gaining temporary air superiority over a chosen spot. That tactic — in fact the only possible one against those odds — was to end in the total destruction of the Luftwaffe in France. But the Normandy battle might have been totally different, and its success delayed if not compromised, could the Germans have deployed in quantity at that time the Messerschmitt 262, the first jet-propelled fighter to become operational during the war. Their appearance in October 1944 on this front created problems owing to their tremendous speed advantage. But the thousand-odd Me 262s that were produced in the last six months of the war arrived too late to save Germany.

In Normandy the Germans had undisputed flak supremacy. It was estimated to be about 20,000 batteries of anti-aircraft guns, ranging from 105, 88, 40, 37 to 20 mm, and not counting the numerous heavy machine-gun sites. Hence, the odds in favour of the enemy stood at 4 to 1 against the number of Allied aircraft. When concentrated on some key points of the battlefront, the odds easily reached 20 or 30 to 1 in favour of the defenders: this explains why up to 95 per cent of our losses in attacks on ground targets were the result of flak defences against a mere. 5 per cent attributed to Luftwaffe intervention.

The final issue of the battle of Normandy remained uncertain during the period covering the 6th of June till the 20th of August, partly because of the fierce German resistance in and around Caen, partly because of the German coup when their armour managed to cut through the American lines and threaten the road to Avranches. When these two attacks had been overcome, the ultimate victory was no longer in doubt. It was plain that the Germans were by then incapable of regaining the initiative at any point of the front. And the reason for that incapacity, although they had better and more armour at the time, was the fact that the Allied Tactical Air Force killed at birth any attempt by the enemy to play a trump card. While the British maintained their pressure on the Caen area, the Americans were able to liberate Cherbourg and Brittany, so that Patton could swing to the east and drive towards Paris, while the British and Canadians raced north-east to free Belgium and southern Holland.

Forty years have elapsed since three main battles were won in Normandy: Caen, Mortain and Falaise. To this day and to my knowledge, no learned historian has assessed with any objectivity the determining factor of Allied victory in Normandy. I firmly believe that it was the role played by 2 TAF in general and by the Typhoons in particular. Bearing in mind that the fire power of a rocket-firing Typhoon was equivalent to a broadside from a light cruiser, it may be understood why less than 400 Typhoons — the average strength thrown daily into the battle during those crucial three months — tilted the balance towards our side. Although far from winning the war by themselves, they certainly made all the difference on the Normandy front, just as the Stukas had done for Guderian's Panzers in 1940 during the battle of France.

For the 2000 Nazi tanks that went into battle in Normandy there was a double, and tremendous, advantage over the Anglo-American armour: firstly, the 88 mm gun that was standard equipment on the Tiger, the Panther and the anti-tank batteries. It completely outclassed the 75 mm cannon used by the Allies. Secondly their armour plating was far superior to ours. Especially in defensive warfare, the German equipment played havoc with Allied tanks and it was not uncommon to see a single Tiger Panzer destroying a squadron of Shermans. Often dug a foot or two into the ground, well camouflaged by the local undergrowth, the Panzers of the 12 Nazi armoured divisions formed a strong, continuous barrier that proved more than a match for the lighter Allied armour.

A first consequence of our air supremacy had been to deny effective movement of German Panzers during the hours of daylight, owing to the heavy losses inflicted on them by our aircraft. Trains bringing reinforcements and equipment were attacked and burned as far as 100 miles from the front line. Even at night, troop transports were easy prey for the intruding Mosquitoes, some 300 of them sharing the task of policing the French roads. But though the 1200 Spitfire fighter-bombers, the 60 Tempests and the 200 Mustangs filled the French sky during daylight to prevent any aggression by the Luftwaffe or to strafe anything that moved, even their 250 lb bombs were too light to halt the Panzers. This part of the muted task fell to the 400 Typhoons that were first based in southern England, then on the newly built airstrips around Bayeux from June 15th onwards. For a short period they escaped the nightly shelling from German batteries by landing back in England at dusk to rejoin the battle at dawn. There was about a fortnight during which our ground crews had a rough time before the area was cleaned up and we occupied our French airfields permanently. Thanks to the 'Cab Rank' system, used as standard procedure, the Typhoons were able to respond in a matter of minutes to any call for assistance by the forward troops. It consisted of direct radio liaison between an RAF controller pilot who went ahead, with the troops either in a jeep or an armoured vehicle with a patrol, and the airborne Typhoon squadron or section. The type and location of enemy opposition encountered was accurately described. Both controllers and pilots used a large-scale map divided into squares and marked horizontally by letters and vertically by numbers. The ground-based controller could call down one or more aircraft from the 'Cab Rank' behind. The guidance became so accurate and the description so precise that a low-flying aircraft could pinpoint even very small targets, such as a sniper in a field or a concealed Panzer in a thicket. This enabled us to operate to within a few yards of our own troops — but it left little room for error. Moreover, the low-level attacks by screaming Typhoons had a grave psychological impact upon the German soldiers and tank crews. It created a 'Tiffy-happy' complex among them, considerably lowering their determination to fight to the end.

Though the enemy air opposition had fallen to such a low level that it did very little to hinder our offensive sorties, flak had become a deadly weapon taking a heavy toll of our low-flying aircraft and causing terrible losses among the aircrew. No Panzer unit would venture into the open without its flak umbrella, and those entrenched were surrounded by numerous anti-aircraft guns of all types. The price the Typhoons had to pay was the highest ever, as shown in the official records released after the war.

The following tables show the strength of 2 ATAF during the months of June, July and August 1944, and cover the invasion period. The total numbers of aircraft engaged are shown, together with types and losses incurred. At the time of publication, the exact numbers of men killed had not been reported.

June 1944

	Aircraft available	Shot down	Damaged beyond repair	Damaged	Total	%
Spitfire	1166	169	107	61	337	29
Hurricane	29	0	1	0	1	0.3
Mustang	233	76	26	14	116	52
Tempest	38	6	0	6	12	31
Mosquito	282	21	11	23	55	19.5
TYPHOON	383	84	58	28	170	44
Total	2131	356	203	132	691	32.6

July 1944

	Aircraft available	Shot down	Damaged beyond repair	Damaged	Total	%
Spitfire	1107	96	112	42	250	22
Hurricane	27	0	0	0	0	0
Mustang	223	29	26	4	59	26.4
Tempest	62	15	0	2	17	27
Mosquito	282	27	8	5	40	14
TYPHOON	354	67	60	23	150	47
Total	2055	234	206	76	516	25

August 1944

	Aircraft available	Shot down	Damaged beyond repair	Damaged	Total	%
Spitfire	1150	102	75	40	217	18
Hurricane	27	0	2	1	3	11
Mustang	217	31	17	6	54	24
Tempest	66	11	3	2	16	24
Mosquito	295	22	9	2	33	11
TYPHOON	365	92	55	24	171	46
Total	2120	258	161	75	494	23
Total losses	out of 3832	848	570	283	1701	44.5 (2)

(1) 'Aircraft available' means aircraft ready to fly after the daily inspection. The total number of aircraft allotted to the 2nd ATAF was probably higher by 10%.
(2) This percentage is calculated over the initial strength on June 6th plus the replacements of July and August.

Those statistics show that the 2nd ATAF deployed an average of 2100 aircraft daily for a period of three months, from 6 June 1944 to 1 September, with the following losses:

Spitfire	804	or 68%	of the initial force of	1166
		and 41%	of the total engaged of	1954
Hurricane	4	or 13%	of the initial force of	29
		and 12.9%	of the total engaged of	31
Mustang	229	or 98%	of the initial force of	233
		and 49.6%	of the total engaged of	462
Mosquito	128	or 45.4%	of the initial force of	282
		and 32.8%	of the total engaged of	398
TYPHOON	491	or 128%	of the initial force of	383
		or 56.2%	of the total engaged of	874
Total losses	1701		amounting to 80.18% of initial force or 44.50% with reinforcements included.	

After 84 days of fighting on the Continent, the losses of 2nd ATAF amounted to over 80 per cent of the initial strength on 6 June.

The rocket-firing Typhoons were chosen primarily to fight the obvious targets: the Tiger and Panther Panzers were top priority, then armoured vehicles in general, followed by flak positions. But convoys, trains, headquarters, barges, bridges and troop concentrations were also daily objectives. Diving from 4000 feet to ground level or going in at nought feet, with speed building up to 400 or 500 mph in a steep dive, the Typhoon achieved great accuracy of fire, thanks to the flat trajectory of its rockets at any range up to 600 yards and the devastating effect of 20 mm cannons firing at 640 shells per minute.

But the approach to the target had to be made through the usual wall of anti-aircraft fire, and our losses were in proportion to the accepted risks. The results obtained were also in direct relation to the determination, keenness and the guts displayed by the pilots.

It should be mentioned that there was a running controversy at the time between the RAF claims and the Army HQ assessments of damage, as well as by whom they were caused. While the front-line troops and the tank crews never missed an opportunity to demonstrate their gratitude and their comradeship, underlining the Tiffies' share of their success, Army HQ sometimes appropriated for their arm many enemy losses sustained from RAF attack. Where rivalry ends and bad faith begins is a matter of opinion. It is extremely difficult to determine with complete accuracy the claims made by each arm in such a confused battle.

Claims by the Royal Air Force were automatically checked by the cameras fitted to the aircraft and synchronised with the guns. This and the thorough scrutiny at debriefing by the intelligence officer after each operation largely contributed to a correct appreciation of the RAF assessment.

There are documents that enable us to have an independent opinion of work done by the Typhoons. They originate from the highest German sources. General Bayerlein, officer commanding the Lehr Panzer division says (Bulletin No. A.H.B./8/15/201): 'Our division was denied the use of main roads and our movements were totally interrupted by daytime, as a result of the heavy losses sustained after the terrible and repeated attacks made by rocket-Typhoons.' Describing the Falaise battle, General Speidel, Rommel's chief of staff says: 'In the Mortain area, during the German endeavour to break the siege of our forces, we were continuously submitted to massive attacks by Typhoons. Our convoys were decimated because the Typhoon tactics were to hit both the head and the tail of our columns, then to wreck the immobilised armour caught in the trap. On that day alone 84 tanks were destroyed, 35 heavily damaged and 21 damaged, while we shot down only three Typhoons.' (Invasion 1944). This is unsolicited testimony. Bayerlein was in charge of the breakthrough crippled by the Typhoons.

As far as I am concerned, as I led several attacks against the bold Panzer manoeuvre of 7 August, I do well remember that having taken advantage of the early morning fog that kept us grounded for several hours the German armour, brushing aside the meagre reserves trying to oppose their drive, smashed through the American lines at dawn and started racing towards Avranches. The artillery positions were bypassed and the road to the sea was wide open with no opposition possible. It must have been around 10.30 a.m. when the fog lifted enough to allow us to scramble and look for the enemy still hidden in the haze. Then suddenly we located the Panzers; the scene was unforgettable — and quite alarming. Like well-disciplined ants, some 600 Panzers, escorted by their mobile flak units, were pressing forward in perfect battle order along a shallow valley, without any noticeable resistance. Then, the next minute, scores of Typhoons were surging from every corner of the sky, adding the danger of collision to the usual hazards of their task. The slaughter began at once; it lasted the whole day and the next. After silencing most of the flak, the Tiffies stopped the enemy advance, then methodically smashed the armour as they ran for safety. When those Germans who were still alive threw their hands in and took advantage of the dark to retreat, the fields were littered with over 400 trackless tanks and armoured vehicles. Crumpled bodies next to the burning wrecks attested to the fierce battle that spelled for the Germans the beginning of the end. A special communiqué issued the same day by American HQ underlined that it was thanks to the Typhoons that near-disaster had been turned into complete victory and General Eisenhower himself visited our airfields to express his thanks. About that unique fight, General Speidel testified in his memoirs: 'That action was maybe the most decisive operation of the air war in Western Europe.'

It will also be remembered that a British fighter-bomber of 83 Group of 2nd ATAF strafed a group of staff cars at a French crossroads on 17 July 1944, killing several officers and severely wounding Field Marshal Rommel. Rommel was later compelled by Hitler to commit suicide. That officer, elevated by the Nazi regime to the highest rank in the hierarchy, respected the rules of war and always behaved like a gentleman: the general feeling among us when we learned of his death was to salute a fallen adversary rather than to rejoice about the end of a hated Nazi.

It is not my proposition that Typhoons alone gained victory in Normandy; to win a war a huge common effort is necessary. But, contrary to Air Marshal Harris's theory, the war could not be and was not won primarily by strategic bombing of Germany day and night. It reduced production, but only for a time. It affected civilian morale, and created many problems of communication. Short of the atomic bomb (which was ready for the Allies only a year later) the war still had to be won by classic means — by beating the enemy on the ground and by occupation of his territory. It is by destroying most of the German armoured forces that the 2nd ATAF aircraft made the balance tilt in our favour during and after the Normandy battle.

From June to September 1944, an average of 380 Typhoons made about 35,000 offensive sorties, launching 265,000 rockets and firing 13,000,000 20 mm shells. This was at the cost of 243 Typhoons lost, 173 severely damaged and 75 less badly hit by flak. During the same period, over 1000 tanks out of about 3000 (reinforcements included) were put out of action by Typhoons. They can also be credited with the destruction of 12,000 to 15,000 vehicles of all types, over 50 trains, about 30 barge-bridges and a great many gun positions. Thousands of German soldiers fell to their fire and liberation of the Channel ports was partly due to the Tactical Air Force.

During the invasion period. The loss of life was heavy amongst the Tiffy pilots. The main reason was obviously the choice of low-flying attacks made on targets defended by many well-trained, accurate flak batteries. To a lesser degree, other causes were the unreliability of the Sabre engine which, although improved, never equalled that of Rolls-Royce. Also, the lack of experience of younger pilots going straight from school into battle. Needless to say, maintenance on newly acquired airstrips, lacking normal facilities and equipment, was done under poor conditions through no fault of our magnificent ground crews, who worked for months without a break. Fine dust choking the big radiators and clogging the cylinders developed into major trouble and was responsible for many engine failures. Finally, though my personal faith in the Typhoon went unshaken to the last day, I think that it was not an easy aircraft to fly, let alone for pilots freshly out of school to fight in. They did not get a proper chance to master the aircraft before getting their baptism of fire. But there was no other solution than to gain 'on the job' experience. Even though the old hands tried hard to pass on the gen and protect their green comrades, the God Moloch claimed his due and many young ones did not attain even five operational sorties before going missing. At a slower rate the veterans went too, after challenging the odds for weeks on end. A look at the statistics shown earlier tells the tale.